Praise for *The Narcissist Next Door*

"[This] well-researched and entertaining study of the syndrome du jour pulls in figures as varied as Lance Armstrong, Kim Kardashian, Jayson Blair, and Steve Jobs. It also names 'exploitativeness' and 'entitlement' as two of the narcissist's calling cards."
—*Slate*

"This thoroughly engrossing book contains a plethora of information . . . anyone interested in psychology will find it an invaluable resource."
—*Library Journal* (starred review)

"Informative and engaging, Kluger's account provides some effective tools for dealing with potential narcissists."
—*Publishers Weekly*

"Narcissists can be captivating people, and *The Narcissist Next Door* is a captivating book: meticulously researched, written with verve, and spiced with irresistible examples from the headlines and everyday life."
—Steven Pinker, Johnstone Professor of Psychology, Harvard University, and author of *How the Mind Works* and *The Sense of Style*

"We are surrounded by narcissists and from afar, they are often easy to like. They are famous entertainers, successful businesspeople, and politicians. The charm wears off quickly, though, if they get too close—your neighbors, friends, or your own family. The brilliant Jeffrey Kluger, one of our country's most admired science writers, has written a book that taught me a great deal, made me laugh out loud on a quiet airplane ride, and forced me to be introspective about myself and the people I love. Kluger gives a lot of himself in this book, deftly weaving cutting-edge science with poignant personal stories that are astonishingly candid, and, at times, very familiar. At the risk of sounding . . .well, narcissistic, I of course wondered if I fit any of the criteria. Chances are you are wondering the same thing. So open the book and find out."
—Dr. Sanjay Gupta

Praise for *The Sibling Effect*

"The science of siblings is well overdue for this kind of attention . . . [*The Sibling Effect* is] never less than interesting, especially to those of us who grew up with siblings or are raising them now, and when Kluger turns to his own band of brothers, the book gains depth and emotional resonance."
—*The Boston Globe*

D0150263

"We—or I, anyway—learn a lot . . . [Kluger's] own sibling history is movingly recounted." —*The New York Times Book Review*

"In each chapter there are gems of advice for parents." —Salon.com

"Like Malcolm Gladwell . . . [Kluger] can fashion something addictively readable out of even the densest list of statistics without dumbing it down . . . Just as his gift for parsing journal articles and master's theses gives the book its intellectual heft, his own experiences give the book its heart." —*Entertainment Weekly*

"[Kluger's] writing about his family is both frank and lyrical, and it's tough not to fall for his spunky tales of brotherly hijinks." —*Slate*

"Honest and vulnerable and caring." —*The Washington Post*

"*The Sibling Effect* is informative and engaging. The stories Kluger tells remind us that the bonds among brothers and sisters are loving, soothing, irritating, sometimes bitter, but always fascinating." —*Science* magazine

"For anyone who has a sibling or wants to better understand their kids' dynamics, this is an extremely interesting read." —*Parents* magazine

"In nostalgic fashion, void of sappiness, Kluger appropriately inserts his personal stories throughout this book. And being the good science journalist he is, the author loads *The Sibling Effect* full with the latest research." —*Psychology Today*

"Masterfully weaving anecdotal passages with academic research and scientific data, the author thoroughly examines the many manifestations of the simple brother-brother, sister-sister or brother-sister relationship, and the dynamic within each . . . entertaining, enlightening and helpful." —*Kirkus*

THE
NARCISSIST
NEXT DOOR

UNDERSTANDING THE MONSTER IN YOUR FAMILY,
IN YOUR OFFICE, IN YOUR BED—
IN YOUR WORLD

Jeffrey Kluger

RIVERHEAD BOOKS
New York

RIVERHEAD BOOKS
An imprint of Penguin Random House LLC
375 Hudson Street
New York, New York 10014

The Library of Congress has catalogued the Riverhead hardcover edition as follows:

Kluger, Jeffrey.
The narcissist next door : understanding the monster in your family, in your office, in
your bed—in your world / Jeffrey Kluger.
p.   cm.
ISBN 978-1-59448-636-4
1. Narcissism.   I. Title.
BF575.N35K58   2014   2014006297
616.85'854—dc23

First Riverhead hardcover edition: September 2014
First Riverhead trade paperback edition: September 2015
Riverhead trade paperback ISBN: 978-1-59463-391-1

Printed in the United States of America
1   3   5   7   9   10   8   6   4   2

BOOK DESIGN BY NICOLE LAROCHE

In keeping with the times:

To me

CONTENTS

CHAPTER ONE

The Mighty I

It can't be easy to wake up every day and discover that you're still Donald Trump. You were Trump yesterday, you're Trump today, and barring some extraordinary intervention, you'll be Trump tomorrow.

There are, certainly, compensations to being Donald Trump. You're fabulously wealthy; you have a lifetime pass to help yourself to younger and younger wives, even as you get older and older—a two-way Benjamin Button dynamic that is equal parts enviable and grotesque. You own homes in Manhattan; Palm Beach; upstate New York; Charlottesville, Virginia; and Rancho Palos Verdes, California; and you're free to bunk down in the penthouse suite of any hotel, apartment building, or resort that flies the Trump flag, anywhere on the planet—and there are a lot of them.

But none of that changes the reality of waking up every morning, looking in the bathroom mirror, and seeing Donald Trump staring back at you. And no, it's not the hair; that, after all, is a choice—one that may be hard for most people to understand, but a choice all the same, and there's a certain go-to-hell confidence in continuing to make it. The problem with being Trump is the same thing that explains the enormous fame and success of Trump: a naked neediness, a certain shamelessness, an insatiable hunger to be the largest, loudest, most honkingly conspicuous presence in any room—the great, braying Trumpness of Trump—and that's probably far less of a revel than it seems.

Contented people, well-grounded people, people at ease inside their skin, just don't behave the way Trump does. They go easy on the superlatives—especially when they're talking about their own accomplishments. Maybe what they're building or selling really is the greatest, the grandest, the biggest, the most stupendous, but they let the product do the talking. If it can't, maybe it ain't so great. They use their own names sparingly, too—even when they're businesspeople who have the opportunity to turn themselves from a person into a brand. There is no GatesWare software, no BezosBooks.com; it's not Zuckerbook you log on to a dozen times a day, it's Facebook. But the Trump name is everywhere in the Trump world—on his buildings, on his helicopters, on the side of every single plane in the fleet that was once known as the Eastern Air Shuttle until Trump bought it in 1989 and renamed it the Trump Shuttle. It's been on Trump Mortgage, Trump Financial, Trump Sales and Leasing, Trump Restaurants, Trump vodka, Trump chocolate, Donald Trump The Fragrance, Trump water, Trump home furnishings, Trump clothing, Trump Books, Trump Golf, Trump University and yes, Trump the Game.

There is presumption in the Trump persona, too—in his attempt to trademark "You're fired," after it became a catchphrase on *The Apprentice*, his top-rated reality show; in his offer to donate $5 million to a charity of President Obama's choosing if Obama would release to him, Trump, his college transcripts. There is petulance—in his public feuds with Rosie O'Donnell ("A total loser"), Seth Meyers ("He's a stutterer"), Robert De Niro ("We're not dealing with Albert Einstein") and Arianna Huffington ("Unattractive both inside and out. I fully understand why her former husband left her for a man . . .").

There is, too, an almost—*almost*—endearing cluelessness to the primal way he signals his pride in himself. He poses for pictures with his suit jacket flaring open, his hands on his hips, index and ring fingers pointing inevitably groinward—a great-ape fitness and genital display if ever there was one. After he bought the moribund Gulf+Western Building in New York City's Columbus Circle, skinned it down, covered it in gold-colored glass, converted it into a luxury hotel and residence, and reinforced it with steel and concrete to make it less subject to swaying in the wind, Trump boasted to *The New York Times* that it was going to be "the stiffest building in the city." If he was aware of his own psychic subtext, he gave no indication.

Donald Trump the person was not always Donald Trump the phenomenon. He began his career in his father's company, building modestly priced rental properties in Brooklyn, Queens and Staten Island, which is to the New York real estate world what Waffle House is to the high-end restaurant industry. He made his move into Manhattan in 1971, and while his interests and appetites were clearly, gaudily upscale, he was, in his own vainglorious way, something of a man of the people. When the city couldn't manage to get Wollman Rink in Central Park renovated on time, Trump offered to take the project over, got it done within months and gave the city change back from its original budget. Yes, the name Trump would forever appear in conspicuous all-caps on the retaining walls surrounding the rink, but a civic good guy deserves a little recognition, doesn't he? He was married to the same woman for fifteen years, they had three children together, and if the first of them was named, no surprise, Donald, well, what of it? We had two George Bushes and two John Adamses, didn't we? He was socially and politically moderate: pro-choice, troubled by the unregulated flow of money into political campaigns, a champion of universal health care. "Our goal should be clear," he said. "Our people are our greatest asset."

It is a matter of historical record that that Trump is no more, that a large, loud foghorn of a man has taken his place, a man whose business acumen is undeniable, but whose public persona has become, to many, unbearable. To call Donald Trump a narcissist is to state what seems clinically obvious. There is the egotism of narcissism, the grandiosity of narcissism, the social obtuseness of narcissism. He has his believers, yes. "Love him or hate him, Trump is a man who is certain about what he wants, and sets out to get it, no holds barred," said one. "Women find his power almost as much of a turn-on as his money." But it was Trump himself who spoke those admiring words, which makes them comical, sure, but troubling as well.

Trump may be an easy target, but he is also, in some ways, a sympathetic one. Narcissism isn't easy, it isn't fun, it isn't something to be waved off as a personal shortcoming that hurts only the narcissists themselves, any more than you can look at the drunk or philanderer or compulsive gambler and not see the grief and ruin in his future. Trump is unlikely to suffer such a fate, but it awaits plenty of other narcissists—and increasingly, they seem to be everywhere.

Narcissists are corrupt public officials, and honest ones too; they are the criminals who fill the jail cells, and sometimes the police who put them there in the first place. They are in industry, in media, in finance, in show business. They are artists, designers, chefs, scholars. They are the people we work with and the people we work for; the people we love and the people we bed; the people we hire or marry or befriend, and soon want to fire or leave or unfriend. They are the people who love us—until they betray us.

The very word *narcissist*—once the stuff of Greek mythology and psychology texts—has entered the cultural argot as a shorthand descriptor for all manner of unpleasant characters, and we recognize each of them. It's the windbag drinking buddy who can go on for an entire evening about himself and his work and his new car and new house, but whose eyes glaze over and whose mind wanders the moment you begin to talk about yourself. It's the mirror-gazing friend who insists on modeling every stitch of clothing she owns for you but never seems to notice—or comment on—whether you're wearing a new dress, a favorite business suit or a giant garbage bag. It's the bombastic relative who sucks the air out of Thanksgiving dinner, holding forth on politics from the pumpkin soup through the pumpkin pie and tolerating neither interruption nor contradiction. It's the lover who charms the pants off of you—literally—and never returns your calls after that.

Narcissists may be ubiquitous—paradoxically commonplace given how exceptional they think they are—showing up in every corner of our lives, but it's the famous ones, the ones with the biggest stages and the biggest soapboxes, we notice before we notice the ones closest to us. That makes sense, partly because they warrant close scrutiny given the kind of impact—usually negative—they can have, partly because there's a can't-look-away quality to their train-wreck behavior. And we've had a lot to look at in the United States of late.

So we get Ted Cruz, the freshman senator from Texas, conducting a twenty-one-hour filibuster—perhaps democracy's greatest "Look at me!" spectacle—in 2013 to oppose a health care law he couldn't repeal, couldn't defund and wouldn't sit down quietly to try to amend and improve, because that would mean weeks and months of collaborative work in private rooms with no cameras rolling or headlines flashing, and where's the fun in that? So we get Marlin Stutzman, a back-bench congressman who helped engineer the two-and-a-half-week federal shutdown that followed Cruz's spectacle and who, when asked why he and the rest of his faction wouldn't back down despite the cost to the nation, answered, "We're not going to be disrespected. We have to get something out of this. And I don't know what that even is." Because when 800,000 federal employees aren't allowed to go to work, when food inspections are being canceled, when the country is losing over $1.5 billion a day, what really counts is whether the politicians themselves are feeling the love.

So we get New Jersey governor Chris Christie, longtime political bullyboy, on whose watch the entire town of Fort Lee, New Jersey, suffered through four days of gridlock when most of its access to the George Washington Bridge was cut off, an act of professional payback after the town's Democratic mayor declined to cross party lines and endorse Christie in a reelection bid he was certain to win by a landslide anyway. Christie's marathon 109-minute press conference after the story broke was less *mea culpa* than personal lamentation, a catalogue of the ways he'd suffered as a result of the incident.

"I am a very sad person today," he said. "That's the emotion I feel. A person close to me betrayed me. . . . I probably will get angry at some point, but I got to tell you the truth, I'm sad." Christie also shared that he hadn't been sleeping well as a result of the scandal and that he felt "humiliated" and "blindsided" and found it "incredibly disappointing to have people let [him] down this way." *The Washington Post* ran a word count on Christie's first-person references in the course of his long, on-camera ramble and reported 692 uses of *I*; 217 repetitions of *me*, *my* or *mine*; and 186 uses of *I'm* or *I've*. Thousands and thousands of Fort Lee residents suffered, but the big story to Chris Christie was, apparently, Chris Christie—and that hurt him badly. "I had a donor say well 'Who gives a shit about you?'" said one GOP finance official, according to Politico.com. "What about all the people who are stuck on the bridge?"

We have had, too, Miley Cyrus, who from childhood never had to look far for a camera or an audience, because she was practically born with them in front of her. Her twerking and grinding and stroking herself with a foam-rubber finger in a live TV performance left critics and fans slack-jawed. Most people concluded her performance was an effort to demonstrate to her fans that she had, you know, grown up and was, you know, no longer a child—a rite of passage as inevitable for her as for anyone else, but somehow newsworthy because it was happening to Miley. This played out in the same summer that Lady

Gaga—she of the meat dress, which may or may not have had much fashion merit, but undeniably drew eyeballs—released a song called "Applause," in which she repeats over and over the lyric "I live for the applause, applause, applause," as frank an admission and as powerful an anthem of the age of narcissism as you could imagine.

There is Bernie Madoff as well, a man whose multi-decade Ponzi scheme made him exceedingly rich, but at the cost of $65 billion in other people's wealth, stolen from a victim list that, in the government's records, ran 165 pages long. Hedge funds and banks made up much of that inventory of the wronged—admittedly, nobody's idea of sympathetic victims—but there were also pension funds and charities, as well as individuals like Jack Cutter of Longmont, Colorado, a seventy-nine-year-old oil industry worker who was living with his wife on $1 million in retirement savings, a nest egg that vanished in Madoff's care, forcing Cutter to take a job stocking supermarket shelves. Madoff may not have known Cutter, but he did know there would be hundreds or thousands of other Cutters among his victims—indeed, his scheme depended on that fact—and every morning he could nonetheless get out of bed and say, "Yes, this is all right, these are good decisions."

Narcissists are the vanity presidential candidates—the likes of Herman Cain and H. Ross Perot, people with more money and name recognition than governing skills, but who fancy themselves up to the task of being the most powerful person on earth because, well, how could they not be? It doesn't even require wealth to go on that "Vote for me or at least pay attention to me" ride. Did anybody believe Ron Paul or Dennis Kucinich had any chance at all of ever taking the oath of office—did they even believe it themselves?—or was it just the naked craving to be on the presidential stage? In 2000, Ralph Nader ran quixotically for president on the Green Party ticket, winning 2.8 million votes nationwide—and 97,488 of them in Florida, the large majority of which surely came out of Al Gore's hide. That Florida haul would have been more than enough to overcome the paper-thin 537 votes by which Gore lost the state to George W. Bush and, ultimately, the presidency. Yet when Nader was asked afterward if he felt like he had cost Gore the election, his answer was succinct: "I think that Al Gore cost *me* the election."

Narcissists are athletes, too, and if anything, they're worse than the politicians, since they don't even have to affect humility, freeing them up to enjoy their posses and their bling and their SUVs, and to indulge in their magisterial habit of referring to themselves in the third person because, apparently, a mere pronoun is so unsatisfying when you have the opportunity to speak your own name aloud. "I wanted to do what was best for, you know, LeBron James, and what LeBron James was gonna do to make him happy," said, well, LeBron James about his 2010 decision to leave the Cleveland Cavaliers for the Miami Heat—or, as he put it, "to take my talents to South Beach."

"If they don't sign me, sorry, but I must go. That's what Carlos Zambrano thinks," said, yes, pitcher Carlos Zambrano when he was in contract negotiations with the Chicago Cubs. "Rickey wants to play another year, and he thinks he wants to play for you," said baseball Hall of Famer Rickey Henderson near the end of his career when he called to chat with the general manager of another team. And Rickey was *job hunting* at the time.

Few of us will ever rise to the self-adoring heights of LeBron or Madoff or Miley or Cruz, but we're kidding ourselves if we don't think we may have been bitten by the same narcissistic bug that infected them. It's not merely the "Notice me" roar of the Facebook age—with 1 billion of us updating our status and uploading our photos of such who-cares minutiae as what we had for dinner, because, really, how could our friends not want to look at a glamour shot of the farfalle with peppers and shrimp we just made? It's not just the 500 million of us on Twitter, trained in the urgent art of posting 140 characters of absolutely nothing. ("Just had a Krispy Kreme! Yum!") It's not merely Foursquare that lets us check in when we go somewhere—anywhere, really—so that we can report the late-breaking news that we just drove past Fenway Park or the Gateway Arch or our old elementary school. It's not even the *reductio ad absurdum* site Threewords.me, which allows—indeed, invites—your friends to sign up so they can choose the three words that best describe you, and you in turn can describe them. That's all there is to it—really. If the site accepts hyphens, how many uploads of "self-absorbed twit" do you think they'll get?

Our narcissism has other expressions, too: the symbiotic exhibitionism and voyeurism of the reality show. *Look at me while I, um, live in a house on the Jersey Shore, and maybe one day you can get a show and people will look at you living in a house too!* Yes, there's money to be made from being a reality star, but it's a simple truth of commerce that the things a culture rewards are the things it values, and in twenty-first-century America, spending your life before the camera is a growth industry, with both consumers and providers willing to contribute to it.

Those cameras don't even have to be wielded by TV producers. We can do it very well ourselves, thank you very much, giving rise to our culture-wide sexting habit, with videos and cell phone images forever getting shot and saved and shared, because what good is a vigorous sexual romp unless other people can watch it play out and what good is the pleasure you take in looking at your own hot bits if other people can't look along with you. Preposterous ex-congressman Anthony Weiner may be the poster boy—or poster something—for sexting, but with 80 percent of college students saying that they sext and 20 percent of the rest of the population admitting they do, too, he's got plenty of company.

It's starting earlier and earlier, this pandemic of simultaneous showing off and mirror-gazing—in the everybody-gets-a-trophy ethos of the grade-school track meet, in the well-intentioned song preschoolers are taught to sing to the tune of "Frère Jacques": "I am special, I am special, Look at me, Look at me." Well, maybe you are, but as with the 1981 study that found that 82 percent of people believe they're in the top 33 percent of drivers—a statistical impossibility—if everyone's special, by definition no one is. Only in Lake Wobegon are all the children above average. Mister Rogers sold the same idea of pre-K exceptionalism decades ago, but with an important twist: "You are my friend, you are special, you are my friend, you're special to me," he sang. The specialness lay in the connection to Mister Rogers—and, by implication, to all the other friends the child was learning to make—not in some factory-loaded excellence that's standard equipment in all of us.

Some of this is natural in kids. "If you go into a classroom and say, 'How many of you are good at math?'" observes Brad Bushman, a professor of psychology and communications at Ohio State University, "kids under eight will raise their hands even if they suck at math. The same is true of singing and other skills. Before age eight, people think they're good at everything." But what starts as a sort of naïve conceit is too often hothoused into full-blown grandiosity.

It's hard to say when Americans finally, fully gave themselves over to the cult of love-me-ism—or at least openly acknowledged it—but December 2006 is often pointed to as a sort of benchmark. That was the month one of *Time* magazine's most-talked-about Person of the Year issues was published. In all the decades *Time* has existed, it has accorded the honor to a host of history's giants: Lindbergh, Gandhi, Eisenhower, Sadat, Gorbachev, Churchill (twice), Franklin Roosevelt (three times). Monsters have been chosen, too—Hitler, Stalin, Khomeini—abiding by the magazine's self-imposed rule that the sole standard for selection be the person who most influenced world events in the previous year, for better or worse. Whole groups have gotten the honor: Hungarian freedom fighters in 1956, Baby Boomers in 1966, American women in

1975. In 1988, the Earth itself was named Planet of the Year as a nod to the perilous state of the environment; in 1982, the personal computer was named Machine of the Year—a choice that turned out to be prescient given that there wasn't even a publicly available Internet yet.

In 2006, however, everyone got the track-meet ribbon. *Time*'s Person of the Year was, simply: *You.* "You. Yes, You," the cover line read. "You control the information age. Welcome to your world." The conceit of the story was that in an era of user-derived content, we were all now running the cultural show. "For seizing the reins of the global media," *Time* wrote, "for founding and framing the new digital democracy, for working for nothing and beating the pros at their own game, TIME's Person of the Year for 2006 is you." To make sure that the congratulatory message got through, the cover included a piece of reflective Mylar—a hand mirror to match the self-adoration theme of the story.

As a longtime *Time* staffer—someone who looks at the red border the way Yankee players see their pinstripes—I wish I could say I questioned the choice, raised my hand and asked if that really, truly was the statement we wanted to make. But I didn't. The fact is, I cautiously applauded the idea, thought it captured the zeitgeist in a fresh and interesting way—and I still think it did. The problem was, it also endorsed that zeitgeist, validated it, gave cover to people for whom the "I am special, Look at me" refrain was more than a song lyric. It was the animating idea of their lives.

In the years since, the tidal wave of first-person love has only climbed higher. Our careful curation of our Facebook pages has become something of a cultural art form, as we post only the prettiest pictures, the sunniest news, the funniest observations—grooming our image for a following that we convince ourselves gives a hoot. We have become artists of the selfie, the first-person photo taken with a smartphone held at arm's length—an immediately recognizable posture that may become the signature pose of our era. The Vine website allows us to post eleven-second video clips—the visual equivalent of Twitter—doing whatever we've convinced ourselves the world wants to watch us doing.

Amazon.com now lists nearly 70,000 book titles under the "Self-esteem" rubric—and that's only in paperback. More than 3,700 such books are aimed at kids and more than 300 of those, incredibly, at the birth-to-age-two group—or precisely the stage of life in which kids need absolutely no help to believe they sit at the center of the universe. The titles achieve a certain redundancy after a while—*I Like Me*; *The Best Part of Me*; *You Are Important*; *Happy to Be Me!*; *The Lovables in the Kingdom of Self*—but they all sell the same ego-puffing product. Self-esteem is undeniably important, and plenty of people—especially kids—with rough lives or troubled psyches need a boost. But surely not 70,000 books' worth of boost.

Calling all of this narcissism can be something of a stretch. Physical and emotional conditions tend to slip in and out of vogue, with a lot of sloppy diagnosing of ourselves and of others coming with it. We find it awfully easy to label a moody friend "bipolar," notwithstanding the fact that only 2.6 percent of the world's population actually suffers from the condition, according to the National Institute of Mental Health. Ditto obsessive-compulsive disorder, which everyone on the planet seems to think they have at some point or another—even reducing the label to an adjective ("I'm so OCD!")—simply because they like to keep their desk neat. But if you're not part of the 2 percent of all people who actually have a clinical, diagnosable case of the condition, you're probably just tidy. As for hypoglycemia? Please. Unless you're diabetic and have just injected yourself with insulin and skipped a meal, odds are you're just tired, hungry and looking for an excuse for a snack. So eat a Snickers and pipe down.

It is much the same way with narcissism. The actual incidence of true narcissistic personality disorder (NPD) is just 1 percent in the general population, sneaking up to 3 percent in certain groups—such as people in their twenties who have yet to be humbled a bit by the challenges and setbacks of adult life. The numbers climb much higher among self-selected populations of people who have already entered psychotherapy for some emotional condition, ranging anywhere from 2 percent for the average therapy patient to 16 percent for institution-alized patients.

The behaviors that characterize the narcissistic personality are spelled out starkly by the *Diagnostic and Statistical Manual (DSM)*, psychology's universally relied-upon field guide to the mind, which defines the condition as, in effect, three conditions: a toxic mash-up of grandiosity, an unquenchable thirst for admiration and a near-total blindness to how other people see you. But those are only the broadest features. There is, too, a lack of empathy in the narcissist—an utter inability not only to understand what other people are feeling but how they may be responsible for those feelings, especially when they're bad.

Narcissists are afflicted with a bottomless appetite as well—for recognition, attention, glory, rewards. And it's a zero-sum thing. Every moment a narcissist spends listening to another party guest tell a story is a moment in which the stage has been surrendered. Most people welcome that give-and-take; it's the social part of socializing, and listening can provide a welcome break from the performance demands of telling a story or otherwise holding court. In the karaoke cycle that is life, we all get our turns on the stage and our turns in the crowd. The narcissist withers in—and rages against—any dying of the light.

Entitlement is another part of the narcissistic profile—a sense that attention and rewards are not only expected but owing—accompanied by an always-ready rage when those goodies aren't delivered. "Perhaps the worst expression of narcissism is that sense of entitlement," says research psychologist Robin Edelstein of the University of Michigan. "It usually exists side by side with a terrible exploitativeness, a willingness to take advantage of other people, but a brittleness and defensiveness if they feel someone is taking advantage of them."

Adds Brad Bushman of Ohio State University, "I'm an aggression researcher, and when it comes to narcissists, nothing sets aggression off so much as that sense of entitlement."

Narcissism is not a stand-alone condition. It's part of the suite of ten personality disorders, which also include paranoid, borderline, histrionic, antisocial, dependent, avoidant, rigid, schizoid and schizotypal personalities. (The last two, as their names suggest, include features of schizophrenia but are not the same as that full-blown condition, which is in a diagnostic class almost by itself.)

Personality disorders are among the most stubborn conditions psychologists treat, because they're what is known as "egosyntonic"— which is shrink-talk for the idea that the patients buy into what their minds are telling them. You're not paranoid, people really are after you; you're not pathologically rigid, there really are certain ways all things must be done at all times; and you're not narcissistic, you really are more talented, more important and just plain better than everybody else.

Anxiety conditions, such as phobias and OCD, are what's known as "egodystonic." The person with a morbid fear of spiders or snakes or elevators knows it's nuts but can't control it. The obsessive-compulsive who devotes three hours a day to hand-washing or checking to make sure the stove is turned off recognizes the madness of the behavior and would much rather be doing other things, but the psychic pull of the rituals is too great. When anxiety sufferers come into therapy, they deeply want to change. When people with a personality disorder at last enter treatment, it's typically because family or friends push them there. Absent that kind of coercion, they really see no need to change. This is especially true of narcissists, who not only don't think they need a doctor but are convinced they're smarter than the doctor.

Not every case of narcissism is the clinical, capital-N kind. Like all personality disorders, it exists on a sort of continuum, with people with ordinary self-esteem at one end, the floridly narcissistic at the other and uncounted little gradations in between. A whole lot of people are now moving up that scale, developing cases of subclinical, or lowercase-*n*, narcissism that may not shut down governments but may cause plenty of personal harm to the people around them.

In 2008, a team of researchers published a study in the *Journal of Personality* looking at narcissism among college students over a twenty-seven-year period, from 1979 to 2006. Their paper was what's known as a meta-analysis, a recrunching of the data from eighty-five separate narcissism studies covering a collective 16,475 subjects. All of the people surveyed had been administered the Narcissistic Personality Inventory (NPI), a forty-item questionnaire that requires subjects to choose between such essentially opposite statements as "I insist upon getting the respect that is due me" and "I usually get the respect that I deserve"; "Sometimes I tell good stories" and "Everybody likes to hear my stories"; "I can read people like a book" and "People are sometimes hard to understand"; "I am more capable than other people" and "There is a lot I can learn from other people." (See page 259.) In some cases, both statements can be true—you may in fact be more capable than other people and still have things to learn from them—but the "forced choice" nature of the questions is designed to make people own up to the traits that best describe them, even if that's not all there is to them.

The average person scores slightly below 16 on the NPI. Move above 20 and you're flirting with narcissism. Broadly, people diagnosed with narcissism can be divided into three groups: the power group, the special-person group and the grandiose-exhibitionist group, depending on the mix of descriptions they choose for themselves—but all of them are still narcissists. Since 1979, the 2008 study found, there has been a 30 percent increase in overall NPI scores in the sample population, with more than two-thirds of contemporary college students scoring higher than what the mean score was from 1979 through 1985. "The exact same test has been given every year," says Bushman, who was one of the coauthors of the study, "and the narcissism rates are increasing over time."

Like all psychological surveys, the NPI will never be as empirically accurate as, say, a blood test or a cholesterol count. But when tools like this stick around as long as this one has, and when they're used as widely as this one is, they've usually proven their powerful if imperfect merit. What's more, even before people take the test, both experts and non-experts can often predict who will score high, based on their tell-tale behavior.

Narcissists thrive when there's an opportunity for glory but are uninterested in the collaborative work that leads to greater good for a larger group; they bristle and bitch when their talents are challenged, but never consider the possibility that those talents may be less than they believe them to be or that there is at least room for improvement. For narcissists, setbacks are not opportunities to learn; they're problems caused by somebody else who got in their way or sabotaged their plans.

"Narcissists tend to blame others, rather than to own it," says Nathanael Fast, professor of management and organizational behavior at the University of Southern California. "There's a fragility to the narcissistic personality, a pressure to be superior and the implicit need to prove how great they are."

It's that pressure, that panic, that drives narcissists to cut corners and break rules—the plagiarist or the academic cheater whose shame at acting unethically or fear of being caught is no match for the thrill of the unearned A+ or the fraudulent byline. "Narcissistic students have higher levels of academic misconduct and we think that's because they don't feel guilt," says psychologist Amy Brunell of Ohio State University at Newark, who has studied narcissism and academic dishonesty. "We asked them about their impressions of other students and they felt that other people were cheating more than they actually

were. But people who merely have high self-esteem as opposed to narcissism don't cheat as much."

That kind of behavior takes its toll on everyone. By the time the
cheater has aced the course and moved on, she's thrown off the curve
for the rest of the class and perhaps won the internship or postgrad job
that honest students were gunning for, too. By the time the woman
who falls in love with a narcissist realizes he will never adore her nearly
as much as he adores himself, she may already have given up her apartment, moved into his and never suspected that he's cheating with the
new account executive in his office whom he insists he doesn't find the
slightest bit pretty. By the time the human resources department realizes that the VP it hired to manage an office of two hundred people is
a raging narcissist, he's probably browbeaten dozens of employees,
filched credit for work they've done, and led the firm to a quarterly
loss because, never mind what all the trained analysts told him about
why he shouldn't invest in new product development till next year, he
reckoned his judgment was better and smarter and bolder than theirs.

There can, surely, be profound good that comes from narcissists—
or at least from their works. However wise and humble and spiritual
Mohandas Gandhi and Martin Luther King, Jr., were, they surely got
a charge out of rousing hundreds of thousands, even millions, of people with the sound of their voice and the power of their ideas. Had
they been more timid men, less inclined toward—or delighted by—
the power that comes from leadership, they might never have stepped
up to lead at all. Jonas Salk and Albert Sabin saved the world from
polio with their competing and very different vaccines. But it was the
race to be first—to be the man who would be celebrated for beating
the disease—that helped impel their work. Dwight Eisenhower led
the Allies to victory during World War II, and for that he was rightly
celebrated. But if you don't think he quietly enjoyed wearing an
explosively beribboned uniform and a title like Supreme Allied Com-

mander, you don't know much about human nature. It is the same confidence—sometimes arrogance—that has allowed inventors and industrialists like Steve Jobs, Bill Gates and Elon Musk to press on in improbable ventures against extraordinary odds and create things that improve the world in big and meaningful ways, even if they make few friends doing it.

Still, the heroic narcissist, the ingenious narcissist, the courageous narcissist are not the most common breeds. It's the everyday, self-obsessed, pay-attention-to-me narcissist who is. Almost anywhere you look in your world, you have an ever bigger chance of finding one of them: in your office, in your social circle, in your arms—in yourself. If you don't know how to recognize them in time—to avoid them if you can or to manage them if you're already entangled—the price can be high. And it can be higher still if the narcissist is you.

For too many people, the very idea of love—that greatest and most other-directed of human impulses—is folding in on itself, with admiration turning to exhibitionism, charity to greed, altruism to appetite. We are more and more living in a mirror world—with the most prominent sight being the reflected one. And too many of us like that view just fine.

CHAPTER TWO

The Monster in the Nursery

I was once a sociopath. I didn't know it at the time, and I wouldn't have cared much even if I had known, a fact that really just makes things worse. It's hard to say exactly when I crossed the line from mere incivility into true social savagery—with the exploitativeness and indifference to the rights or suffering of others that that implies—but I'd have to say it was probably the day I decided to clobber a strange man on the head with a boat.

In fairness, the boat was a toy—though it was a big one, made of hard, heavy plastic. And in fairness too, I was only four years old. Still, I had a very clear idea of the crime I wanted to commit and I set about carrying it out with patience and quiet deliberateness. The man was a complete stranger. He had come to our house that day to pick up a babysitter and was sitting in our den while she put on her coat and collected her things. I didn't know if he was the sitter's brother or husband or even father; to me all adults still fell into one large, undifferentiated age group. What I did recognize immediately was that he was bald, with a horseshoe rim of hair around the sides and back of his head and a mesmerizingly shiny scalp on top.

I had never seen a bald head up close before and I stared at him intently, which surely made him uncomfortable—something that didn't trouble me a bit, either. What did interest me was a question: If having hair protects the top of your head from cuts or bumps, wouldn't *not* having hair make you extra-susceptible to injury? Even the slightest blow would have to hurt a lot more on a completely hairless scalp, right?

The idea intrigued me, and the only way to test it was to run the experiment. I had an available subject, and looking around, I realized that I had the necessary equipment: the toy boat lying on the floor within easy reach. The whole thing was really nothing more than a rudimentary exercise of the scientific method—not a bad concept for someone so young to stumble across, even if I was about to execute it in a decidedly criminal way.

I picked up the boat, hefted it once and found it suitable, then raised it above my head and advanced wordlessly on the unsuspecting man. He had been looking away, but finally he turned his attention toward me and realized what I was up to. "Uh, uh, uh," he scolded. "No, no, no."

I hesitated just in front of him, and he held out his hand. I gave him the boat without argument, he put it aside and I walked off to busy myself with other things. I don't know if the man ever told the sitter or my parents what had happened, but I suspect not, since I surely would have had to account for myself if he had. And my response to being questioned would just as surely have been to shrug. I felt no regret or contrition over what I'd nearly done, though I was slightly piqued that I'd never get to test my theory.

There was not a single thing about my behavior that day that ought to be acceptable in a civil society. It was an attempted battery—willful, premeditated, indifferent to the consequences. But there was not a single thing wrong with it, either.

Small children, by their very nature, are moral monsters. They're greedy, demanding, violent, destructive, selfish, impulsive and utterly remorseless. They fight with playmates and siblings constantly—biting, hitting and kicking at will, but screaming in pain and indignation if they're attacked in return. They expect to be adored but not disciplined, rewarded but never penalized, cared for and served by parents and family without caring or serving reciprocally. They are, in any meaningful respect, incapable of functioning in civil society, which is the reason that from the time they're born till the time they reach their preteens, they are never allowed out without a parent or other adult keeping them on-leash.

All of this is psychopathology of the first order—and narcissistic pathology in particular. There is the entitlement of narcissism, the egocentrism of narcissism, the bottomless appetite—for attention, applause, rewards—of narcissism. And there's the utter, narcissistic numbness to how others may suffer from your behavior. You don't throw a punch or land a kick unless you either assume that your victim doesn't experience the attack the same way you do, or you don't think about it at all—neither one good. You don't demand without asking or take without thanking if you give a fig about the person who has just provided you with the goodies. And you certainly don't try to hit a strange man on the head with a boat to determine what he'd feel, without perversely ignoring the fact that what he'd be feeling would be pain—quite a lot of it.

"We're born with this idea that we're the center of the universe," says Aaron Pincus, professor of psychology and director of clinical training in Penn State University's doctoral program in psychology. "We think everything responds to us. There's a pervasiveness to it, a sense that the world serves you, and kids behave accordingly. There's a reason infants drop a pen a million times and make you pick it up. That seems boring to you, but they're making you do stuff."

In many ways, babies begin making you do stuff even before they're born. For all the drama, romance and seeming magic of childbearing, what happy expectant parents are really celebrating is nothing more than a parasite-host relationship. At the moment of conception, an effectively alien creature commandeers the mother's womb and uses it as a sort of beachhead from which to seize control of her entire body. Mothers get nothing from this arrangement physically; babies get life itself, and they will stop at nothing to ensure their own survival, often relying on deceit of the first order.

While an unfertilized ovum is an immunologically benign thing—wholly produced by the mother's body and thus very much a home-team player—the sperm that seek it out are interlopers, even if, in the case of parents who are trying to conceive, they're invited interlopers. The lucky sperm cell that wins the conception race is safely subsumed into the larger body of the egg and the rest of the millions-strong swarm soon die off, so any threat to the integrity of the mother's system ought to be over. The sperm's genes survive, however—indeed, mixing them with the genetic material of the ovum is the whole point of conception—and the embryo that results will thus always be 50 percent foreign. So much outside genetics, even in a single cell, ought to be enough to stir the mother's immune system to attack—and attack it would if the newly created organism didn't have some clever defenses.

Almost immediately upon conception, the fertilized egg generates masking proteins that conceal the paternal DNA and allow only the mother's genetic material to show. That bit of nothing-to-see-here sleight of hand blinds the mom's immune system, even as the father's genes go on doubling in density every time the cells that make up the new embryo divide. This strategy works for a while, but once the embryo implants itself in the uterine wall, even masking proteins wouldn't be enough to conceal the alien mass of growing tissue. So the placenta steps in and helps the baby boost its game.

A temporary organ that serves as the bridge between mother and fetus, the placenta quickly begins releasing the hormone chorionic gonadotropin, which more powerfully repels the mother's immune system, actually killing vital T-cells. The gonadotropin also triggers the release of the hormone progesterone, which stimulates the growth of feeder capillaries from the placenta outward into the uterus and directs maternal capillaries to grow inward toward the womb in return, rooting the outsider more firmly in the mother's interior and tapping into its energy and nutrient grid. Other hormones expand the diameter of maternal arteries supplying the womb and suppress the mother's ability to regulate blood flow, and with it, her own blood pressure.

At the same time, the placenta begins generating a hormone called placental lactogen, which raises glucose levels in the maternal bloodstream in order to satisfy the nutrient needs of the growing fetus. The mother responds by increasing insulin output—and the fetus sees that and raises it by calling for more glucose. Other proteins pour forth from the placenta that swirl through the mother's bloodstream and dissolve the very calcium in her bones, diverting it to the womb, where the baby takes it up and uses it to build its own skeleton.

The result of all of this is a mother who goes into pregnancy perfectly healthy and approaches the end of it suffering from symptoms of hypertension, diabetes and osteoporosis. Her pelvis will have come unhinged to accommodate the growing baby, her very organs will have repositioned themselves to make room for her swelling womb— the bladder flattening, the intestines compressing. Her breasts are engorged, her abdomen is distended, and the truly grueling finale to it all, labor and childbirth, is still to come. Mom has given all she could, and what her body didn't surrender willingly, the baby simply took. It is a process as selfish as it is involuntary, as heedless as it is mindless. The baby has no idea about the sublime self-centeredness of its own actions. But it's difficult all the same not to see a sort of existential greed in the way a fetus takes hold and grows—and that's a view even scientists find it hard not to take.

Evolutionary biologist David Haig, for one, famously described the

placenta as a "ruthless, parasitic organ existing solely for the mainte-
nance and protection of the fetus, perhaps too often to the disregard
of the maternal organism." It's no wonder, either, that the less scientific but decidedly more readable team of mothers and authors behind
the book *Sh*tty Mom: The Parenting Guide for the Rest of Us* take an
even less sentimental approach: "The first few hours after the baby
comes, you will be in a blurry, ecstatic state, flush with new mama-
love and painkillers. Then the anesthesia and epidural will wear off.
You'll need to pee. The bathroom will be four feet away and you'll
need a walker. During this trek, you will understand that your vagina
is being held together by stitches. If you had a C-section, there is a
thin-lipped smile across your midsection. You will look like what you
are: a childbirth survivor."

And when all this is done—when gestation and childbirth are at last
over—the baby will demand only one thing: to have its every need
tended immediately, fully and around the clock. It feeds every two or
three hours, must be changed a dozen times a day, sleeps sporadically,
cries constantly and brooks absolutely no deviation or delay in the
satisfaction of its needs, on pain of a high-decibel wail evolutionarily
engineered to cut through parents like a knife. As for the needs of the
parents themselves? Please.

"It's an evolutionary imperative for babies to be selfish and narcissistic at birth in order to get their needs met," says developmental
psychologist Mark Barnett of Kansas State University. "They're not
helpless but they are dependent. Life is set up so that they get what
they have to get to survive."

"They want everything you have, and they want it now," write the
Sh*tty Mom moms. "They don't care about ruining your abs or killing
your sex life, and they sure as hell don't give a shit that you only slept
four hours last night. . . . They are the animal kingdom's most mean-
spirited young."

That idea—expressed only slightly more charitably—is one that parents, caregivers and, more recently, parent-bloggers have grown wise to, and they have latched on to an idea that neatly captures it all. "Your Baby Has Narcissistic Personality Disorder" reads the blunt headline of a post on the deliciously named website CrassParenting .com. The headline appears above a picture of a baby in a high chair with a bib around her neck and a spoon hovering at her mouth; she stares at the camera with what looks for all the world like weary disdain. "Have you ever put a baby in front of a mirror?" asks the site's mom-blogger. "They are so self-absorbed. They can look at themselves for hours. . . . They use their mothers as food sources and make them dispose of their waste and dribble. [They literally] crawl over other people." Author Lesley Garner, in her book *Everything I've Ever Learned About Love*, makes the same charge, describing babies as creatures "drawing in love from every source and developmentally incapable of the acts of reaching out, self-restraint and empathy that recognise that they are not the centre of the world."

Early psychologists made the same point, though in a far more arid and academic way. In a 1914 essay appropriately titled "His Majesty the Baby," Sigmund Freud wrote that the earliest stage of a baby's life is defined by what he called "primary narcissism." Freud, of course, who could find sexuality in a bowl of chicken noodle soup, found it here, too. "We call this condition narcissism and this way of obtaining satisfaction auto-eroticism," he wrote. In adolescence, Freud explained, that same auto-eroticism expresses itself far more literally as masturbation, with young teens turning their own bodies into what he termed "love objects"—an idea that to the hormone-addled adolescents themselves would surely qualify as overthinking things a bit.

Freud's followers built on his theories. Hungarian psychologist Sándor Ferenczi described babies as living in a "monistic" world—one in which all things are distilled down to a sensory need to eliminate the unpleasant and acquire the pleasant: exchange the wet diaper for a dry one, a hungry belly for a full one, an empty room for one that has

Mom within it. The idea of "dualism," he wrote—or the ability to tolerate less than optimal circumstances with the understanding that comfort will come eventually—is entirely off the table. The baby's needs are the first concern—and since the baby's survival is on the line, they really should be the only concern.

Twentieth-century Austrian psychologist Melanie Klein was even harder on babies. They are raging megalomaniacs, she believed, consumed by their sense of omnipotence and intolerant of anything that challenges that primacy. She went so far as to label them "paranoid-schizoid," with the paranoid part involving vigilance against harm and the schizoid involving the rejection of the bad and the ravenous pursuit of the good and the comforting.

Calling any of this survival-based behavior true narcissism is, of course, nonsense. Gestation is a mindless process, with the fetus no more consciously running the show than the mother is. And the more sentient baby is similarly moved less by guile and will than by mindless instinct.

But that doesn't mean that the seeds of the behaviors that turn into genuine narcissism aren't scattered throughout the baby's temperament at birth—just like the seeds of other personality disorders are. Babies are crazily histrionic creatures, for example, given to all manner of behavioral extremes. Slowly, over time, they get their emotions in harness. But if they don't—if the same extravagant delight, purple rages and unchecked crying jags that are age-appropriate for the baby persist into adulthood—psychologists would diagnose histrionic personality disorder, which is a whole different matter. Ditto the binary craziness with which small children treat parents, caregivers and other children—clinging or rejecting, hugging or hitting, craving love and attention but growing furious if it doesn't come at exactly the right time and in exactly the right way. That hate-you-love-you whipsaw may play out all the time with kids. But when it's exhibited in an adult, you'd call it borderline personality disorder and you'd truly want no part of it. There's a lot to be learned by watching how all those behaviors are expressed by the baby—and how the kids themselves slowly bring those tendencies under control.

Lack of empathy is easily the most important of these disagreeable traits, and in many ways is the hardest for babies to overcome. Not only does the mind of the infant not allow for considering the feelings of others, it doesn't even fully grasp that people or things exist at all once they pass outside the baby's sight or hearing.

A six-month-old child who drops a spoon from a high-chair will not look down on the floor for it because of the assumption—a perfectly reasonable one from the baby's point of view—that if it's passed out of view, it's passed completely out of the world, so there's no point in trying to pull it back. Infants don't experience separation anxiety the same way toddlers do, for the same reason. Adults are perishable, interchangeable, flashing out of existence like subatomic particles the moment they leave the room, only to be replaced by another particle-person a little while later. Mom and Dad can thus slip out for the evening and leave an infant in the care of a babysitter because Mom and Dad are fungible. A dry diaper, a warm bottle and a long cuddle can be provided by pretty much anyone. But try the same parental date night when the baby is a year or two old and you'll have a howling, shrieking meltdown on your hands.

"This concept of object- or person-permanence doesn't even begin to emerge until the child is about six months old," says Barnett. "That's when kids begin to understand that there are things or people outside of their world and outside of themselves. It's only at that point that they start to get sensitive to others."

But that awakening comes very slowly. Even when children begin to understand that people and objects exist outside of their reach, they still don't grasp the idea that knowledge does, too. Acquiring this so-called theory of mind—the understanding that what's in your head is not necessarily in other people's heads—is a slow slog. In behavioral studies, toddlers who watch an experimenter hide a toy in a cabinet or drawer will automatically assume that anyone who walks in the room later will know where it's hidden, too. The phenomenon becomes even more obvious as children acquire a sophisticated command of language. I would marvel at this assumed familiarity even when my daughters were seven or eight years old and would tell me about a TV show they'd seen that they knew full well I hadn't.

"So the same girl walked in the door as before," one of them would say, "except it was the smaller door and she was wearing red shoes instead of blue and that boy who was mean to her last time is nice." What girl? What door? What mean boy? I could follow her eyes as they flicked around slightly, scanning the TV scene that was clearly still in her head, but I could not begin to follow her story.

When children do start to acquire a theory of mind, it often, encouragingly, shows itself in the first green shoots of empathy—understanding that someone else is sad or suffering even if the children themselves are not. Even then, however, the toddler will behave egocentrically. "A small child will try to comfort his mother the same way he would want to be comforted," Barnett says. "That may mean giving her his teddy bear or some other toy he likes." Funnily, this usually works—though not for the reason the toddler thinks. The naïve tenderness of the gesture will be irresistible to parents and a genuine smile and hug will result. For the toddler, the initial assumption is thus confirmed: Yep, teddy bears make sad moms feel better, too.

Some scientists have observed empathic sparks in babies who are much younger still—in newborns, in fact. At just one or two days old, Barnett says, babies will react differently to the sound of a real baby crying in a nearby crib from how they react to a recording of a cry, even if the two sounds are indistinguishable to the adult ear. The brain, it seems, is hardwired to tease apart the genuine from the counterfeit and to respond more sensitively to one than to the other. And to the extent that babies react at all to a recorded cry, they seem to care less when they hear the sounds of themselves played back to them than they do the sounds of another baby. It's impossible to know why this is so, but it may simply be that they know they're fine themselves—fed and dry and warm for the moment—so they can ignore their own wails. But what about that other suffering child? If narcissism is partly the inability to care about the welfare of someone other than yourself, this kind of sensitivity to the suffering of another person is a first tiny step toward something better and deeper.

"There's a sort of emotional mimicry going on," Barnett says. "Babies take in what another baby is feeling and they mirror it. This isn't true empathy, but it's a start."

That start can turn quickly into something much more complex, as a 2012 study illustrated. Working with a sample group of 824 babies of different ages—fourteen, twenty, twenty-four and thirty-six months old—researchers at the University of Colorado and four other institutions staged little scenes in the lab and in the babies' homes, designed to trigger whatever empathic capacity the children had. In the course of the experiment, both the mothers of the babies and a researcher would fake a minor injury of some kind—banging a knee, tripping over a chair, slamming a hand in a drawer or pinching a finger in a clipboard. The adults were told to pantomime pain for sixty seconds, but not to engage the babies directly in any way.

Broadly, the babies would respond in one of several ways: Sometimes they'd simply approach the injured person and watch with what appeared to be concern, sometimes they'd offer verbal comfort and sometimes physical—patting the pinched finger or the bumped knee. They might also take a punitive—if still indirectly empathic— approach, hitting the drawer or chair that caused the accident. In the less empathic alternative, they might run away or simply laugh. In general, the older the children got the likelier they were to react empathically, with the kind of help they offered—from staring to verbally soothing to offering hands-on comforting—growing more sophisticated, too. But the empathy arc wasn't smooth. A wild card in the children's behavior was verbal skill.

The higher the babies scored on a language test taken before the experiment began, the likelier they were to be capable of an empathic response. In general, girls scored higher on both metrics than boys, which would hardly come as a surprise to parents who have long observed that their daughters acquire language earlier than their sons and tend to show more compassion, too. But the larger rule—speech breeds empathy—applied to both sexes in the study. "Talking about feelings is a way of modeling them," says Barnett. "Even without thinking about this, parents seem to know it instinctively, which is why when they read a storybook to a small child they'll so often discuss the feelings of the characters. Children who can describe the feelings can understand and communicate them better."

LACK OF EMPATHY is hardly the only thing that makes most babies unalloyed narcissists—even if they're age-appropriate narcissists. Lack of impulse control contributes too, and indeed, that one's a lot harder to overcome. The empathic response comes on kids slowly, usually with little effort, and it costs them nothing to act on it; indeed, parents may reward them when they do. Impulse control is a whole different matter.

The ability to want something and not take it—or at least to put off taking it—is something human beings struggle with their entire lives. Play must come second to work, gluttony must yield to restraint, and all manner of other pleasures must be passed up entirely if they violate marriage vows, the law or simple common sense. None of that is easy, and we often fail at it miserably.

"The heart wants what it wants," said Woody Allen in a supremely narcissistic moment, as he blithely explained away his decision to ditch his longtime partner, Mia Farrow, in favor of her twenty-one-year-old daughter, Soon-Yi Previn.

"Well, that's what I did," is how Ponzi king Bernie Madoff shrugged it off to a fellow inmate who offered the hard-to-argue-with opinion that stealing money from old ladies was a "fucked-up thing to do." Both Madoff and Allen wanted and they took. Full stop.

The idea that desire equals license is something that comes factory-loaded in all of us, and is the reason babies are not just sad or disappointed when they're denied something, but downright furious. They are moved equally by the fact that they want the cookie they've got their eye on and the belief they have a right to the cookie—are *owed* the cookie—and woe betide the person who tries to deny it to them. And as for asking babies to police themselves—to keep their hands off the plate of snacks or their playmate's belongings? Not a chance. The heart wants what it wants.

It was in the 1960s that Stanford University psychologist Walter Mischel first conducted his landmark study in impulse control that became simply and universally known as "the marshmallow test." Working with a sample group of four-year-olds, he offered each of the kids a deal: They could have one marshmallow right away or, if they waited fifteen minutes while he stepped out to run an errand, they could have two upon his return. When he did leave the room, he left the single marshmallow on a plate in easy reach of the child.

A remarkable two-thirds of the four-year-olds held out for the full fifteen minutes—but it wasn't easy. They distracted themselves by singing, talking aloud, looking away from the marshmallow or even covering their eyes entirely. When Mischel returned, they got the promised reward. Maybe the kids who succeeded at the test were innately strong-willed, or maybe they got lucky that once, but if it was indeed luck that was involved, the experience taught them an indelible lesson. When Mischel and his colleagues followed up with the same children fourteen years later, around the time of their high school graduation, he found that the ones who did well on the marshmallow experiment scored higher on behavioral tests that measured assertiveness, social effectiveness and the ability to cope with frustration. They also scored, on average, 210 points higher on their SATs than the kids who'd jumped at the single marshmallow so many years earlier.

Contemporary studies have expanded on Mischel's work, using a toy instead of a marshmallow, and testing kids at a variety of ages, though mercifully making them endure just three minutes of waiting instead of fifteen. The difference just a few months of maturation made was remarkable: At 18 months old, the babies were able to hold out for just ten seconds before they caved in and grabbed the toy. At 24 months, they made it for a minute; at 30 months they got to two and a half minutes. Not until they were 36 months old, however, did they last the full three minutes. Breaking down the numbers, the researchers found that any one child will gain about two seconds of impulse control for every month of age.

It's not just automatic maturation that strengthens the restraint muscles. Parental teaching and social learning play a role, too. In a 2012 study, a team led by cognitive scientist Celeste Kidd of the University of Rochester reran the marshmallow test but divided the kids into two groups: those who had been conditioned to believe that the researchers were honest and that their word could be trusted, and those who were given reason to doubt that. The effectiveness of the marshmallow test, after all, rests on the children being able to trust that if they resist eating the solitary treat, the experimenter will come back and make good on the bargain they struck. That kind of constancy is a feature of some kids' worlds much more than it is of others'—and outside the lab, that can make a very big difference in cognitive development.

"Consider the mind-set of a four-year-old living in a crowded shelter, surrounded by older children with little adult supervision," Kidd and her colleagues wrote. "For a child accustomed to stolen possessions and broken promises, the only guaranteed treats are the ones you have already swallowed."

To test this premise, the researchers recruited twenty-eight children between three and six years of age, all from stable homes. The first step of the two-part study was a priming exercise. The kids were all presented with either a small, half-used set of crayons or a solitary sticker. Both groups were told that if they didn't touch those rather modest art supplies for a few minutes, the researcher would return with a whole carousel of crayons and brushes or whole sheets of colorful stickers. In some cases, when the researchers returned, they delivered the goods as promised; in others, they returned with nothing but an apology: "I'm sorry, I made a mistake," they'd say. "We don't have any more supplies after all. But why don't you just use the ones you have instead."

All of the kids then took the marshmallow test—and, perhaps no surprise, the ones who had learned in the earlier exercise that the researchers could be trusted showed much better impulse control than the ones who hadn't. In the group that had learned to trust, the median wait time before giving in and scarfing up the solitary marshmallow was a respectable 12 minutes and 2 seconds. In the unreliable group, it was just 3 minutes and 2 seconds.

Admittedly, this is only the poorest approximation of the larger world. It takes just a single broken promise from a researcher in a lab for a child to conclude that that same adult is not to be trusted. It's hardly as straightforward a thing for a child in a shelter or an unstable home to reach a broader conclusion—that the lessons of unreliability they learn where they live are applicable to other situations in life. Still, kids do make that leap, and when they do, impulse control can be powerfully affected.

THE HANDMAIDEN of both lack of empathy and lack of impulse control is lack of remorse. It's hard to be a successful glutton for goodies or manipulator of people if you constantly feel lousy afterward about what you've done. Better to remain numb to the wrongness of your behavior if you plan to keep it up. Both children and narcissistic adults feel bad when they're punished, but non-narcissists may feel bad beforehand, too.

When Rhett Butler is attempting to comfort the sublimely narcissistic—and quite drunk—Scarlett O'Hara in *Gone With the Wind*, as she confesses her fear that she's going to hell for one of her many bad acts, he laughs knowingly. "If you had it to do all over again, you'd do it no differently," he says. "You're like the thief who isn't the least bit sorry he stole but he's terribly, terribly sorry he's going to jail."

Real-world narcissists and nearly all kids are gifted practitioners of this kind of too-late contrition, remaining wholly untroubled by their bad behavior unless they've gotten caught. Even then, they flip the victim script, claiming not only that they have done nothing wrong but that a powerful injustice is being done to them. It's no coincidence that the outraged cry of *unfair!* is such a common refrain when small children are being marched off to a well-deserved time-out. In the grown-up narcissist, the lament remains the same.

"How could they do this to me?" demanded John Edwards of his staff when he first saw the *National Enquirer* story reporting—accurately—that he had cheated on his cancer-stricken wife. "How could they fucking say this?"

Richard Nixon made the same point in a more maudlin way during his teary farewell to his White House staff after he resigned the presidency in 1974. "Always remember that others may hate you but those who hate you don't win unless you hate them. And then you destroy yourself," he counseled. They were words better suited to a president who had been unjustly hounded from office by a vindictive mob, rather than to a man who had engineered his own destruction by his own criminal acts.

And then—again and always—there's Madoff. "Fuck my victims," he said in an interview from prison with *New York* magazine in June 2010, slightly less than a year after he received his 150-year sentence. "I carried them for 20 years and now I'm doing 150 years."

It would be an unusual child who would frame things precisely Madoff's way, but Bernie and the baby nonetheless see the world similarly—even if the baby grows out of it. A wonderfully revealing study conducted in 2009 by University of Iowa developmental psychologist Grazyna Kochanska explored just how—and how early—toddlers display remorse, and what they do to manage those feelings.

Kochanska and her colleagues assembled a sample group of fifty-seven children, all roughly two years old, and gave each one a toy. The children were told that the toy was exceedingly special, that it belonged to the experimenter and that she had had it since she herself was a baby. That was not true. In fact, the toy was special in just one way: it was rigged to break into pieces the second the child touched it. When it did fall apart, the experimenter would respond with a carefully calibrated expression of distress—saying only "Oh my," which was just enough to confirm that, yes, something bad had happened, but not enough to have much influence on how the babies responded.

For the next sixty seconds, the researcher would simply watch. Some of the children would seem untroubled, playing with the remains of the toy, apparently indifferent to its condition. Others would be more visibly upset, covering their eyes, turning away from the researcher, hugging themselves for comfort. It was, in some ways, a nasty bit of research, and after it was published in the *Journal of Personality and Social Psychology* and later written up in *The New York Times*, the online reaction was scathing.

"Ethics research that is itself unethical," wrote one angry reader. "Let's make babies feel bad!"

"The experimenters would not be permitted to slap the toddlers, so why is it all right for them to inflict emotional pain?" wrote another.

For those babies, the long minute of suffering was indeed no fun, but it did end, and it was followed by an equally staged absolution. The experimenter would collect the pieces of the toy and leave the room saying she was going to see if she might be able to fix it. She would then return happily with a duplicate toy, this one in perfect working order.

Significantly, Kochanska's work, like Mischel's, did not conclude with just a single trial. She kept up with her subjects, checking back in with them when they were seven years old. Those who had shown the most discomfort during the exercise also later exhibited the fewest behavioral and academic problems. Those who had shrugged off the guilt of the busted toy were more likely to shrug off the idea of breaking broader social rules, too. That says a lot about the adaptive value of guilt and shame. Both feel lousy, but they're supposed to—and they wouldn't have the civilizing power they do if they didn't hurt.

"I believe guilt has gotten a bad rap over the years," says Barnett, "provided you don't overdo it."

THE NARCISSISM that babies exhibit, of course, is a much simpler, coarser kind than what shows up in adults, and in the majority of kids, it's a phase that usually passes—but it can take time. I may never have gotten the chance to follow through on my planned attack on the bald stranger, but there was nothing to stop me from later committing the Great Ant Slaughter of the kitchen steps. One afternoon in my pre-K years, I was sitting on the concrete stoop outside our kitchen door, playing with a little toy dinosaur—a plastic stegosaur that fit comfortably in my very small hand. I looked at the pitted surface of the steps and noticed a swarm of ants racing around it.

I contemplated them for a moment, and something about the three orders of scale intrigued me. I was a giant compared with the stegosaur; the stegosaur was a giant compared with the ants. Disparity in size means disparity in power, and I began to exercise that considerable difference, crushing the ants individually under one of the flat, plastic feet of the stegosaur. I don't know how many ants I killed that day, but the attention span of a child being a fleeting thing, I probably lost interest after wiping out only a small share of them and then moved on to less murderous play.

It was only in later years that I became troubled by what I'd done that day, which in some ways had things backward. When I was a child, I assumed ants had fears and feelings and some capacity for grieving their dead, even if it was all a lot simpler than ours. It was only in later years that I came to the understanding that awareness and emotion are much more complicated concepts, and if ants are conscious at all—which is not a certain thing—it would be only in the most flickering way. Yet it's now that I wince at what I did and it was then—when I assumed I was causing deep suffering—that I didn't care.

Somewhere along the way I went from a coldly curious being to one with a more complex capacity for shame and regret and respect for others—even insectile others. That doesn't make me unusual or remarkable. Indeed, what is unusual and remarkable is when that transition does not occur. But it often doesn't—and when that happens, more than a swarm of ants suffers.

CHAPTER THREE

The Narcissists Break Free

Science will never want to study Charlie Sheen's brain. It would not look very different from any other human brain—three pounds or so of wrinkled, grayish-white tissue about the size of a cantaloupe. Somewhere, invisibly encoded in its trillions of neural connections, would be the circuitry that makes Sheen the deft comic actor he is. Somewhere, too, would be the wiring that makes him a drinker and drug abuser. And somewhere else would be the circuits that make him a narcissist.

There's no telling simply by looking exactly how any of that wiring got laid down in the first place—genes, environment, some combination of both—any more than looking at the lines of code in a piece of software would tell you how they were composed or who typed them in. But neither the computer nor the brain could operate the way either does without such primal circuitry.

Sheen's narcissism was on jaw-dropping display in 2011, after he had undergone another in a series of rehab stints—his third in twelve months—and begun feuding with his onetime creative partner Chuck Lorre, the producer of his still-popular TV show, *Two and a Half Men*. Sheen took their private quarrel public, granting a round of interviews in which he described his former friend as "a clown," "a punk" and a "stupid, stupid little man." The thing about producers, however, is that they're also employers, and Lorre did what any boss would do if someone who worked for him called him a stupid, stupid little man, which is to say he fired him.

The ordinary employee might have known that was coming and might have avoided saying something so provocative, or at least, having said it, might apologize and plead for the public's forgiveness—to say nothing of his boss's. But Sheen wasn't ordinary. He was special, he was different, and he went on national TV to say so—a multiday spectacle that was equal parts train wreck, performance art and a sort of field guide to the narcissistic personality.

"I'm sorry, man, but I've got magic. I've got poetry in my fingertips," Sheen said at the opening of one of his media sit-downs. "I'm different. I have a different constitution, I have a different heart. . . . I'm tired of pretending I'm not special. I'm tired of pretending I'm not a total bitchin' rock star from Mars."

Sheen's misbehavior was not his own fault, he explained, it was the fault of the other, smaller people in his life. As with all great men, it was his curse and burden that he was forced to move among them. "Look at what I'm dealing with, man. I'm dealing with fools and trolls," he said. "They lay down with their ugly wives and their ugly children and just look at their loser lives and then they look at me and say, 'I can't process it.'"

There were a lot of other things Sheen explained about himself as well. Never mind his history of substance abuse, for example, he didn't really need rehab. AA was "the work of sissies," he said, "people that don't have tiger blood and Adonis DNA." Never mind, too, the seemingly manic nature of his behavior—which looked for all the world like the impulsive outbursts of a man at the high end of a bipolar cycle. "Wow. What does that mean? I'm bi-*winning*." He had survived all of his years of high living and hard partying—so far, at least—for a very

simple reason: "Because I'm me. I'm different. I have a different brain."
And about that brain—that melon-sized mass of gray-white tissue that
would look more or less like anyone else's? "If you borrowed my brain
for five seconds, you'd be like, 'Dude! Can't handle it, unplug this bastard!' It fires away in a way that's maybe not from, uh, this terrestrial
realm."

It's easy to take shots at Sheen. For narcissism researchers he's a
piece of decidedly low-hanging fruit. But Sheen is in some ways as
special as he says—a uniquely good lab rat for his particular psychic
affliction. He has a brother and he has a father, after all—Emilio Estevez and Martin Sheen; they're both actors like Charlie, they're both
famous like Charlie and they're both rich like Charlie. Martin was
once even a drunk like Charlie. But Martin has been sober for more
than twenty years, and both he and Estevez have distinguished themselves as well-behaving family men—model Hollywood citizens, with
no rap sheets, no TV rants, no claims of special brains or special blood.
So what made the difference? What kept father and brother grounded
while Charlie went up in a ball of self-adoring smoke?

Across families, across industries, anywhere narcissists roam, that
question regularly arises. Why do similar causes, similar circumstances, give rise to radically different effects? You can be a political
wunderkind like Marco Rubio—a young senator from Florida and
possible presidential candidate who works hard, minds his manners
and in his first several years in Washington deflected any questions
about his future with all the right "I'm just focusing on serving my
state" demurrals. Or you can be Sarah Palin, a rare and incandescent
talent who burst on the national stage, grew seduced by her crowds and
consumed by her approval ratings, and seemed wholly uninterested in
the briefing-book drudgery of actually learning how to govern.

You can be a National Football League flameout like Ryan Leaf,
the number two player picked in the 1998 draft, who was out of the
league entirely by 2002 after four years of indifference, poor play and

multiple ugly public incidents including an infamous moment, caught on videotape, in which he stood over a frightened-looking sports-writer who had apparently asked the wrong question, screaming, "Just fucking don't talk to me, all right? Knock it off!" Or you can be Super Bowl winner Peyton Manning, picked number one in the same year Leaf was drafted, who has spent the better part of two decades winning games and smashing records and whose only scandalous moment in his long career was . . . well, never mind. There never was one.

So what makes the difference between a Palin and a Rubio, a Leaf and a Manning, a Sheen and, say, a Michael J. Fox—whose nice-guy image was established back in the days of his star turns on TV's *Family Ties* and in the *Back to the Future* movies, and whose grace in battling Parkinson's disease has simply confirmed the high opinion most of the world had of him? Genes, certainly, may play a role. Nearly all psychological disorders have some heritability component. For obsessive-compulsive disorder—one of the best studied and most easily diagnosable anxiety conditions—the average incidence in the population is about 3 percent. If you have any blood relative at all with OCD, your probability quadruples to 12 percent. If both parents are obsessive-compulsive, the risk ticks up again, to 20 percent. And if you're part of an identical twin pair and your matching sibling has OCD, your risk is as high as 47 percent. For depression, the heritability numbers are similarly high: 42 percent for women in a family in which depression is common and 29 percent for men, according to a 2006 study by Virginia Commonwealth University.

And narcissism? Is there such a thing as self-adoration genes? A 2000 study conducted by the University of Oslo compared the incidence of all the conditions in a large sample group of identical and fraternal twins—which is almost the perfect way to test for these things. Twins who grow up in the same household have more or less matching environments throughout their childhoods—born into exactly the same family circumstances and typically leaving home at exactly the same time, eighteen years later. If environment were the only determinant of narcissism, then in nearly all cases both twins either would or would not have the condition, and that would be true of both identicals and fraternals. But if genes play a role too, identical twins should be more similar to each other than fraternals—either for better or for worse. Just how much more similar is the measure of the condition's heritability.

The Oslo researchers found that the average heritability of all of the personality disorders was 58 percent, but condition by condition the scores were very different. Paranoia was the least heritable of the group, with genes conferring a 30 percent increased risk. Schizoid and avoidant personalities were next at 31 percent. Dependent personality disorder clocked in at 55 percent, histrionic at 67 percent and borderline at 69 percent. Narcissism was near the top, with a whopping 77 percent heritability, second only to rigidity and perfectionism, at 78 percent. An earlier, more frequently cited study from 1993 pegged the heritability of all of the disorders a bit lower, but put narcissism at the very top this time, at 64 percent.

Results like that seem awfully conclusive, but not everyone is sold on such deterministic numbers. "There are no biological determinants for narcissism," says social psychologist Jerome Kagan of Harvard University, "none that are known, at least."

Kagan bases his beliefs on a range of factors. For starters, the twin studies gather their raw data via questionnaires, which rely on the subjects to rate themselves and, harder still, to do so honestly. This is true no matter who the subjects are, but when they're twins things can get skewed further, since fraternal siblings, as a rule, try harder to distinguish themselves from each other than identical twins do, and that response bias may show up in their answers.

What's more, Kagan says, in genetic studies, in which actual genes as opposed to mere behaviors are identified, biological heritability rarely turns out to account for more than 10 percent of the variability in any trait—a statistical light-year from the supposed 77 percent in the case of narcissism.

Kagan, however, has his own doubters. Steven Pinker, professor of psychology at Harvard University and author of numerous books, including *The Better Angels of Our Nature*, defends research based on questionnaires—and for good reason. It may lack the empirical absoluteness of, say, a blood test, but it is a powerful tool psychologists have used for generations, and has built up a robust record for reliability. Throw out the questionnaires and you gut well-proven science.

Pinker also believes Kagan has it wrong when it comes to the 10 percent variability determined by genes. "Gene-hunting studies cannot identify genes which collectively account for more than 10 percent of the variance in a trait," he says. "But that doesn't mean that the heritability of it is 10 percent; it just means that there is 'missing heritability,'" explained by a long tail of common genes, each with tiny effects, which collectively can add up to a big effect.

Still, whether the influence of genes is great or small, they will always be only part of the narcissism mix, as Sheen's florid narcissism so vividly suggests: If genetics were all there was to it, his father or his brother would be struggling with the condition as well—especially with an ostensible heritability as high as 77 percent.

Upbringing is the next big x-factor in planting the seeds of narcissism. Since the days of Freud, psychologists have argued about what role parents play in shaping the self-adoring personality. Freud and his adherents, even comparatively modern ones, belong to what is known as the mask model school of thought: The self-adoring narcissistic pose, they say, is adopted as a way to conceal its exact opposite—feelings of deep worthlessness and self-loathing. Such shattered self-esteem, according to those thinkers, is not congenital but instead is painfully and perhaps permanently learned.

"Narcissistic personality disorder is likely to develop if parents are neglectful, devaluing or unempathetic to the child," wrote celebrated

Austrian psychoanalyst and theorist Heinz Kohut, who studied medicine at the University of Vienna in the 1930s, during the hothouse years of Freudianism. "This individual will be perpetually searching for affirmation of an idealized and grandiose sense of self."

The mask model has never gone completely away—indeed, it retains a lot of believers. As recently as 2008, a multi-institute study led by psychologist Jennifer Bosson of the University of South Florida took a long historical look at the mask-model theory in the journal *Social and Personality Psychology Compass* and concluded that while there are other ways to explain the clinically narcissistic personality, it's hard to get away entirely from the idea that narcissists are urgently, almost desperately, trying to cover up something else.

"The mask model offers an appealing answer to why narcissists behave as they do," she wrote. "Narcissists self-aggrandize, manipulate, derogate and exploit because deep down inside they actually dislike themselves. Not only does this answer make intuitive sense to many, it also fits nicely with current thinking about people's introspective access to their own inner selves."

Nothing in David Letterman's biography suggests that he suffered through the kind of esteem-crushing parental behavior that leads to mask-model narcissism, but nothing in his adult life suggests he is a particularly happy man, either. For someone fabulously rich and fabulously famous to be fabulously grim or dissatisfied in private is not unusual—plenty of celebrities are living lives of solitary crankiness or even depression. But Letterman—with his widely discussed reclusiveness and his wildly public life and career—seems to capture that teeter-totter existence better than most, and to suffer a fair bit of self-loathing in the bargain.

There is a much-told story from early in Letterman's career—in the 1980s, during his phase as both cult phenomenon and rising star—when actress Teri Garr was appearing on his show. During a commercial break, Garr asked him how he was doing but had to shout to be heard over the studio band. Letterman, rather than shouting back, scribbled his answer on a piece of paper. "I hate myself," he wrote. Garr demurred, reassuring him that he was a talented and good man. He took the paper back and simply underlined his original statement—twice.

Mask-model narcissism can arise in another, more sudden way—though one that doesn't exactly fit with Letterman's backstory, either. Sometimes, psychologists argue, a person who's already narcissistically predisposed may be tipped over the edge by a single setback—a defeat or disappointment that so deeply touched who they are and how they define themselves that they may spend much of the rest of their lives trying to fill the hole that's left. This so-called narcissistic wound is sustained by a lot of people. Think of the high school basketball star who never even makes the college team, a disappointment that puts his dreams of a pro career—and his vision of himself as someone special—forever out of reach. Think of the young novelist whose first book is blistered by critics and who never writes again. Maybe they adjust and learn, maybe they move on to something else—or maybe they do neither.

"No matter how much we want to achieve, sometimes the world doesn't cooperate," says Penn State psychologist Aaron Pincus. "A nonpathological person knows how to respond, channeling those disappointments and frustrations into socially acceptable ways of coping—I'll try harder, I'll learn more. Pathological narcissists fall apart. They lack a resilience, and that's when psychotherapists see them."

Other theorists reject the mask and wound models entirely, believing that narcissism stems from a completely opposite dynamic. Far from being denied praise and applause, they say, narcissists get so much validation and enjoy so much success early in life that they are gobsmacked later when they enter a world that doesn't think they're entitled to still more. That idea is consistent with the likes of Sheen, who grew up as Hollywood royalty, thanks to his father's stardom, and got waved into his own acting career when he was just nine years old, making a brief appearance in one of his father's movies. It's certainly consistent with real royals, particularly of the British variety—a group of cosseted kids who spend their childhoods indulged and adored and who may become modest, well-behaving adults (think Prince William), but who just as often go on to make a hash of their lives—at least early on—with all manner of scandalous and even illegal behavior. Will's little brother, Prince Harry, didn't get photographed naked in a Las Vegas hotel room in the company of multiple women because of a *lack* of self-esteem or entitlement. He didn't wear a Nazi uniform to a costume party—complete with a swastika—because he assumed he was subject to the same standards of social opprobrium as everyone else.

It is also of a piece with the disproportionately high number of sports stars who wind up getting arrested on DWI, drug or domestic abuse charges—and are often arrested again and again, particularly in the National Football League. Spend your early life getting waved through high school, then college and on into the pros, often earning credit for classes you barely attend, much less pass, and it's no wonder you develop a sense that you live outside the rules. Quarterback bust Ryan Leaf, like most highly sought athletes, received a lucrative signing bonus just for agreeing to terms with his team—collecting $11.25 million and becoming instantly wealthy before he had ever done a single day of paying work in his chosen career.

So bad has the professional football crime wave become that *The San Diego Union-Tribune* has actually launched an NFL Arrests Database, which it updates every time a player is busted for any offense more serious than driving over the speed limit. You can organize your search by name, team, position or incident—and it's handy to have those kinds of tools available, since from 2000 through 2012 alone there were 623 entries, or a tidy 48 busts per year. And while the NFL and other sports leagues may eventually tame some of the narcissists on their rosters, they typically have a harder time than any other industry, including Hollywood—and with good reason.

"A key dimension of narcissism," says psychologist Brad Bushman of Ohio State University, "is believing you're better-looking and more athletically gifted than others." Bushman overstates his case a bit here. Plenty of people become full-blown narcissists without a lick of athletic ability, or a lick of self-deluded belief that they have any. But if athleticism and physical attractiveness are on the table at all—if narcissists can make even a colorable case that they possess those attributes—they'll simply roll them into their larger collection of natural gifts. For pro athletes there's no such self-delusion necessary. They are indeed the most physically talented person in almost any room they enter, and they're often the most gorgeous, too. Any wonder so many of them come to grief?

Then, too, there's the possibility that a combination of both kinds of parental malfeasance is responsible for narcissism in kids. A trio of studies in 2006 that analyzed both the current personalities and developmental pasts of college-age narcissists found that a significant number of the subjects reported having been raised by parents who both praised them too much and appeared to love them too little—applauding their accomplishments and indulging their wishes, but never really showing them terribly much warmth or quiet attention. The children thus got conflicting—indeed, wholly contradictory—messages about their worth and grew up in a state of ego paradox, uncertain if they are greater or lesser than other people, and thus exhibiting both the entitlement of kids who think they're better than others and the mask-model overcompensation of people with low self-esteem. The children of Tiger Moms like Amy Chua could become the living examples of this push-and-pull, turning into miserable, double-dip narcissists—even if they can play Rachmaninoff when they're still in preschool.

———

ALL OF THESE narcissistic x-factors have always been around. Our genes have been part of us since we were pond bacteria. Parents have either pampered or mistreated kids as long as they've been having them. And the world has always been filled with the privileged and entitled—pharaohs had royal children, Greece had temperamental actors, Rome had NFL-class gladiators. So what's behind the modern narcissism boom?

For starters, it's not so modern. It's been coming, by some estimates, for about six centuries. "If you take just the last 600 years of human history, we've gone from communal, religious societies to individualistic, secular ones," says Kagan. "First comes Martin Luther, then comes Adam Smith, then the Declaration of Independence, then diverse societies like the U.S. and Europe, where nobody can agree on the same set of values."

It's not for nothing, Kagan argues, that the United States, the most powerful and prosperous country in the history of the world, established life, liberty and the pursuit of happiness as among its highest aspirations—compared with Canada's much more modest "peace, order and good government." It's not for nothing either that our guiding philosophy was adopted by so many of the younger democracies that followed. "If you can count on one thing in the human genome," Kagan says, "it's that everyone wants to know that they're ahead and winning."

In the United States, the past sixty years have turbocharged our me-first tendencies. American babies born just after World War II were not around for any of the sacrifice or sorrow that came with that years-long bloodbath, but they surely enjoyed its fruits. The U.S. industrial engine emerged from the war intact—indeed, bigger and more productive than it had ever been, thanks to the military manufacturing boom that began after Pearl Harbor—while the factories and distribution chains of other countries, even victorious ones like the UK and the USSR, were smashed to rubble. The GI Bill guaranteed college, jobs and easy access to mortgages for returning vets, and a fat and happy population did what fat and happy populations have always done throughout history, which is to say they bred—a lot. Young American couples cranked out 78.3 million babies from 1946 to 1964 and had everything they needed to raise them well. There was plenty of food, there were plenty of toys, the bills were always current and Dad always had a good-paying job.

The wealth that kept the kids in relative splendor and the increasingly liberal parenting that followed from raising them in safe, suburban paddocks found a perfect voice in pediatrician Benjamin Spock, whose mega-bestseller *The Common Sense Book of Baby and Child Care*, published the very year the Baby Boom began, set the tone for how so many of those new and privileged arrivals would be reared. The book's kindest and most confidence-boosting line was directed at mothers specifically and promised them simply: "You know more than you think you do." And what mothers knew better than anything, Spock argued, was that babies are very much individuals, ones who deserve to be heard, understood, and deeply, richly loved. That idea seems head-scratchingly obvious now, but it was a huge departure from an era in which the first job of any parent was simply to feed and manage the kids—disciplining them, instructing them and letting the love leak into the spaces that were left.

Spock blew up all that old thinking. Indeed, never mind fears of spoiling kids, he was not above indulging them, provided that it was done in the right ways and at the right moments. "Perhaps a child who is fussed over gets a feeling of destiny," Spock argued. "He thinks he is in the world for something important, and it gives him drive and confidence."

Spock's detractors—and there were plenty—skewered him for beliefs like these. This was exactly the kind of thinking, they argued, that would give rise to a generation of self-adoring princesses and princelings, children driven more by their impulses and pleasures than by a larger sense of community, sacrifice and responsibility, and they would pass the same values on to their own children. During the social and sexual upheaval of the 1960s and 1970s—led by those same Spock kids—the critics thought their case had been made. But the young Boomers who had such a ribald and rollicking time during the Summers of Love grew up to be much more conservative and traditional than anyone reckoned. They surrendered to the gravity of community, coalescing into just the kinds of nuclear families their parents had created and producing up to 80 million babies—or Echo Boomers—of their own.

To the extent that Baby Boomers carried anything with them from their militant and hedonistic past, it was, in some cases at least, an elevated sense of selflessness, perhaps nurtured in the social justice and civil rights struggles that defined their age. Retired professor Robert Mosier of the University of Wisconsin–Stevens Point studied the Boomer generation and divided it into two groups: early Boomers, born from 1943 to 1960, and late Boomers, born in the narrower window of 1960 to 1965. On the whole, he found that while a fair swath of both groups grew up materialistic and ambitious—becoming the often insufferable yuppies of the 1980s and the Wall Street sharks of the last two decades—they also excelled at teamwork, were more involved in parenting than their own parents had been and were more inclined to enter the helping professions, creating an entire industry of neighborhood medical clinics, legal aid offices and public-interest research groups that barely existed before they came along. It was the Echo Boomers who became the real heirs to the me-first lives that people predicted for their parents, and perhaps the biggest reason is also a very simple one: play—or the lack of it.

Get a group of Baby Boomers talking and they will inevitably begin going on about the sweetly feral nature of their youth. Their neighborhoods, they will tell you, were multifamily playgrounds. The kids would swarm from their houses on weekend mornings, pedal away on their bikes together, return home at midday for a bowl of soup and a grilled cheese sandwich, and then scatter again till just before sundown. There were no GPS trackers clipped to their bikes, no cellphone check-ins every hour, and there were surely no parents puffing along on bikes behind them, hollering at them to put on their knee pads, buckle their helmets and quit wiping off the sunscreen already.

The recollections are real, as far as they go, and so are the chills they give parents today. The fact is, a child without a helmet and pads is a lot likelier to wind up in an emergency room than a well-protected one. And while child abductions are still mercifully rare, once the face-on-a-milk-carton trend got started after the kidnapping and killing of six-year-old Etan Patz in New York City in 1979, parents were determined to reduce that low risk of tragedy to something closer to zero. But something was lost in all that protectiveness. Once impromptu play was transformed into the playdate, once pickup games were codified into soccer leagues and independent exploration became the guided hike with the trail-safety ranger, the civilizing power of wild play was lost.

"Social play is the most egalitarian activity people ever engage in," says psychologist and child development specialist Peter Gray of Boston College. "Play, by definition, is cooperative and collective. It's always voluntary, which means you're free to quit if you're not happy. What's more, if you don't treat your playmates well, they're free to quit on you, too."

That kind of unspoken behavioral contract creates a sort of low-level tension in any playgroup—but it's a socializing tension. In a Little League game, with adults on the sidelines and first place in the division at stake, you press your competitive advantage whenever you can. A pitcher facing a weak hitter is supposed to bear down and throw heat, looking for a quick out before moving on to the bigger bat in the on-deck circle. In a pickup game, a smart pitcher does just the opposite.

"If a little kid comes up to bat you pitch more softly, which you have to do or all the little kids would leave and then the game would be over," says Gray. "You care less about winning than having fun—and having fun means you have to keep the other kids engaged."

Those younger children get a different kind of socialization in return. Not only do they learn what fair play looks like, they learn that there are limits imposed on their own behavior. Throw a tantrum at home and you'll either get your way or you won't, but the worst that will happen is you'll be sent to your room; your parents are hardly going to banish you from the family. Do the same in a voluntary game and banishment is a real possibility. "Kids learn that there are consequences to losing control of themselves," Gray says. "They learn to perceive the needs of other people and to contain their own emotions and conduct."

Then, too, there's the lesson of collaboration. Parents applaud a child who can play quietly and alone for hours—lost in a fantasy world of her own creation. My younger daughter has always been a bit better at that than my older daughter, and after she has emerged from her room following a long solo play session, I'll sometimes go discreetly in and look at the little world she's built—with the Polly Pockets figurines lined up in parade formation, a couple of Barbies sitting at a tea table, even a Little People farmhouse from her first-grade days pressed into service as scene setting—and try a little fantasy forensics to see if I can figure out what kind of story she has dreamed up. I dare not ask—or even worse, look in on her while she's playing—lest, like Schrödinger, I kill the cat.

But that mistress-of-the-universe ethos is exactly what's not called for in group play, in which individual identity must be secondary to collective identity, and solo goals must give way to group goals. Yes, the very same collective values are stressed in organized, adult-supervised play—the no-I-in-team bromide, the eternally repeated refrain that sportsmanship and fair play are more important than winning. But the very fact that those ideas are being taught makes the lessons far less powerful than ones acquired on the fly. "It's much more effective to learn these things on your own than to have them taught by a coach," Gray says.

Gray's thinking runs well beyond the boundaries of childhood. Egalitarian play, he believes, builds egalitarian cultures—even if they're not the kinds of cultures we consider mainstream. In the world's surviving hunter-gatherer societies—particularly the !Kung of the Kalahari, the Hadza of the Tanzanian rain forest and the Aché of eastern Paraguay—he sees the fingerprints and the rewards of play especially vividly.

Hunting in hunter-gatherer societies, for example, is framed as a voluntary activity—something enjoyable and exciting but not mandatory. Stay home and you still get to share in the catch, with no social opprobrium attached. Competitive games popular in the developed world don't exist in the hunter-gatherer culture, Gray reports; in their place are more collaborative ones. When the occasional field scientist has tried to introduce soccer to the tribes, the game quickly devolves into a group exercise in which all of the players stand around in a circle and pass the ball from foot to foot, trying to keep it aloft for as long as possible.

Playful teasing is a central part of hunter-gatherer dynamics too, valued for its ability to humble the vain and empower the weak—and the expectation is that the target of the teasing will laugh along. Indeed, a member of a hunter-gatherer band who has particular reason to preen—for bagging an especially big animal, say—will be the likeliest target of a leveling round of teasing. Gray cites the writings of Canadian anthropologist Richard Lee, who became famous for his in-depth studies of the !Kung. To thank the band that had been so welcoming to him during his time in the field, he bought them a 1,200-pound ox for a grand feast, and expected a grand round of thanks in return. He didn't get it. The tribe instead laughed at the gift, describing it as "a bag of bones," with nothing edible on it but the horns—then fell to and ate it with just the gusto Lee had hoped they would. Their gratitude was expressed in their behavior, not in their words. To the !Kung, the teasing had been genuinely funny—and genuinely important—and if Lee had been a tribesman, he'd have thought so, too.

"Hunter-gatherers grow up to be people who are the opposite of narcissists," Gray says. "They've taken the human propensity for play and enhanced it in a way that's essential to their way of life. Our human ancestors were so focused on achieving dominance that they could never engage in this kind of behavior—and most modern humans are the same. Hunter-gatherers are the only exceptions."

THE END of unsupervised play was only one of two very big engines driving the rise of the modern narcissist. The second was the self-esteem movement—and if ever there was a case of good intentions run amok, this is it.

Time was, it was easy to tell the winners from the losers at a grade-school track meet or swim event: There were three ribbons distributed at the end of the day and they came in three colors—gold, blue and red, for first, second and third. Finish fourth or below and you went home empty-handed. That wasn't fun, but at least you knew where you stood.

No more. Beginning in the 1980s, competitive events became strangely, blandly uncompetitive. Yes, there were winners, but there were, oddly, no losers. The gold, blue and red ribbons were joined by yellow for fourth place, maroon for fifth, green for sixth and on down to gray and light blue for ninth and tenth. There were participant ribbons and sportsmanship certificates and even small trophies distributed simply for completing the entire course. At a recent track meet my older daughter attended at her school, I watched in wonder as the children no sooner crossed the finish line than they dipped their heads to have a medal draped around their necks. The prize came before the hugs from the parents, before the needed gulps of water— before the panting children had even fully stopped running at all. As with so many cultural trends, there's an industry behind this bonanza of honors.

"Quick school ribbons are wonderful for instilling confidence and excitement about school in young minds," says the website Ribbons Galore, only one of many such commercial operations. "These event ribbons come in a variety of styles for common school events, ready to personalize."

The name alone—particularly the *galore* part—suggests a cheapening of a once rare tribute. And when the marketers say "common" school events, they're not kidding. There's a ribbon for reaching the 100th day of the school year—not successfully, not productively, just punching the clock and putting in the time. There's a ribbon for doing your best, for taking pride in your work, for "being caught doing something good," even for pledging to remain drug-free—the key being that you're not necessarily actually remaining drug-free, just promising to do so, which, as any addiction counselor will tell you, is kind of the easy part.

"I'm fascinated by where we've landed as a society. Is it better or worse to be a young person today? I honestly don't know the answer," says early-education expert Erika Christakis of Yale University. "Ironically, the goal of the 'Good Job!' school of child development was to give every kid a chance to succeed. But our embrace of everybody's issues, the sense of entitlement and specialness we're fostering in kids, may produce a generation of young adults lacking resilience relative to previous generations." The tens of thousands of different self-esteem books are just one more expression of this everyone-is-special trend.

Certainly, there's a lot of good that can come from kids carbo-loading on a little free-of-charge self-esteem. Schools are psychically savage places, where children found wanting by their peers—because of their clothes, their looks or simple shyness—may be taunted merci-lessly. Best to armor up with a lot of self-love before you step into a war zone like that. What's more, those are only the mainstream kids, the ones without learning or behavioral challenges that put them at a disadvantage before they ever set foot in a classroom. Children who do wrestle with such issues would once have been marginalized not just by their peers but by the schools themselves, sent down the off-ramps of the educational system into poorly funded special-ed programs where the expectations were low and the kids—no surprise—lived down to those standards.

"Let's not forget what it looked like a generation or two ago," says Christakis. "There was a tendency to view children not as unique individuals but as a monolithic category of people to be managed, con-trolled and often ignored. For every embarrassing example of excess, there's a counterexample of a child who would have been crushed or ignored in previous generations."

Still, the downside of all this supportive goodness is impossible to deny. When children in the 1950s were administered the Minnesota Multiphasic Personality Inventory (MMPI)—an exceedingly detailed survey that requires subjects to answer hundreds of true-false ques-tions measuring personality on multiple dimensions—only 12 percent agreed with the statement "I am a special person." By the late 1980s, the figure had exploded to 80 percent. Other studies in the 1990s showed similar high numbers of kids agreeing with such statements as "I have often met people who are supposed to be experts who are no better than I." A 2012 meta-analysis of results from the American Freshman Survey, a personality inventory that has been administered to a collective nine million incoming college students in the United States over the past forty-seven years, has found that in every one of five different personality dimensions tested—drive to achieve, intellectual self-confidence, belief in leadership ability, social self-confidence and belief in writing ability—scores have been steadily on the rise, with up to 75 percent of kids believing they are above average. For any one student that's a good thing, and no parent would want a child heading off to college laboring under the burden of low self-esteem. But it does say something when 75 percent of an entire demographic segment believes, impossibly, that it sits above the 50 percent line.

"Our culture used to encourage modesty and humility and not bragging about yourself," Jean Twenge, San Diego State University psychologist and author of the book *Generation Me*, said in a 2012 conversation with BBC News when the Freshman Survey study was released. "It was considered a bad thing to be seen as conceited or full of yourself. The fact that that is no longer the case means a generation that is not only becoming increasingly arrogant, but that is doomed to disappointment too."

Grade inflation has only made things worse. According to a 2008 study by Twenge and several other researchers, only 27 percent of the entering classes at American colleges and universities in 1980 had maintained an A average through high school. By 2004, that number had jumped to 48 percent. And while the simple expedient of working harder and studying more could—indeed should—have accounted for the improvement, other surveys covering much of the same period showed that the amount of time kids spent at the books had actually fallen, with 47 percent of college freshmen saying they devoted at least six hours per week to studying in 1987, compared with 33 percent in 2003.

That working-less-but-getting-more phenomenon continues straight through the college years. A massive and regularly updated survey of colleges and universities, conducted by Stuart Rojstaczer, a retired professor of geophysics at Duke University, found that from 1991 to 2007, the grade point average at 247 schools rose from a mean of 2.93 to 3.11. The grade inflation, distressingly, was worse not at publicly funded colleges where tuitions are usually lower, but at top-dollar, high-prestige schools where the standards, in theory, ought to be tougher.

At Auburn, for example, a public university once known as the Agricultural and Mechanical College of Alabama, the average GPA from 1975 to 2006 barely budged, going from 2.71 to 2.75, or up 1.5 percent. Princeton, by contrast, jumped from 3.09 to 3.30, or 6.8 percent. The Community College of Philadelphia crept up from 2.38 to 2.50, or 5 percent, while Harvard soared from a 3.05 GPA to 3.45, or a whopping 13 percent. And even as the kids at the highest-status universities were being fattened up on such high-fructose grades, many of them seemed to conclude that if anything, they deserved more. In her 2008 paper, Twenge reported that 30 percent of college students questioned in one survey agreed with the statement "If I show up to every class, I deserve at least a B."

AS A CULTURE CHANGES, so do the kinds of entertainment it demands. It's always tempting to try to determine where the cause and effect begins here, and it's usually impossible to say. Did the forced sobriety and the resulting speakeasy culture of the Prohibition era give rise to the musical rule-breaking of jazz, or did jazz encourage flouting the no-drinking laws? Did the sexual and political anarchy of the 1960s spark the guitar-smashing rock of that age, or did the onstage frenzy stir up the kids in the streets? It's likely, surely, that it's a two-way process, a back-and-forth sloshing in which art and culture influence each other. That's no less true in the narcissism era.

In 2011, Twenge, along with psychologists C. Nathan DeWall and Richard Pond of the University of Kentucky, and Keith Campbell of the University of Georgia, published a study of *Billboard* magazine's Top 10 songs for every year from 1980 to 2007—a total of 280 songs. The researchers were not terribly interested in the music—indeed, they weren't interested in it at all—but they cared mightily about the lyrics.

Using a nifty piece of software called the Linguistic Inquiry Word Count Program, which scans text for specific types of words, the investigators went searching first for all first-person, second-person and third-person pronouns—both singular and plural—in the songs. In addition to those occurrences of *I, me, you, us, my, mine, ours* and the like, they looked for the frequency of words indicating social connectedness (*mate, talk, child, love, nice, sweet*) and anger or social alienation (*hate, kill, damn*).

Together, the 280 songs included 88,621 words—or about 315 each. That seems like an awful lot for a genre that's known for the simplicity of its lyrics, but the key is that these were not necessarily 315 different words. Repetition counts for a lot in determining the message of a song, and it matters a great deal if the word "love" appears once or 21 times. Ditto telltale words of self-absorption like "want," "me," or "money."

Algorithms like this aren't perfect, especially since they can't code for irony or social commentary. "Diamonds Are a Girl's Best Friend" is a cold ode to acquisitiveness and greed—at least if all you know of it are the words. But watch it performed, and you realize it's meant to be sold with a wink—literally, when Marilyn Monroe did it. The Beatles' song "I, Me, Mine," which includes the refrain "I, me, me, mine" over and over and over again, would have practically broken the needle in any first-person word-counting program, but the software could not know that the song was intended as a critical commentary on avarice and narcissism, not a celebration of it.

Still, most songs say what they mean, and the results of the 2011 study were revealing: Over the course of nearly thirty years, the *Billboard* hits showed a 30 percent increase in the use of the first-person singular, while the more collective first-person plural—most notably the shared possessive *our* and *ours*—plummeted 40 percent. There was a 21 percent decline in themes that spoke of social connectedness and a 75 percent increase in words suggesting alienation and solitariness.

"Popular song lyrics are a window into understanding U.S. cultural changes," Twenge and her colleagues wrote. The songs "serve as cultural artifacts of shifts toward self-focus, social disconnection, anger, antisocial behavior, and misery."

The same sour turning inward is evident in the language in books on the bestseller lists, a category that goes well beyond just the self-esteem books. In 2012, Twenge, Campbell and University of Georgia psychologist Brittany Gentile conducted another, even larger survey (software-aided, of course) of 766,513 American books published from 1960 to 2008, looking for a similar rise in the language of selfishness and individualism, and they found it—in a very big way.

The use of words suggesting individualism and, significantly, excellence (*self, standout, unique, independence, individual*) increased 20 percent, as did individualistic phrases like "all about me," "I can do it myself" and "I get what I want." It was the pronouns, however, that once again told the real tale. Use of the first-person singular increased 20 percent, while use of the second-person singular and plural (*you, your, yours, yourself, yourselves*) exploded by 300 percent. This was not a reflection of readers' looking outward, focusing on the perspective of others, but of writers speaking directly to readers, addressing their concerns and needs—how *you* can lose weight, how *you* can make more money, how *you* can find a new job. Even novels, like Jay McInerney's *Bright Lights, Big City* and Tom Robbins's *Half Asleep in Frog Pajamas*, employed the unusual device of writing in the second person. Individualistic phrases and terms rose as well, by 42 percent, easily outdistancing communal terms like "it takes a village" and "community spirit."

Finally, ultimately, the me-first culture—like everything else—went online. Books and music are one thing, but if there was ever something that was going to collect the nation's self-absorption and spin it down into true weapons-grade narcissism, it was the rise of social media sites—particularly Facebook and Twitter. Once social exhibitionism no longer actually had to be social—once you could sit at your laptop and post any stray thought you had or any flattering picture someone had just taken of you—even the innately modest would become self-absorbed. Or at least that's always been the thinking.

Campbell and University of Georgia colleague Laura Buffardi were among the first serious researchers to consider the narcissism-fueling effect of social media when they explored the then-new virtual community in 2009. It's a measure of the fast-forward speed at which the online world moves that even those few years ago, Facebook was still terra incognita—at least in the social sciences world—and it was still in competition with sites like MySpace and Friendster, once-thriving online communities that are now ghost towns. Buffardi and her colleagues volunteered to explore those strange lands and then file dispatches back to the psychologists left behind in base camp.

"Social networking Web sites are built on the base of superficial 'friendships' with many individuals and 'sound-byte' [sic] driven communication between friends (i.e., *wallposts*)," the authors patiently explained. "A Facebook page utilizes a fill-in-the-blank system of personalization. All pages share common social characteristics, such as links to friends' pages . . . and an electronic bulletin board, called the *wall*. . . . Many users have hundreds or even thousands of 'friends.'"

OK, so the wide-eyed language seems comically outdated, but the narcissistic science remains sound. Campbell and Buffardi recruited 1,567 college students—all with Facebook pages—and administered the forty-question, forced-choice Narcissistic Personality Inventory to them. They then surveyed all of the subjects' profile pages and analyzed them on four different scales: number of friends, number of posts, number of groups joined and, critically, number of lines of text in the "About Me" section.

To those objective measures, the researchers added subjective analysis. They rated the overall tone of the "About Me" section as self-absorbed, self-important, self-promoting or—the opposite of all three—self-conscious. The profile picture the subject chose to post was rated on how much or how little clothing was worn, and whether the image seemed vain, sexy, modest or exhibitionistic. The overall attractiveness of the picture was also rated, though here Campbell and Buffardi had to apply a somewhat complex standard. They could not consider simply the qualities that make up a pretty or less pretty face, since these are hardly within the subject's control. Instead they looked at how studied the pose, lighting and composition of the picture were. The subject who posts a random picture snapped at a picnic or an amusement park simply because she looks happy in it is likely a different sort of person from the one who posts a studio portrait or a glamour shot.

Last, the researchers looked at the "Favorite Quotes" section of the page. Here the analysis was something of a bank shot, since the quotes are not ones of the person's own composition but rather sound bites plucked from history or literature. But there's a lot to be learned by whether someone chooses Eleanor Roosevelt's celebrated observation about how much better it is to light a single candle than to curse the darkness or Muhammad Ali's declaration that "'impossible' is just a big word thrown around by small men."

Up and down the line, the page analyses revealed a powerful link between narcissism and online exhibitionism. Subjects who scored higher on the NPI tended to write longer and more self-promotional profiles, to post sexier and more affected pictures, and to talk more about themselves in their posts. The quotes chosen also tended to be less clever and entertaining and more cocky and self-promoting.

So the study was solid, the methods were sound and the results were clear—and yet the ultimate conclusions? Ambiguous. Narcissists may be more attracted to Facebook than non-narcissists, but that doesn't mean that Facebook actually made anyone more narcissistic. Rather, the site may have simply been what tequila is to the drunk or cheesecake is to the glutton—a high-density form of the indulgence they'd be seeking out anyway.

"Individualism and narcissism started long before the Internet arrived," Twenge told me. "In some ways, Facebook's influence has been overstated. Narcissists do have more friends on Facebook, but being on Facebook can also lead to political participation. The data reveals both extreme individualism and collectivism—to becoming more absorbed in yourself or getting outside of yourself."

Facebook, agrees research psychologist Joanna Fanos of Dartmouth Medical School, doesn't necessarily foster people's narcissism, but "it *reveals* their narcissism. In a face-to-face conversation you can disguise the narcissistic intent more, but on Facebook it's more evident."

The ultimate expression of this kind of online baring all is a literal baring all—in the form of the sext. Sexting as an act was as culturally inevitable as the minting of the word itself was linguistically inevitable, with *sex* and *text* destined for a mash-up once the right technology came along. But just because we have a word for an act doesn't mean we can always define it—which makes studying how widespread sexting is difficult. Does suggestive flirtation count? Explicit phrasing? A beach picture taken in a skimpy bathing suit? Or must it be bared breasts or fully bared bits? What's more, does it make a difference if the exchange is between two virtual strangers, two people who are casually dating or a committed couple with a healthy, ongoing sex life?

Most studies, like one the PEW Research Institute conducted in 2009, define sexting as "sending a sexually suggestive nude or nearly nude photo or video," which pretty much rules out the more innocent, clothed or inadvertent kind of cyberflirting and includes people of all degrees of intimacy. Still, even with a good definition of what the act is, solid data about who's performing it is hard to come by, since sexting studies rely on self-reporting, and kids—not to put too fine a point on it—lie like rugs, especially when they're doing something that could land them in the deepest kind of parental trouble.

All the same, a whopping load of studies into the phenomenon have been conducted and that large body of research, plus the fact that the results of most of the studies come down in the same numerical range, suggests that investigators are managing to get at the truth. In general, 20 to 25 percent of teens have sexted, with the receivers exceeding the senders, though things break down differently along gender lines. More girls than boys send (one study put it at 65 percent versus 35 percent), but more boys than girls request. In one survey, 51 percent of girls who sent a nude or semi-nude picture of themselves said they did so because a boy asked for it; only 18 percent of boys said they had been asked to serve themselves up this way. College students and young adults sext more than high school students, but the numbers tail off after that.

It's hard not to see the hand of narcissism at work here, though it's important not to overstate the link. Anthony Weiner—the compulsively sexting former New York congressman and 2013 mayoral candidate—has skewed any rational measurement of the connection between narcissism and sexting in much the way the likes of, say, Bill Gates throws off the curve when you try to define rich. The constant downward focus of Weiner's camera did suggest a consuming, self-admiring pleasure with what he saw, and his need to share that fine view certainly was not the act of a modest man. But Weiner's full motivation—to say nothing of his full psychological makeup—is impossible to determine just from his public behavior, and it's frankly not fair to try. Authoring the end of your own career in the reckless and almost wantonly self-destructive way he did speaks to a type of emotional turbulence best left to Weiner and the people who know him best. His narcissism may have been the rain, but there probably are a lot of other parts to his internal storm.

For people who have less at stake, however, it's hard not to see a powerful strain of narcissism in the nude selfie that is then sent wide—especially since once the picture is out of your control it can be forwarded, posted and seen by anyone at all. In at least some cases, that potential wider audience might be perceived not as one of the risks but as part of the thrill.

"I would posit that people high in narcissism are definitely more likely to sext," says Twenge. "A few years ago, the *Today* show interviewed some high school students about sexting. One girl commented that if you boost girls' self-esteem they'll sext less. The problem is that low-self-esteem girls are the least likely to sext and seek attention in the first place. It's those high in self-esteem, and especially in narcissism, who would do it. They are thinking, 'I'm hot, and I want everyone to see that.' And I don't buy the argument that some people who are physically attractive but not narcissistic would sext simply because they're comfortable with themselves. If you're hot but not vain, knowing you're hot is enough—you don't need to show it to everyone else."

Campbell sees one dimension to sexting that could militate against the narcissism component a little. "There can be an interesting anxiety or insecurity element here," he says. "That is, some people who are insecure about a relationship could sext to keep the other partner interested. But when the sexting is more about gaining power or getting positive attention, then my guess is that it's linked to narcissism."

That, surely, is true about all online showing off, whether it's sexting or merely an attention-seeking Twitter post. Facebook never could have blown past its campus-only demographic, growing from 175 million users in 2009 to a staggering one billion in 2012, if it and other forms of cyberexpression weren't somehow appealing to a cultural appetite to display, to exhibit—to forget about simply finding a place in the spotlight and instead just carrying one with you and keeping it shining in your face all the time. That's a lot of weight to lug around and a lot of constant heat to endure, but to narcissists, the benefits easily exceed the burdens.

CHAPTER FOUR

The Schmuck in the Next Cubicle

When you're telling lies, it helps to be charming. Anyone can make stuff up, but if you want to be believed—which, after all, is the whole point of telling lies—you'd best know how to look honest and earnest and nice while you're doing it. It's a lot harder to dupe people who don't like you or trust you.

Take Lance Armstrong, the disgraced cyclist and confessed juicer who faked his way to seven Tour de France titles over a nearly twenty-year career, hectoring, abusing and even suing anyone who suggested that he might be taking performance-enhancing drugs—which he was. That aggressive defense may have silenced some critics, but it only emboldened others, who pursued him with an Inspector Javert–like persistence, determined to bring the nasty bastard down if only because he deserved it. Eventually, a lot of people took part in that job, as eleven of Armstrong's ex-teammates publicly rolled on him, testifying that all of the stories over all of the years were entirely true. When Armstrong finally accepted that the jig was up and embarked on the inevitable apology tour, he earned not a shred of public forgiveness. Instead he found himself shunned and shamed, a bad-tempered character who richly deserved his public banishment.

The same was true of Richard Nixon, a man of black moods and stubborn grudges, who stood in almost surreal contrast to his existential opposite, the boundlessly charismatic Bill Clinton. Both men faced impeachment and both were guilty of the things they had been accused of doing. Clinton's misdeeds were far, far smaller than Nixon's, but his case actually proceeded further, to a full trial in the Senate, while Nixon got out of Dodge before articles of impeachment could even be voted out of the House.

It wasn't shame that drove Nixon to resign—though the underlying self-loathing and profound insecurity that impelled him to commit his crimes surely contained an element of that. Rather, it was something closer to narcissistic calculation: His presidency was doomed no matter what. Better to walk out than be carried out, and preserve some scrap of historical dignity in the process. Clinton was short on shame too. If he had had more of it—particularly the corrective kind of shame that stops people from doing things like cheating on a spouse when they've already been caught at it multiple times before—he wouldn't have gotten into his impeachment mess in the first place. But it's the glowering Nixon who slipped into the historical shadows while the sunny, seductive Clinton—the man you want to believe is telling the truth even when every instinct you have is screaming that he's selling you a bill of goods—survived politically.

The power of the disarming manipulator is evident everywhere—in the entrepreneur who charms seven-figure financing out of credulous investors with his tales of a sure-thing payoff; in the broker who sells you securities you don't really need and can't really afford, then promptly sends an e-mail to a colleague boasting about the dog of a stock he just unloaded on some customer whose name, frankly, he can't quite remember. It was vividly evident, too, in the twin cases of ex-reporters Stephen Glass and Jayson Blair—the Castor and Pollux of journalistic fraud—who made their names first as wunderkind reporters, then as suspected fabricators and finally as reportorial fabulists of the first order.

Blair, who worked for *The New York Times* from 1999 to 2003, and Glass, who wrote for *The New Republic* from 1995 to 1998, were liars both, inventors both, and brilliantly good at it both. At least twenty-seven of the forty-one stories Glass wrote for the magazine were shot through with manufactured scenes, imagined quotes and vivid characters who existed nowhere but in the author's mind. Blair was an even more prolific counterfeiter, inventing interviews, scenes and sources in at least thirty-six of the seventy-three articles he wrote in a span of seven months—a case of perverse productivity if ever there was one.

The two young men covered different kinds of news and wrote very different kinds of stories—Glass the longer-form, tale-telling kind of journalism that is favored by *The New Republic*; Blair the straight-up, just-the-facts reporting that is the *Times'* meat and potatoes. Both of them were as sloppy as they were prolific, leaving a bread-crumb trail of inconsistencies and suspicious behavior throughout their careers that eventually caused a lot of people—at least the ones who were watching closely—to suspect they were no good. And both of them survived to lie some more—surrounding themselves with people who liked them or at least believed in them, and helped look out for them, too. The reason was simple: Like Nixon and Armstrong, both of them were narcissistic exploiters and attention-seekers—but unlike Nixon and Armstrong, they were charismatically good at it.

Glass was especially adept at gathering people to him, and he did it in a number of ways. For one, he seemed to be an eager listener—inquiring about his colleagues and learning all he could about them, which hardly seems of a piece with the narcissistic poseur, unless there's a larger strategy at work. Said former *New Republic* senior editor Margaret Talbot in an exhaustive article about Glass, published in 1998 in *Vanity Fair*, which served as the basis of the later movie *Shat-*

tered Glass: "There are so many assholes in journalism, so many brag-
garts and arrogant jerks. [Then] someone comes along who appears to
have talent, is self-effacing to a fault, and is sweet and solicitous."

It was the self-effacing piece that was especially effective. Glass had
an odd habit of denigrating his ideas for articles, dismissing them as
rubbish even as he was pitching them, though both he and his listeners
knew they were brilliant. During happy hours after work, he would
similarly hold the floor, telling elaborate stories that may or may not
have been true, but were always entertaining and, more to the point,
always framed him as the foil, often clownishly so. The ploys worked,
leading even competitive colleagues who might be gnashing their
teeth at how bloody good his articles and anecdotes were to like him
despite themselves.

"He had this puppy-dog, protect-me charm," one former colleague
told me, requesting anonymity so as not to pile on Glass years after
the fact. "In the movie he's not suave or smooth, but he's shown as a lot
suaver and smoother than he was in real life. He was also incredibly
solicitous and nice and well-mannered." The film and the *Vanity Fair*
piece also make much of Glass's habit of routinely asking people if they
were mad at him, a question that was as odd and even irritating as it
was disarming. But it was an accurate portrayal of his behavior—and
that was only part of it. "In one instance, there was some really, really
minor thing that he thought I was upset about," said the former colleague. "He left me an apology note in my mailbox, and it was the kind
of thing that wouldn't even have required a verbal apology." This may
have been genuine—if excessive—contrition, the act of a deeply insecure man intolerant of not feeling well-liked. Or it may have been social strategizing. Both fit comfortably within the behavioral profile of
the narcissist and both served his larger scheme.

Blair was not above blandishments and humility in the service of his
larger mission, either. He had a clever habit of praising fellow reporters for an artful phrase or a well-researched fact in a recently pub-

lished piece—which is nice, but not all that unusual in the field. However, in his case the detail he chose to praise always seemed, at least in retrospect, to be less genuine than tactical. "It was something far down in the story, so you'd know he read it," said *Times* columnist David Carr, speaking about Blair in the epic *mea culpa* the newspaper published after the scandal broke. "He had charisma, enormous charisma."

That interpersonal artfulness was selectively deployed, however. Unlike Glass, Blair was not necessarily trying to be liked by the people who could not do him any good, only by those who had a direct hand in advancing his career. He spent the summer of 1998 as a *Times* intern and in that span wrote nineteen published articles—an enormous total for someone so green. He arrived at work before all of the other interns, left later, and took the time to help them with their work as well. Nonetheless, the other interns admitted that they never much cared for him—that he seemed to see them all as competition. The editors, however, loved him, applauding his output, tenacity and collegiality and seeing in him the makings of a true *Times*-man.

"My feeling was here was a guy who was working hard and getting into the paper on significant stories," said then executive editor Howell Raines in the *Times* story. After Blair was hired, one of his bosses even took it on himself to look after the prodigy. Noticing that Blair was developing the newsman's habit of drinking too often, smoking too much and eating poorly, he pulled him aside and told him he could not go on living on a diet of cigarettes, scotch and vending-machine Cheez Doodles. Then he shooed him off to continue his work, which typically involved inserting one more byline—and many more fabrications—into the Newspaper of Record.

Glass's world came undone in 1998; Blair's five years later in 2003. And both fabulists followed similar patterns. Once too many invented facts raised too many eyebrows and uncomfortable questions started getting asked about their work, they donned the cloak of victimhood.

Glass insisted that he was the one being duped by his sources, not that the magazine and its readers were being duped by him, and that his editor, Chuck Lane, was failing to support him the way a better boss would. "You know, Chuck, I feel really attacked," Lane recalled Glass saying, according to *Vanity Fair*. "I feel really hurt. You're my editor and you're not backing me up."

Blair fumed less directly. When scolded by the Metropolitan editor for his unacceptably high error rate and instructed to write an e-mail explaining it, Blair complied, then told a colleague he had done so while holding his nose. He huffed that he was considering reporting the incident to "the people who hired me—and they all have executive or managing editor in their titles." It was Blair's belief that the very people he had deceived the most would surely take his side. In some ways, both Blair and Glass achieved the perfect narcissist's trifecta: an abiding conviction that they were too good to be caught, an indifference to the harm they were doing to other people—in this case, not just colleagues but millions of readers—and a profound sense of grievance when it all came crashing down. And crash down it did, as both young men were fired for committing what is widely thought of as journalism's death-penalty crime.

There is, as people outside the field sometimes complain, more than a little pretension in the way journalists themselves view their work and their mission. Reporting and analyzing the news are crafts like any other. They're vital crafts, certainly, and require honesty and integrity, but the pose the practitioners sometimes strike as guardians of the truth and protectors of the public square can become more than a little self-important—professionalism sloshing over into pretension. Still, both Glass and Blair knew those were the standards to which they'd be held, and by violating the principles of the industry in so outrageous and shameless a way they were both effectively expelled from it.

Both, too, began their postfraud careers with a sense—perhaps intended, perhaps not—of both irony and arrogance. Glass wrote a poorly received novel based on his experiences, titled *The Fabulist*—a sort of meta-fiction atop the real-life fiction he'd lived. He later completed law school, passed the bar exam, and began a years-long campaign to be admitted to the California State Bar Association, trying to persuade officials that a man best known for lying spectacularly could be trusted in a profession whose central mission is the search for truth. So far, his applications continue to be denied—though, as before, he has won supporters and even champions along the way. Blair has gone on the speakers' circuit, discussing his experiences and what he learned from them, and offering his audiences advice about how to recover from personal disaster. His preferred, if unofficial, post-scandal title? Life coach.

NARCISSISTS FIND their way into almost any business organization, where they succeed brilliantly, crash spectacularly, thrive and die and charm and alienate in seemingly equal measure—often in the span of a very short stay before moving on. People with true, clinical narcissistic personality disorder may represent no more than 3 percent of the population, but they—along with people with milder, less febrile cases of the condition—turn up in high-profile, high-power positions more often than their numbers would suggest. The reason is simple: no one lands a job without acing the interview, and that's a setting in which many narcissists—with their incandescent smiles and their glad-handing ease—have a pronounced edge over the nervous, sweaty-palmed rest of us.

Interviewing for a job is all about what business experts and psychologists call impression management. The people in your world are free to think anything they want about you, but if you know what you're doing, you can shape those beliefs for them. That's a high-stakes game with an equally high risk of failure—as you've learned every time you've said something you thought was charming or clever at a meeting or on a date and then flushed red when the *bon mot* bombed, wishing with every particle of yourself that you could wind the moment back. Narcissists experience that kind of thing less frequently simply because they bomb less, and when they do, they often don't even notice—an obliviousness to their own gaffes that allows them to move on without the self-consciousness that can otherwise cause one bad moment to lead to another and another.

A 2011 study conducted at the University of British Columbia defined four basic qualities necessary for effective impression management: self-promotion, ingratiation, supplication and intimidation, every one of which is a basic part of the narcissist's toolbox. Glass was a master of supplication; clumsy narcissists like Armstrong go heavy on the intimidation. But in a job interview, it's ingratiation and, critically, self-promotion that make the real difference. And narcissists self-promote in remarkable—and sometimes very dangerous—ways.

The British Columbia investigators recruited ninety-four undergrads and had them participate in a simulated job interview for a research–assistant position in a psychology lab. The subjects were all administered the Narcissistic Personality Inventory first and also took a fifty-question multiple-choice test to determine their general knowledge of the field of psychology. Only then did they sit for their interview—though not all of the subjects got the same kind of inquisitor. Some were told that the person asking the questions was an English major who "doesn't know much about psychology." Others were told they landed someone with more exacting standards: a graduate student in psychology who is an "expert in the field." In truth, all of the interviewers were psych students.

The entire sample group of subjects were asked the same set of questions by the researchers—including some about psychological concepts that just don't exist. How you answer the unanswerable question can reveal a lot about you. In everyday life, we all bluff a little: Someone at an academic gathering asks you if you read *Les Misérables*, which you did—but only if the fifty pages you got through before you dropped the French lit class you took in college count. You did see the movie, however, and can riff a little about rebellion, prosecutorial obsession and nineteenth-century France. In a job interview, the stakes are much higher—and the risk of being caught lying is much greater. Any undergrad applying for a job in a psych lab can fake a good response to a question about Jung or Freud or cognitive-behavioral therapy. But it takes a special kind of brass to improv persuasively when you're asked about, say, Bünche or Kleinhaus or compensatory impulse triggering, entirely authentic-sounding—and entirely made up.

The British Columbia researchers predicted that not only would the people who scored highest on the NPI keep right on answering any question they were asked with the same seeming confidence no matter how much they had to fake it, but that they would actually be likelier to do so when being interviewed by a psychology grad student than an English major. It's always more gratifying to fool an expert than a non-expert, after all. The results of the study confirmed that surprising hypothesis.

In the non-expert scenario, all of the subjects were willing to fake an answer with more or less the same frequency—with about 2.5 invented responses in the course of an interview for the non-narcissists compared with 3 for the narcissists. In the expert scenario, however, the two groups went in opposite directions, with the narcissists averaging nearly 4 faked answers for every 1.5 tallied by the non-narcissists. Something similar held true in an earlier study by many of the same researchers in which narcissists and non-narcissists were asked to rate, on a scale of zero to six, how familiar they were with terms such as "Manhattan Project," "plate tectonics" and "particle accelerator," which do exist, and a few like "choraline," "ultralipid" and "plates of parallax," which don't. The narcissists scored sixes across the board, even on the nonsense terms, while the non-narcissists bailed with a zero when they had no idea what they were talking about.

"The fact that narcissists seem to truly believe their claims of superiority suggests that their self-presentational style goes beyond impression management to a form of self-deceptive enhancement," the researchers wrote in the later study. "Accordingly [they] may sustain or even increase their self-enhancing behaviors."

That dangerous strategy very often works. Real-life job interviews are typically not scattered with deliberate land mines set to trip up frauds, so narcissists who know little but vamp well can often find themselves landing jobs that would have better gone to more qualified people who simply don't perform as effectively in a face-to-face meeting. That, however, presents another puzzle: Why in the world would you want a job you know you're not qualified to perform, especially since every day will only present another test of what you don't know, and ultimately you're going to be found out?

One of the great mysteries of the Glass case was the amount of effort he had to exert to keep his masquerade going. He would routinely turn in stacks of fraudulent notes, travel receipts and other backup material to *The New Republic*'s fact-checkers, all of which were painstakingly created to look authentic and, critically, to jibe well with what was in his story. And since no article is without any mistakes at all and any one that looked too clean would raise the suspicions of fact-checkers, he even included a few small errors in every piece to help deflect attention from the very big ones that were hiding in plain sight. All that seems like a lot more work than just going out and reporting the story for real.

But Glass had a problem, which was that—not to put too fine a point on it—he wasn't any good. "Yes, it's more work to make up a story than to report it, but only if it's reportable," says the former colleague. "If the story isn't out there, then it's easier to make it up."

Glass's gift, he says, wasn't his prose—indeed, his work was often re-written by well-regarded senior editors like the columnist Andrew Sullivan. His talent "was that he seemed to be able to do this eye-popping, unique, entertaining reporting. He was coming up with stuff that was so different and unusual and appetizing to his editors." Those kinds of scoops, however, come along only rarely, so if you're going to keep serving them up, you often also have to make them up.

That's not how the non-narcissist would do things, of course. If you want to be a basketball player more than anything else in life, but you just don't have the height, you suck it up and find something else to do. Ditto if you want to be an architect or a senator or a celebrated jour-nalist, but you don't have the spatial sense or the speech-making skills or the narrative ability. In all of those cases, you bid good-bye to your earlier ambitions—sadly, to be sure—and move on. For the narcissist who becomes fixed on a goal, however, the ego isn't just bruised by the prospect of failure, it's annihilated.

"Life hands us these setbacks all the time," says Penn State psy-chologist Aaron Pincus, "and sometimes they're big ones. You lose your capacity to do what you do best—the athlete who suffers an ac-cident or injury, for example, and can no longer play. You also might find that you never really did have the ability to do what you thought you did best in the first place. Learning from it, suffering through it and changing course is the only healthy way to survive it."

The narcissist, who would be utterly hollowed out by giving up, may choose to cheat instead, and once that cycle starts it's hard to stop. Indeed, not only do narcissists operate under the illusion that the rules don't apply to them, when they do get tripped up but somehow sur-vive, it may only embolden them to cheat some more.

Psychologist Keith Campbell of the University of Georgia likes to point to studies he conducted in 2004 in which subjects were adminis-tered the NPI and then took on-screen trivia tests, which offered them the chance to bet a small quantity of money on each question. They

learned after every one if they had gotten the correct or incorrect answer and how much they had won or lost. They could then decide how
much they wanted to bet on the next one.

This, for the non-narcissist, is a perfect real-time feedback system—a
way to evaluate your performance as you go along, pull back your bets
if you see you're not doing well and press them if you are. The people
who scored highest on the NPI, however, pursued exactly the opposite
strategy. "They overpredicted their performance," Campbell says.
"Even when they lost and were continuing to lose, they didn't learn
from it."

The study included an element that actually quantified precisely
how overconfident the narcissists were. After placing a bet and answering a question, all of the subjects were asked to rate the likelihood that
their response was correct—from 50–60 percent, 61–70 percent and so
on in increments to 98–100 percent. For non-narcissists, confidence
rose or fell more or less in lockstep with performance. For narcissists,
confidence level always exceeded performance—with an average score
on the 101-question test of 73.5 percent and an average confidence of
80 percent. That 6.5 percent difference may not be much in raw numbers, but when you're poised on the edge of either making a bet or not
making it—pushing a $500 chip into the circle at a blackjack table even
though you've lost the last five bets—it may be more than enough to
make you keep right on playing. The same is true if you're deciding
between filing one more in a string of fraudulent stories, or taking
your undeserved winnings and at last cashing them in. "Narcissists,"
Campbell observes, "pursue a top-down strategy for self-assessment:
'I am good, therefore I will do well on this task, did do well and will do
well in the future.'"

COCKINESS, CHEATING and overclaiming knowledge are not the
only disagreeable traits narcissists bring to an organization. So is

exhibitionism—the social kind, that is—and for colleagues forced to endure it, it can be more tiresome than all of the others.

I thought about this a lot the day I got a congratulatory e-mail from a man I'll call Dennis. I rather like Dennis; more important, I respect him, and chances are, you do too. Dennis is one of the best reporters I know—tireless, smart and thorough. He has developed a significant following over the years, remains one of the best-known journalists on the beat he covers and a few years ago broke a Washington scandal that shook a former president and resulted in a lot of people having to do a lot of explaining.

But none of that means he isn't hard to take. Years ago, when Dennis and I worked together, he'd sometimes drop by my office to chat and the drill would always be the same: He'd tell me what new story he was working on, share an anecdote or two about his life outside the office and then, when I began to speak, would pick up a newspaper and begin leafing through it—intermittently glancing up and muttering, "interesting, interesting," in a pantomime of listening that revealed only that he was not interested at all. About a week after my first daughter was born, Dennis, who had preceded me into fatherhood and clearly knew a thing or two about the total-immersion madness of those early postnatal days, called me at home, offered his pro forma best wishes, and then mentioned that he'd be in my neighborhood doing a public reading of his work that evening and wondered if I might like to attend, provided the baby was asleep. The assumption presumably was that that would be the way I would want to spend the sweet relief of a quiet moment, and that my wife, one week postpartum and entirely sleep-deprived, would not have other ideas about my stepping out.

So Dennis has kind of a thing for Dennis, but I never realized how much of a thing until the congratulatory e-mail. Another reporter and I had just won a well-respected journalism award that most people have never heard of but that reporters in certain circles know well.

Among that small group, word went around fast. Dennis sent his congratulations to both of us straightaway, which seemed gracious—at first. But no sooner had he offered his kudos than he added that it really was a shame he hadn't been allowed to submit his name for the same award, since the publication for which he worked at the time did not permit such competition among its reporters. "Anyway," he concluded, "couldn't have gone to two more deserving." Except, the unspoken postscript said, for him.

If there was a whole lot of unapologetic narcissism in Dennis's behavior—and there was—there's also a certain churlishness in my annoyance over it, since this all occurred years ago. But while the behavior perhaps should no longer grate, it still mystifies. Dennis is the real deal, a man whose hard work and talents have earned him justifiable recognition. So why the ceaseless self-promoting? One reason might be that he simply can't help it.

The craving for the spotlight, so great a craving that even when it's shining on someone else, narcissists are still trying to take hold of its blazing white face and turn it their way, consumes them, and it's not a pretty thing to observe. And yet narcissists are often tolerated all the same because many of them, like Dennis, do have the chops. In 1996, when the boundlessly self-adoring Barbra Streisand released her film *The Mirror Has Two Faces*—in which she served as both director and star—critic Janet Maslin grumbled about Streisand's repeated habit of shooting herself sumptuously lit and in loving close-up, literally casting herself in a different light from that of her costars. Still, Maslin conceded, Streisand's "diva appeal" was undeniable. "The camera does love her," she memorably wrote, "even with a gun to its head."

In the close quarters of an office, that kind of talent—the kind that may be worth tolerating despite the fact that it comes bundled with ceaseless showing off—is particularly noticeable, given the intimate setting of a meeting or work group, in which leaders and laggards inevitably emerge. "Narcissists are actually quite good at energizing groups of workers," says Peter Harms, professor of personality psychology at the University of Nebraska, Lincoln. "They like talking first and they like talking a lot, and this can break the ice when the members of a team are just getting to know one another. Their confidence helps a lot here."

It's not just confidence that narcissists bring to these situations; it's drive. Even if they're not in the talent class of a Dennis or a Barbra, narcissists are often the most motivated people in a group—powerfully driven by the prospect of praise and recognition. That means that from the outset, they're determined to make a mark, especially when they know that higher-ups will be watching. Not for them the surreptitious texting or sideways clock glancing of the less ambitious colleagues who just want to wrap the meeting up and get back to their desks. For them it's all about the energetic doing—and the hope of being seen in the process.

"Narcissists are often brought in because a unit is cratering," says Wayne Hochwarter, Florida State University professor of business. "They come in full of piss and vinegar and say rah-rah we're going to save the world, and it does get everybody motivated. These traits make them seem pretty favorable."

The problem here is that when the meeting adjourns, not everyone comes away with the same impression of whose contributions were really the most valuable. Harms cites studies in which sample groups of college students are brought together, administered the NPI, and then set to work on a simple project—solving math problems, say, or trying to come up with multiple uses for an ordinary object like a paper clip. Afterward, all of the members are asked to evaluate how much they contributed to the group and how much everybody else did.

No surprise, the subjects who score highest on the NPI tend to give themselves rave reviews and lowball the work of the other members, but those scores often do not accord with what the others report. And even when everyone is in agreement—that the narcissist really was an effective leader—just how effective is a matter of dispute, with the narcissists' self-ratings often much higher than the score the rest of the group gave them. This remains true, remarkably, even when the individual group members' contributions are empirically quantifiable in some way—by counting who came up with the most uses for the paper clip, say. Narcissists may score near the bottom, but that doesn't change their opinion of themselves.

"They'll say that they facilitated the conversations that helped other people be more productive," Harms says. "And they'll persist in that position even if you show them videotapes of the group that prove otherwise."

All that would be tolerable, except that in many cases, it's only the first part of a behavioral two-step. It's not enough for some narcissists simply to succeed; it's necessary that the people around them fail—or at least succeed less conspicuously. This is most evident in brainstorming meetings, when ideas or pitches are being tossed out and debated. In most gatherings like this, attendees fall into one of three groups: the indiscriminate praisers—those who applaud pretty much every idea they hear, perhaps because they simply like the coworkers who proposed them and want to give them a hand, perhaps because they are just easy to please. Indiscriminate praisers are sweet and they're generous and everybody likes them—and they're often useless in the greater effort to find truly good ideas. Next and best are the tough but fair graders—folks who tolerate no sloppiness, find the genuine flaws in any proposal but quite frankly hope they find none at all because they're invested in the success of the people and the enterprise around them.

The third group are the picnic skunks—those of the disdainful shrugs and barely concealed eye rolls, who find disqualifying short-comings in even the niftiest idea. It's unoriginal—even though no one else in the room seems to think so. It's not interesting—even though everyone else in the room seems intrigued by it. It's unrealistic—even though it seems eminently achievable and it's been well thought out. Something is being served here that has nothing to do with the company's larger mission and everything to do with the critic's smaller one—the belief that professional recognition is a zero-sum game, and that every little success one coworker enjoys is somehow subtracted from your own.

"This is a dangerous game to play," says Hochwarter. "You really have to be careful about being so obvious, since all of the capital you acquired can be spent very quickly. It's in the nature of the narcissistic beast that they start off being well liked until me-ism begins to ooze out of their pores. If they're smart they'll try to put that off as long as possible."

Hochwarter knows what he's talking about, partly because of the ravenous way he works—always on the hunt for volunteers to fill out surveys about their behavior in the workplace and that of their colleagues so that he can add to his data pool. And since he speaks to a lot of business groups and has a lot of grad students willing to conduct fieldwork, he has amassed a research inventory that is many thousands of surveys strong. While he doesn't score his respondents on narcissism specifically—the NPI is time-consuming and people often consider it intrusive—he does ask them questions that tease out self-serving temperaments, which, he says, "can be considered a proxy for narcissism, if not in a clinical sense."

Those bank-shot results reveal a lot. A whopping 44 percent of his respondents, for example, agree with the statement "When others at work receive recognition for a job well done, I get extremely jealous." Another 37 percent agree that "I make sure that I receive the recognition I deserve even if it is a bit exaggerated." And 51 percent cop to this unattractive tendency: "If I am sure I can get away with it, I seek opportunities to get credit for success I had little influence on."

Surely, 51 percent of all Hochwarter's subjects do not suffer from clinically diagnosable narcissistic personality disorder, but subclinical narcissism is a much more common phenomenon. And the business world, with its premium on aggression, achievement and recognition, self-selects for this trait in a way that more other-directed fields like nursing or social work don't. People who enter a service field are inclined to want to give; those who enter the corporate world are at least a little likelier to want to take.

If recognition is the narcissist's drug of choice, it's no surprise that very bad things happen when they're denied it. In fairness to even the worst of the me-firsters, this can be true of all of us. Hochwarter likes to remind business leaders that subordinates often respond with more enthusiasm to public shout-outs and open statements of praise than they do to many kinds of material rewards, including a small bonus in their paychecks, which is literally enriching but entirely anonymous. That's a rather pleasing feature of the human character that reveals just how highly we value the good opinion of the people around us. But it also means we react badly when we don't get the praise we think we deserve.

Jonas Salk, whose eponymous vaccine was developed with the help of a dozens-strong research team toiling away with him in a University of Pittsburgh lab, was never much of a credit grabber or fame seeker. He made clear from the start of his work that he would take no patent on whatever he might develop and would accept no more compensation than the university salary he was already earning. He was not opposed to granting interviews when reporters asked for them, but he preferred to limit that access to the local Pittsburgh press, and he made a point of asking reporters to stop describing what he was working on as the "Salk vaccine" and instead refer to it as the "Pitt vaccine." Aware that editors are always looking for short words in headlines so that they'll fit into the small column-wide space available, he even pointed out that *Pitt*, with its three skinny letters, actually took up fewer typographic picas than *Salk*. The newspapers would have none of it—preferring an individual's name to humanize the story—but Salk made the effort, and it was consistent with the collaborative, shared-credit atmosphere with which he'd run his lab from the beginning.

All the same, on April 12, 1955, after a massive field trial had finally proven the vaccine a success and a triumphant media event was called to make the announcement, it was Salk whom the crowd most wanted to hear from and Salk who received the rock star's reception. He stood before the newsreel cameras and the cheering reporters and did what most people do in that situation, which was to begin handing out thanks—to the university, the foundation that funded his work, the drug companies that manufactured the test vaccine, the dozens of children who volunteered to take the earliest formulation of it, the hundreds of thousands who later stepped forward as guinea pigs for the final version, nearly anyone who had even brushed up against the enterprise in the long years that had preceded that day. And yet somehow—oversight, nerves, an overweening ego at last showing itself (his critics preferred that explanation)—he never mentioned a single member of his lab team, the people who had done more than anyone else to make the vaccine a reality. It would be like a Super Bowl–winning coach acknowledging everyone but the players, a victorious general thanking everyone but the foot soldiers. For the stunned lab workers sitting in the audience, the day turned instantly to ash.

"Young man," legendary CBS newsman Edward R. Murrow said to Salk when he buttonholed him in the back of the hall after the presentation, "a great tragedy has befallen you. You've lost your anonymity." Salk's shocked lab workers kept theirs—and even half a century later, some of the survivors never forgave their former boss.

The push-pull between the innate satisfaction that comes from doing something applause-worthy and being recognized for having done so plays out not just in the workplace. Consider: It's a cold, wet day, you see a homeless man on the street and instead of merely walking by or, perhaps, giving him a dollar, you go into a nearby deli and buy him soup, a sandwich and a cup of hot coffee. Good for you! Now I dare you to keep it to yourself—to go home and not tell your family about the kindly thing you just did. Is the good deed unobserved even worth the bother?

In the delightful movie *Kate & Leopold*, the time-traveling duke of the title appears in twenty-first-century New York and, of course, finds romance there. After making a surprise breakfast for the woman he is wooing, he is advised by a friend not to turn on the dishwasher until she is there to witness it, since if a man washes a dish and no one sees him do it, did it really happen? Kids similarly prefer it if Mom and Dad actually witness them cleaning their room as opposed to simply seeing the results; and if the boss is passing by, employees would definitely rather it happen when their desk is piled high with work, as opposed to a few hours later when the work is actually done and the desk is clean.

The problem with this universal tendency is that for some people, especially narcissists, earning that recognition is all—or nearly all—that matters. Leopold would have washed the dishes no matter what, and the employee who has a lot of work to do had better get it done regardless of who's watching. Not so for many narcissists—who often let others carry the workload if there will be little or no individual recognition for it. The phenomenon is called "social loafing" in most venues, and "dogging it" in the world of sports, and in any of those places, it's an ugly thing.

"I play when I want to play," is how NFL bad boy Randy Moss explained his habit of actually seeming to take certain plays off during a game, barely jogging his way through them if a pass—and the possible glory that would come with catching it—was not clearly heading his way.

"It's practice, man! We're not talking about the game. It's practice!" exclaimed Allen Iverson, superstar point guard for the Philadelphia 76ers, during an infamous 2006 press conference in which reporters

questioned why he had failed to show up for scheduled drills—
something that was mandatory for all of the other players on the team
but not, he seemed to feel, for him. There are, after all, no spectators
at drills. The phenomenon is so common throughout all of sports that
ESPN.com even created a Dogging It Club for athletes who quit trying when the attention is on someone else. That ignominious group
had ten charter members when it was inaugurated in 2010—marquee
names all—from the NBA (Allen Iverson, Shaquille O'Neal and Ra-
sheed Wallace); the NFL (Randy Moss, Terrell Owens, JaMarcus
Russell and Deion Sanders); Major League Baseball (Manny Ramirez
and Andruw Jones) and even the PGA, improbable since golfers are
solo performers and share the spotlight with no one. Still, ESPN gave
a nod to John Daly, who won the PGA championship in 1991 but
dogged it through the 2000s, content to play and coast but not truly
compete.

To test how much effort both narcissists and non-narcissists will
exert when there is a chance for recognition on the line, a group of
researchers at Case Western University recruited 238 subjects, administered them the NPI and set them to work on a series of tasks, the
first of which involved the wonderfully nonscientific business of playing the manual-dexterity game Operation—using tiny tweezers to
remove tiny plastic body parts from the cartoon outline of a person on
a battery-charged board. Touch the tweezers to anything but the
target part itself and a buzzer sounds. To raise the ego stakes on this
stakes-less game, the participants were told that their first round
would be a practice round. On the second round, they could win
money if their score improved. Some of the subjects were told that
improvement was quite easy and very common among subjects who
had practiced; others were told that only the best and most dexterous
players ever improved on their initial score. For that group, there
would thus be glory, albeit a vanishingly tiny bit of it, in showing improvement. To the narcissists, however, that seemed to be enough.

Among people who had scored low on the NPI, there was usually a small improvement between the first and second round whether they'd been told that that was likely or not. This was also true for people who scored high on the NPI and had been told that improvement was common. Those narcissists who had been told that improvement was difficult or impossible, however, did a whopping four times better on the second round than those who believed improvement was routine. Clearly, they weren't innately more dexterous than all of the other subjects, but they were innately more hungry for glory.

A second experiment with a second sample group essentially repeated the first test, but used math problems instead of Operation. This time, the researchers not only found that narcissists did better when they were told the task was especially hard, but that non-narcissists actually did worse, apparently discouraged by the prediction that they would not do well and thus fulfilling that prophecy.

The third trial in the study went more directly at the social-loafing idea. The subjects were told they were part of an experiment that would test their creativity. They would be given twelve minutes to write down as many uses for a knife as they could. The quality of the ideas didn't matter, only the quantity. Some of the subjects were told that their answers would be entirely anonymous—that neither they nor the other group members nor the experimenters would know how any one person did compared with everyone else. Others were told that the experimenter would know who did best, but no one else. And still others were told that the results would be made completely public.

All of the subjects, regardless of NPI scores, performed in a similar range of about twenty ideas in the twelve allotted minutes when the results were either anonymous or known only to a researcher. But when the results would be made public—when there was a chance to do well in a way that everyone else would have to recognize—the highest-scoring narcissists blew the doors off the non-narcissists, coming up with an average of forty-four ideas compared with just fourteen. The researchers called the narcissists' performance on the nonpublic task flat-out "lazy" compared with how they did in the public scenario—another word for social loafing if ever there was one. Their high score on the public test, by contrast, was the product of "self-presentational exhibitionism," pure and simple.

This kind of "Look at me or else" behavior plays out in offices not just in ways that are bad for morale, but can be bad for the bottom line, particularly if other people are logging paid overtime to complete work that a social loafer is letting slide. "You hear the 'Hey, I need a couple of days to get up to speed on this' sort of thing from the narcissist," says Hochwarter. "It's a kind of shirking. It doesn't continue forever, of course. Eventually, the rest of the team has an aha moment. One person in the group sees what's going on and the information spreads to the rest." By then, the collegial and collaborative team has become a restive and resentful one—and that's pretty much the mood they'll start out with the next time they're stuck in a project with the narcissist.

ONE OF THE WORST THINGS about narcissists in the workplace is that their unlovely traits emerge even when things are going well. Profits may be up, products may be thriving and there may be nothing but praise to go around—and yet the self-promoters are still angling to get more than their share of credit and deny others theirs. Things get much worse when there's a problem, when a project goes south or a product has flopped and the narcissist is one of the people taking the heat.

The best strategy for anyone being blamed, even in part, for a problem is to be honest about what went wrong. Owning up to screwing up is a hard skill for any employee to learn, but there's something brave and even dignified about the well-timed *oops*, something that gets the hunt for responsible parties over with quickly and lets the whole company start cleaning up whatever mess was made. If that mess wasn't too big, the mere fact of your candor may ultimately earn you admiration—especially if you've taken a bullet for your team or subordinates. None of that is in the narcissist's skill set. Indeed, not only do they not accept blame, they usually deflect it to others—and they often actually believe what they're saying.

"Ego protection is of the utmost importance for a narcissist," says Harms. "So when they fail, it's attributed to something external: There's something wrong in the organization, someone didn't get me the information I needed, I've got to do everything myself."

Adds Campbell: "This is something we see a lot in people, but especially in narcissists. It's what we call self-enhancement bias. You fail a test and you blame the test—it wasn't your fault. You ace the test and you credit your studying. Either way, you're covered."

The real danger in cases like this is that the dysfunction spreads beyond the narcissist and the people being accused directly. Blame is radioactive. Nobody wants to accept it or handle it, especially if it's undeserved, so we react to it the way we do to anything that's too hot to touch, which is that we flip it away fast. When a narcissist is in trouble for botching a deal but blames a colleague for failing to send along an important e-mail, that person may immediately react by blaming a subordinate for, say, failing to flag the e-mail as urgent. The subordinate may then claim never to have received it in the first place, flipping the blame down to the person who was supposed to have sent it. The phenomenon is known by organizational psychologists as a blame contagion, and it spreads in just the wide-ranging, viral way a real infection does. As with an infection, too, it's possible to pass on the pathogen involuntarily and entirely unconsciously, as Nathanael Fast, of the University of Southern California, proved in a 2010 study.

In the first step in his multipart study, Fast had a group of college students read one of two news stories about a special election that former California governor Arnold Schwarzenegger called in 2005 in order to push through four referenda he supported. The public, suffering from ballot fatigue after a 2002 off-year election, a 2004 presidential election and no shortage of the special elections so peculiar to the state, pushed back, decisively rejecting all four of the initiatives. The whole misbegotten idea cost the already cash-strapped California $250 million, and Schwarzenegger was roundly pilloried for it. All of that actually happened, but the news stories the students were given to read were invented.

Half of them read a faux clip in which the governor manned up and took the blame for the mess. "Schwarzenegger said the responsibility for the election rests solely with him," the piece reported. " 'The buck stops with me,' he said. 'One shouldn't shy away from that. It was my idea to have the special election and I said this is the year for reform. However, the people of California did not like what I proposed and now we must move forward.' "

The other subjects read a clip that featured a decidedly pettier governor: "Schwarzenegger blamed bitter political partisanship for the results of the special election. 'It is unfortunate that certain special-interest groups can think only about their own interests. I do not blame anyone on my team or myself for what happened. For the reasons mentioned, the election didn't work out.' "

Afterward, Fast and his colleagues gave the subjects what is known as a filler task, asking them to complete a survey indicating how familiar they were with certain professional baseball players. That exercise had nothing at all to do with the study, but served as sort of a cognitive palate cleanser that got them thinking about something else. Finally, the investigators asked the subjects to write a short essay about a failure in their own lives in which they were to describe what had gone on and, significantly, why it happened. The essays were then read by outsiders who knew nothing about the study and were asked simply to rate the responses on a one-to-five scale—with one meaning that the subjects accepted complete blame for the failure and five meaning that they rejected it completely and attributed it to someone else.

On average, the people who had read the Good Arnold story, in which Schwarzenegger accepted full responsibility, scored a 1.84 on the blaming-others scale, while those who read about Bad Arnold scored a 2.41. That's 31 percent higher, a number that, in statistical terms at least, is more than enough to prove the power of the blame contagion.

The experiment, surely, isn't perfect. The baseball filler task, while well-intentioned, might not have been enough to wipe the Schwarzenegger story from the subjects' conscious minds. Still, the other parts of the study explored the same idea in different ways and came up with similar results. In a later trial, subjects read news stories about college students who blamed either themselves or the tough economy for not being able to find a job, and then again wrote essays in which they described a personal setback. The results were close to what they were in the Schwarzenegger study—with 27 percent more finger-pointing among students who'd been primed by a blame-laying news story. That the scores weren't even higher was something of a surprise, since it's a lot easier for a group of students to empathize with another group suffering through the grind of looking for work than with a governor who has suffered a political setback. They thus might have been expected to mirror the blaming behavior in even greater numbers. Still, 27 percent remains a big statistical gap, suggesting that the subjects had indeed caught the blame bug, even if they contracted a milder case than expected.

"The self-image protection goal is extremely contagious," says Fast. "Even if you're not a narcissist, you still carry that impulse in a sort of latent way. When we see other people pursue it in an open way, we copy that, if only to protect ourselves. Latent then becomes active across the whole organization, and everybody pays a price."

If both of those parts of Fast's study showed how stubborn the blame contagion can be, the final part showed a way out of it. In that experiment, students read about a foundation director who refused to accept responsibility for the failure of some of his grants—blaming the recipients themselves. Half of the subjects were then asked to write a brief essay describing one of their talents—something they do well and, significantly, are proud of doing well. Those who had a chance for this kind of self-affirming interlude broke the blame contagion, accepting significantly more responsibility when they later wrote their essays about a personal failure. The ones who'd read about the foundation director and hadn't had the chance to self-affirm went right ahead blaming others.

The problem of narcissists in the workplace is not going away, and nor are the benefits—fraught as they are—of having them around. The high-energy, ice-breaking, approval-seeking employee can, like it or not, be something of a tonic in most offices—at least until that tonic turns toxic. Often, narcissists will flush themselves out of the company's system, either getting fired for some kind of egregious behavior or leaving in various degrees of huff when they decide their surpassing talents aren't being fully appreciated. Before they go—and, ideally, before they drive other people out—they can still be an asset.

"If you're a boss, you've got to figure out how to leverage your narcissists," says Harms. "Get the most out of them. Narcissists will do a lot if they think it will enhance their image, so give them a challenge, move them around to new situations. It also helps to frame any criticism to them carefully. 'You're great, and now here's a way you can be even better.'" That constant cycle of being applauded and starting anew not only plays to the best of the narcissists' skills, but also relieves one team of what can be their increasingly abrasive company, shifting them to another situation in which their good first-impression skills may actually be quite welcome.

Ultimately, of course, there's no one left to impress. Ultimately, too, the boss gets tired of having to manage the narcissist's ego—offering the dog-yummy of a compliment before daring to venture a criticism. All that's left then is a strutting, boasting, blame-laying, selectively lazy employee whose only remaining contribution to the company would be the leaving of it. Narcissists are the volatile compound in the chemistry set of any workplace: they flare brightly and often quite beautifully, but only for a while. Then, inevitably, they either blow up or burn out. Either way, it does not end well.

CHAPTER FIVE

The Beast in Your Bed

Having sex is the second most presumptuous thing you'll ever do in your life. The most presumptuous is expecting it in the first place.

Human beings are highly social, highly affiliative creatures. But we're also keep-your-distance creatures. We crave breathing room and personal space as much as we crave touch. A handshake, a hug, an arm around the shoulder are warm and lovely and among our most powerful ways of expressing connectedness. But they're also transitory, exceedingly fleeting and very explicitly chosen.

This is not so with other kinds of touch—the press of bodies in a crowded subway, the too-close brush in a packed elevator, the accidental jostle in a busy store. The angry cry "Watch where you're going!" may sometimes be the result of being bumped in a startling or even painful way, but just as often it's a reaction to the fact that we've been bumped at all. Sometimes we don't even need actual physical contact to feel encroached upon: the person who moves too close during a conversation, who reaches across you at a table, who merely blocks your view at a meeting or in a movie, all may make you bristle. The sense is not one of merely being inconvenienced, but of being violated. And all that is when we're in public, in control and—not insignificantly—fully clothed.

Sex is another matter entirely. If we can often be touch-averse, we're exponentially more ick-averse. We are predisposed to find some things safe and touchable and some not, and the way we draw the distinction often makes no rational sense. You may think nothing of picking up a dollar off the sidewalk or touching the door handle of a taxi, even though, likely as not, they're crawling with germs. We don't worry too much about that because those objects pass a threshold test: They're hard and they're dry and they have no smell.

Now think of something wet, something sticky, something that gives off a scent of some kind, whether pleasant, unpleasant or neutral. The presumption here is that these are things that warrant some caution. Watch a one-year-old eat a cookie: bliss. Watch the same baby eat an unfrosted piece of chocolate cake: more bliss. Now add frosting and everything changes. The baby pauses, inclines her head, and if she touches the gooey stuff at all, does so only cautiously, then pulls her hand away and regards with distaste the way the frosting sticks to and spreads between her fingers. The bright colors, the sugary smell and the adjacency of the cake, which touches and thus vouches for the frosting, ultimately prevail over the primal suspicion, but it's a close case for a little while.

This, of course, is an ingenious bit of hard behavioral wiring. Germs may live on rocks and coins, but they can't survive there too long. They thrive and divide in goo. Bacteria and viruses incubate in human and animal bodies and are then excreted, sneezed, spit, bled or exhaled into the world. As long as they're wet, they're relatively fresh, and as long as they're fresh they could spell trouble. Sometimes other keep-away cues are added. There's a reason that we perceive the smell of vomit and feces—animal or human—as so singularly revolting, and that's because of their very close relationship to food. Not all that long before, they *were* food, which means that we might be inclined to taste them. So they give off a smell to which our brains assign a powerful, repellent value, and we learn even before we know why that these are things we ought to leave alone.

"We are keenly attuned to the tactile properties of substances that are likely to infect us—curdled, gooey, lukewarm, moist, mucky, oily, scabby, slimy, slithery and squishy," writes Jeffrey A. Lockwood, professor of natural sciences and humanities at the University of Wyoming, in his book *The Infested Mind*. "These are the textures of feces, mucus, lesions, innards, worms, snakes, cockroaches and maggots." Lockwood's book deals with humans' relationships with insects specifically—a source of disgust if ever there was one—but his roots-of-revulsion premise is a well-established one.

The same kind of strategic value judgment is at work when we choose what we find beautiful and what we don't—particularly in one another. Clear, unblemished, unwrinkled flesh signals both the absence of disease and, more important, fertility, and that's something that's exceedingly appealing—not to mention exceedingly important if the species is going to survive. Wrinkled, mottled or blemished flesh signals possible illness and lack of fertility and so we call it ugly—or at least unlovely—and pass it by. The youngest flesh of all, baby flesh, inspires a wholly different—and faintly disturbing—reaction. Anthropologist Sarah Blaffer Hrdy of the University of California, Davis, thinks it's no coincidence that some of the most common terms of endearment we use when we address babies—honey, muffin, cupcake, sweetie, sugar pie—are foods. For a carnivorous species like ours, flesh that is fatty, free of markings and belongs to a creature that is utterly helpless makes an awfully tempting meal. When you nuzzle a chubby six-month-old and say in that only-to-a-baby voice we all use, "Ooh! I could eat you up," you're not kidding.

That cannibalistic impulse, of course, is buried many layers deep in our behavioral repertoire, and it emerges only in symbolic ways. But sex is different. We do it, we crave it, and yet in theory we ought to recoil from it. The mere act of kissing, to say nothing of actual by-the-playbook sex, to say even less about all of the à la carte variations on it that are limited only by our imaginations and our agility, violate nearly every anti-yuck, anti-contamination rule we have. It's a flat-out assault on all five senses—sight, sound, touch, taste, smell—in ways we wouldn't tolerate in nearly any other situation. It may have taken until the AIDS epidemic came along before the term "body fluids" became something we consciously considered dangerous, but the deeper, survival-driven regions of our brains have been screaming that warning to us for as long as the species has existed.

Procreation and the survival of humanity, however, rely on our getting over that base aversion in this particular case, and in 2012, a team of researchers in the Netherlands explored how this disgust override happens. The scientists recruited a group of ninety women and divided them into three groups: one watched an erotic video that tastefully sidestepped some of the more explicit raunch that men don't seem to mind but women generally abhor; another watched a sports video; and the third watched a neutral clip of a moving train. All three groups were then asked to perform yuck-inducing tasks that included eating a cookie that had been lying on a plate next to a worm, cleaning their hands with a used tissue and touching a tray of used condoms. In trial after trial, the women who had watched the sexually arousing video tolerated the tasks better and completed them more dependably than the others.

"The findings indicate that . . . the impact of heightened sexual arousal on subjective disgust . . . will act in a way to facilitate the engagement in pleasurable sex," wrote the authors of the paper. In other words, turn the sexual thermostat up and, for a while at least, you turn the revulsion response down.

Fine, so science can run a crude simulation of one small part of the sexual arousal cycle, which in turn helps explain the improbable appeal of sex and all its variations. Still, that doesn't mean it doesn't require an equally hardwired arrogance to go on the prowl for a sexual partner in the first place. You may have already decided that you're willing to tolerate someone else's manifold sensory offenses. But taking it as a given that someone will tolerate yours, to accept them and even absorb them, to enter, or—more violatively—to be entered by you, is in some ways grandiose in the extreme. Yet that's the offer we put on the table every time we walk into a singles bar—and that's the offer that at least in some cases gets snapped up. Without self-adoration, without an underlying narcissism, there would be no sex.

Still, the self-confident liberation we feel isn't total. Even when the sexual deal has been struck, after the sex has actually begun in fact, we retain a measure of I'm-not-worthy self-consciousness. The goal of complete sexual abandon—of losing yourself in the moment and the experience—might be nice in principle, but in the real world it doesn't happen as often as we might like. The first time we have sex with a new person there is a brainstorm—literally—of natural opiates that can feel very much like chemical intoxication. As relationships go on, they move through predictable stages, including a sort of quieting down, a discerning evaluation of the new partner, an inevitable power struggle as the rules of the romantic union are hammered out and ultimately a commitment or a separation.

That first time, however, the sexually intoxicated time, we like to think the thrill will be total, but it isn't. We still find ourselves wondering: Do I look OK? Am I doing this right? Am I better than, worse than, about on par with the other people who have performed these particular acts with this particular person before? Our own pleasure is tempered by our fretting over the other person's, and enhanced when—*yes!*—that person seems to have been transported by the experience. And no sooner is even a wonderfully satisfying encounter over than the self-consciousness comes creeping back: Plenty of people may be proud—even exhibitionistically so—about their utterly naked bodies, but more are inclined to pull up the sheets, keep the lights dim, wrap themselves in a towel when they get out of bed. Sex is over and the more bordered and circumscribed world comes crowding back.

All that psychic tension is actually not a bad thing. If a relationship is going to develop into anything more than a one-off romp, it's necessary to establish an emotional, intellectual, power and ego balance, too. That requires humility, perspective and a little distance from yourself, and if it means worrying a bit about how you're doing or how you look in the very moments you should be feeling the unhinged bliss of sex, it's a small price to pay.

Such a system of emotional checks and balances works, however, only if the kind of narcissism you bring with you into the singles bar, the bedroom or the eventual relationship is the lowercase-*n* variety, the mild, manageable, general self-confidence that is the table stakes of playing the dating game in the first place. Capital-*N* narcissism— the charming, beautiful, swaggering, slinking, self-adoring kind; the kind that cares deeply only for the pleasure of the narcissist; the kind that sees bedmates and romantic partners as fungible, expendable, forgettable creatures—is a different beast entirely. Narcissism anywhere—in the home, in the workplace, in the classroom—can be a monstrous thing. But it's in the world of romance that the narcissist's greed, hedonism, self-regard and lack of empathy find their highest and purest expression.

The thrill you experience when the narcissist at a party selects you for attention can hit you like hard whiskey. The most attractive, seductive, sought-after person in the room is actually, unbelievably, seeking you. Your beautiful narcissist is fun and funny and crazily attentive. You talk and it seems like you're being listened to, but the truth is you don't have to contribute all that much to the conversation, because the stream of wit and energy coming at you is more than enough to fill any vacuum. The sex that follows—and make no mistake, sex will follow—is more of the same: It's feverish and exhausting and full of abandon, and you can't quite believe that that body with all its crazily sexy energy is colliding with yours. You'll want more—the sex, the charm, the everything—the next day and the next week and the next forever, since, incredibly, you may just have met the person you were meant to be with and it's better than you ever imagined.

You haven't met anything of the kind. Indeed, you've met the exact opposite. You'll notice that soon enough—when the rush of funny and engaging talk that's always pointed your way leaves you feeling a little worn out; when your lovely lover's eyes go blank with disinterest if you do at last find a bit of conversational daylight and begin to talk about yourself; when those same eyes that once fixed so attentively on you wander every time someone else younger, richer, or simply newer than you walks into the room; when your perfect partner seems unable to admit to even the smallest error or shortcoming that might suggest a bit of human imperfection after all. And you'll notice it inevitably when you learn the full wages of making an alliance with a narcissist: when the lying and the cheating and the sexual disinterest begin, when the only words that come from your partner anymore are angry or accusing ones, and finally, when the relationship itself ends and you wind up stunned and alone and your gorgeous narcissist is back in the world, having already connected with someone else—typically one of those younger, better, newer people who drifted by before—having traded up from you, because the next step, the one beyond the now, is the one the narcissist is always thinking about anyway.

"The pattern is predictable," says the University of Georgia's Keith Campbell. "You meet someone charming and extroverted and confident and you find them very exciting to be around in the short term. But the relationship never translates into intimacy and caring. They flirt with other people and you think 'What's wrong with me?' and the person cheats and you break up. And then you think about it for two years. I call it the chocolate cake model. It's a wonderful rush at first, but after you eat it, you want to kill yourself."

Romantic narcissism knows no meaningful gender boundaries.

Men and women may express self-adoration and lack of empathy differently—particularly in terms of their sexual indiscriminateness—but the underlying pathology is the same, and it cuts across not just gender lines but generational ones, too. As always, it's impossible to diagnose anyone—particularly a celebrity we've never met—just by observation, but someone like Taylor Swift, with her serial boys, surely does seem like nothing more than a different era's and different gender's version of Warren Beatty and his serial women.

"He was the only man I knew who could get to a mirror faster than me," said Joan Collins of the man who was once her lover and, according to a preposterously precise figure in a 2010 biography, slept with 12,755 women in his life. That number may be as hard to believe as it is impossible to prove, but it gained a lot of currency when the book came out—enough that Beatty felt obliged to issue a statement denying it—because it was of a piece with the way he'd spent much of his public life. Beatty's A-list lovers included Natalie Wood, Julie Christie, Catherine Deneuve, Faye Dunaway, Melanie Griffith, Diane Keaton, Leslie Caron, Diana Ross, Goldie Hawn, Candice Bergen, Carly Simon, Michelle Phillips, Madonna and more.

"I remember the first time I ever saw Warren," Keaton once said. "I thought, 'He's so beautiful.' It was like there was a light. He looked at me for a second, and then passed me by." The popular assumption has always been that Carly Simon's song "You're So Vain" is about Beatty, which fits because he so assuredly is. The songwriter herself, while never quite denying that, has never quite confirmed it either, but nobody pretended that Beatty was being unfairly tarred if she was indeed singing about him.

Swift, similarly, has conspicuously helped herself to a long line of pop-world princelings—Joe Jonas, Taylor Lautner, Lucas Till, Harry Styles—men she finishes with and then blisters in the hit songs that follow. "If you're horrible to me, I'm going to write a song about it, and you won't like it. That's how I operate," she said.

Even musician John Mayer, another of her boy toys, but one who is thirteen years older than Swift and earns little sympathy for getting entangled with someone so young, seemed stunned at the song she wrote about him. It was titled, appropriately, "Dear John" and it blasted him as "sick," "dark" and "twisted."

"I know she's the biggest thing in the world," a rattled Mayer told *Rolling Stone* later, "and I'm not trying to sink anybody's ship, but I think it's abusing your talent to rub your hands together and go, 'Wait till he gets a load of this!' That's bullshit."

Maybe, and maybe Mayer got what he deserved for dating so far down the age spectrum, whether Swift is a narcissist or not. But most people who become entangled with a narcissist are less to blame for their own pain than Mayer was. Most of them tumble into a narcissist's world and arms and bed thrilled to be there and drunk at the opportunity. That intoxication fades fast, however, and the emotional hangover that follows can be long and nasty—a pain whose only redeeming feature is that it makes you very, very unlikely to make the same mistake again.

IF NARCISSISM is one of humanity's more stubbornly intractable traits—and it is—it's partly because it facilitates the one basic act likelier than anything else to keep a particular physical or behavioral characteristic alive in the gene pool: breeding. Successful narcissists have a whole lot of sex, which means they're statistically likelier to have a whole lot of babies—at least compared to everyone else. This highly adaptive component of narcissism gives it a big edge over other disorders in getting passed down to the next generation.

"When you're talking about truly pathological narcissism, it's hard to say why it hasn't been eradicated from the gene pool," says Jessica Tracy, a professor of personality and social psychology at the University of British Columbia. "But when you're talking about the more everyday kind, it's equally hard to see how it ever would disappear since it's so adaptive. All you have to do is replicate yourself, and narcissists are very good at doing that."

Male narcissists would seem to have a big advantage here, and they do. For men, breeding is biologically cheap and easy, something they could—at least when they're young enough—do multiple times a day. Women, even if they wanted to, could never remotely keep up with that kind of fecundity. But heterosexual narcissistic males are still trying to bed women, and no matter the men's seductiveness, women remain the more discriminating gender and will still be more selective than men about whom they bed. Even the truly narcissistic male will strike out more than he succeeds. Narcissistic women, on the other hand, have a much easier go of things simply because so many men seem almost incapable of saying no.

Psychology and human behavior students are taught early on about the famous 1978 study conducted on the Florida State University campus in which volunteer male and female subjects approached other students of the opposite sex and recited a carefully scripted proposition: "I have been noticing you around campus and I find you to be very attractive," they said. "Would you go to bed with me tonight?"

The subjects were neither particularly unattractive nor extremely attractive—which is to say they were pretty much the kinds of partners most people do wind up going to bed with. The women's success rate when they made this pitch was a remarkable 75 percent, though no subsequent rolls in the hay actually took place—at least not under the aegis of the study. The male volunteers succeeded with this approach precisely 0 percent of the time. Remarkably, the psychologists repeated the study three more times throughout the 1980s—when the AIDS epidemic made casual sex seem like mortal folly—and about 50 percent of the men were still completely receptive to an anonymous hookup.

In the real world, this pattern holds even when the woman is manifestly bad news—narcissistically or otherwise—someone with volatile moods or a turbulent romantic or personal history. It's not for nothing that the term "hot mess" has gained such linguistic currency, capturing as it does the Lindsay Lohans, Amanda Bynes and, at one time, the Kate Mosses of the world: beautiful, captivating women who also, at least for a while, behave in ways that lead to their own undoing. Men can often spot this and nevertheless respond to overtures all the same. A long-ago issue of *Playboy*—a journal with admittedly less cred than the *Journal of Psychology & Human Sexuality*, in which the updates of the Florida State studies were published in 1989—included a cartoon that captured this idea splendidly. A beautiful woman in a little black cocktail dress is seated at a bar, talking to an obviously entranced man. The word "trouble" is literally written all over her, covering nearly every inch of her exposed skin. Another man stands behind the first and helpfully asks him, "Could I talk to you for a moment?" The answer, likely as not, would have been no. The entranced man had just one thing on his mind—and it didn't involve calmly reflecting on what kind of interpersonal crack-up he was courting.

Women may react to charismatic, bad-boy men in much the way men react to bad-girl women, even if they're not nearly the same sexual pushovers. Multiple studies have shown the seductive power of what's evocatively known as the Dark Triad of personality traits: narcissism, impulsive thrill-seeking and Machiavellianism—or exploitativeness. Men who score high in any of these traits—to say nothing of those who score high on all of them, which some do—also tend to exceed other men in number of sexual encounters in any given week, month or year. At a conference convened by the Human Behavior and Evolution Society in Japan in 2008, Peter Jonason of New Mexico State University, who conducted one of the studies, invoked James Bond as the perfect mash-up of all of the Dark Triad traits—and the successful sexuality that goes with it: "He's clearly disagreeable, very extroverted and likes trying new things—including killing people and new women," Jonason said. The headline for the story of Jonason's study in the UK paper *The Independent* was "Why Women Really Do Love Self-Obsessed Psychopaths."

Like Tracy, the other investigators saw evolutionary value in this behavior, simply because any mating at all can result in successful breeding, launching one more little narcissist across the generational divide and into the future. "The strategy seems to have worked. We still have these traits," Jonason said.

That, of course, raises an inevitable question: Why haven't narcissists ultimately risen to a position of wholesale domination of the species, using their procreative prowess simply to crowd out the less dark, more agreeable majority? Jonason believes that the relative scarcity of true narcissists gives them the advantage of surprise: If most of the charming potential suitors a woman met turned out to be self-adoring, Machiavellian cads, they'd know to avoid them. But since most nice-seeming, charming guys really are nice and charming, the bad ones get to slip in under the radar.

ONCE A ROMANTIC RELATIONSHIP is actually established, there will typically be a golden period. This is the thrilling stage, the dreamy-eyed stage, and it's something narcissists do very well. In fact, it's at this point that they actually perform better than non-narcissists in one very unlikely dimension of a romance: fidelity. The higher a partner rates on the NPI, the less likely—at least at first—that person is to cheat. Campbell demonstrated that improbable connection in a 2005 study in which he recruited 154 volunteers, administered them the NPI, and divided them into two random groups. Half were asked to list ten reasons their romantic partner was highly committed to them; the other half were asked for ten reasons their partners might not be committed. Finally, they all took a survey asking them how receptive they'd be to a romantic overture from someone else.

Many of the people who scored high on the NPI, indicating that they have significant narcissistic tendencies even if they aren't clinical narcissists, had a hard time even coming up with ten reasons their partners weren't wholly smitten with them, but had no trouble at all filling out the list of reasons they were. The non-narcissists did equally well on both. And when asked about their willingness to cheat, the narcissists, on the whole, scored lower, a superficial sign that for them this relationship was the real deal. But the superficiality was the key.

The narcissist's transient fidelity was not due to any innate sense of decency, integrity or commitment, but rather to mere obtuseness. Of all the things that push partners to cheat, one of the most powerful is insecurity. If you suspect your lover may be drifting away or losing interest, you're much likelier to seek comfort elsewhere—to have your ego and self-esteem validated and perhaps even establish your next romantic landing spot before you get pushed out of your current relationship. Narcissists, lost in the self-love that defines them, simply cannot fathom that their partner doesn't feel exactly the same way about them, even if the partner has in fact begun to have doubts and withdraw. The result is that the narcissists' eyes aren't wandering elsewhere—yet. This is consistent with the narcissists' characteristically poor learning curve when it comes to personal performance—the inability to accept, say, that they're terrible poker players and their tendency thus to press their bets stubbornly even after they've lost the previous dozen hands. Sometimes, repeated failures like that at the gambling table, in the workplace or in the bedroom make them sullen or aggressive, but other times they remain sunnily unaware.

"Narcissists are buffered to some degree from negative information regarding their romantic relationships," Campbell said. "They don't always perceive their partners' feelings accurately, even if they actually are becoming negative. Of course, there's a mountain of evidence that

relationships with narcissists frequently suffer. But in the right circumstances, for a little while at least, the narcissist's self-confidence
may actually be an advantage."

The first sign that that golden period is ending is often expressed in
fault-finding, the hunt for—and inevitable discovery of—disqualifying
flaws in a partner. If you're a narcissist, the person who appears beside
you has to be someone whose very presence enhances your own status.
Not for the narcissist the plain-looking wife or the nondescript and
quiet husband—strong and loving and even exceptional people, perhaps, but with a value that's evident only to those who know them
best. The narcissist's partner requires a certain immediately recognizable and calculable worth, typically measured in wealth, appearance
or power.

The most obvious example of this, of course, is the trophy wife—
the serial trading up in appearance and down in age that's so common
among rich, successful men. Newt Gingrich, John McCain and Donald Trump have all trod this familiar path, as has Rupert Murdoch,
who in 1999 left his wife of 32 years to marry a woman 38 years his
junior, a marriage that did last a respectable 14 years, until 2013, when
that one, too, ended. But youth and appearance aren't the only way a
partner's qualities reflect well on the narcissist.

Bill Clinton may be in a dead heat with John Edwards on the NPI
scoreboard, but one of the reasons we like him so much—and forgave
him so readily—is Hillary. Yes, he cheated on her—a lot—and the fact
that she would have him back played a not-inconsequential role in the
fact that America took him back, too. But it's also widely accepted
that Hillary Clinton is almost always the smartest person in any room
she enters—including a room that includes Clinton himself—and the
pride he takes in that is palpable. He has regularly described her as the
most interesting person he knows, and while plenty of politicians say
that about their spouses, Clinton intimates have always confirmed that
it's true, that he is never fully satisfied with an idea or an argument

until he hears Hillary's take on it—and that was the case even before she spent eight years as First Lady, another eight as senator from New York, and four as secretary of state.

One of the most dramatic and reflexively genuine moments ever captured on camera between the couple occurred during the taping of their celebrated *60 Minutes* interview during the 1992 presidential campaign, when they addressed then Governor Clinton's serial infidelities. He confessed to having "made mistakes in my marriage," and Hillary gave him a public pass for it, and that was all most people saw. During one of the setups, however, when the cameras were rolling but capturing nothing of importance, a heavy studio light fell from the ceiling and crashed to the floor. Anyone who had been hit by it would have been seriously injured and perhaps even killed. Both Clintons jumped up, and in an eyeblink she turned to him and he took her in his arms and shielded her with his body. The moment felt and looked manifestly real—so fast and automatic it was impossible to fake. He may have betrayed her in the past, and though no one knew it at the time, he would do it again, but that didn't mean he didn't find her precious and irreplaceable. That reflexive and protective moment showed it.

None of that makes Clinton any less of a narcissist. Indeed, it's naïve to think that—his deep love for his wife notwithstanding—he's not getting his own "Look at me" impulses satisfied just by hanging around with Hillary. Her reflected excellence grows only greater with the accumulation of age, experience and wisdom, and that's no small feat. When the reflected excellence comes from a model whose principal appeal to the partner is that she's young and beautiful, the shine fades fast.

In fairness, it's not just men who are capable of the narcissistic alliance or quick trade-up. Jessica Sklar, Jerry Seinfeld's wife, left her first husband after just a month of marriage when the rich, globally famous Seinfeld came along. Ingrid Bergman divorced her husband of thirteen years, California neurosurgeon Petter Lindstrom, after beginning an affair with the decidedly more glamorous director Roberto Rossellini, with whom she was working on a movie in 1950.

"I felt so terrible for my father," said Bergman and Lindstrom's daughter, the TV and radio journalist Pia Lindström, many years later in an interview I had with her in her New York apartment. "I loved him so much and I didn't understand why she didn't anymore." The fact, however, is that Bergman may indeed have loved her ex—even when she left him. But the self-validating pull of a more glamorous partner may have been greater.

"In most nonromantic situations, our relational needs can be satisfied," says Keith Campbell of the University of Georgia. "You don't have a best friend and then want to trade up to a new one. But narcissists do have that need with their romantic partners." Failure to make that periodic upgrade leaves the narcissist at risk, as Campbell has written, of "being admired by an inconsequential other," a stark piece of phrasing that captures the hard calculus of the narcissist's thinking.

Ordinary, nonfamous narcissists don't have the same freedom famous people have to accept nothing less than a Hillary or a Rossellini or a runway model. But it's not too much to say that they will nonetheless look for a certain suite of traits in a partner and will quickly torpedo a relationship they've begun with a partner who is not quite up to scratch.

Campbell and his colleagues have tried to get a more granular sense of what most narcissists look for in a mate—research that is not always easy to collect since it relies on self-reporting, and narcissists, perhaps more than other people, can be reluctant to admit things to a researcher or anyone that will make them look shallow or foolish. Still, there are ways to tease out the data. In one survey, for example, Campbell asked volunteers to describe the kind of partner they were looking for by checking off descriptions in six broad categories: caring, needy, humorous, admiring, perfect (defined by such terms as "ambitious" and "good-looking") and values (which included "interested in family life" and "moral" as descriptors). The sample group was made up of both men and women who scored in a nicely random scatter across the NPI spectrum.

The results of the overall survey did not break down by gender in any meaningful way, but they did break down clearly along the narcissism fault line. Not surprisingly, only one person out of 102 subjects checked off any traits in the needy category—a good indicator that, narcissist or not, few people are attracted to an overly dependent mate. Only three people checked off any of the traits in the admiring category—surprising given the healthy representation of narcissists, but less so given that narcissists don't always admit to or even realize how much admiration they demand from other people, and non-narcissists don't require that much to begin with. The other categories, however, revealed a lot.

Nearly three times as many narcissists as non-narcissists checked off traits describing a perfect partner, while 67 percent more non-narcissists than narcissists checked off the traits of a caring person. Humor scored much higher in the narcissism category too, and when it was combined with the perfect category, it finished with more than twice the number of votes that pairing got among non-narcissists. The combination of caring and values, on the other hand, scored 40 percent higher among non-narcissists than narcissists. Male or female, it seemed, the narcissists were looking for the equivalent of the sexy Italian director, while the non-narcissists were much more drawn to the gentle California neurosurgeon.

The lack of interest in intimacy and caring is a predictable part of the narcissistic package, but it also seems a little surprising. Even a narcissist who always has one eye on the door and one foot out of it still wants to enjoy the relationship while it's going on, and intimacy and caring are just other ways of describing a partner who is concerned with you, will attend to you and listen to you—all big items on a narcissist's bottomless list of needs.

But intimacy does not come free. It takes work to get another person to invest energy and empathy in you when you're sick or sad or disappointed or preoccupied, and that other person requires a measure of reciprocity in order to get to that point at all. Narcissists have no appetite for the quid pro quo. Intimacy also implies a certain lack of freedom, a limitation not just on your license to flirt or cheat, but even to gather an audience and work a room in the way you're accustomed. That constant foraging for attention may be a key source of the narcissist's emotional nourishment, but it's hard to indulge it with a close mate who, after a certain time, expects to sit down together at a dinner party or, at least sometimes, move through a crowd along with you—one half of a joined team to whom you devote some of your focus and with whom you share some of the attention that comes your way.

"For narcissists, every moment is perceived as an opportunity to be recognized and admired," says Aaron Pincus, psychologist and director of clinical training at Penn State University. "After a while, they don't know when to do it and when not to do it." That, clearly, leaves little room for a mate at your side and the confinement of closeness.

Finally, and a little poignantly, there's the central paradox of many narcissists—at least the mask-model variety: They don't think terribly much of themselves to begin with, and that plays a big role in their avoidance of intimacy. At some frightened level, their compulsive seductions are all a desperate, frenzied, even self-loathing pose, and the closer they get to another person, the better the chance that person has of finding them out. When that happens, it's the narcissist who may be the one who gets tossed over, the narcissist who's found lacking. That kind of experience is hard enough for the healthy, grounded non-narcissist to take; for the narcissist, whose self-adoration was a sham in the first place, it can feel like death.

"[It] is like being hollowed out, mentally disemboweled or watching oneself die," wrote Israeli author Sam Vaknin in his book *Malignant*

Self Love, about how the narcissist experiences rejection. "It is a cosmic evaporation, disintegrating into molecules of terrified anguish, helplessly and inexorably. . . . The narcissist will do anything to avoid it." That doesn't sound pretty, and it can't be fun. If remaining at arm's length from a partner can help you avoid such an experience, it seems like a reasonable precaution to take.

WHATEVER IT IS that pushes your relationship with a narcissist into its terminal phase, what comes next will be painful but sadly predictable. Lying will be a big part of it. In some cases, lying in a relationship causes no real harm, and coming from a non-narcissist it might actually be forgivable. Maybe you tell a partner you're home with a headache and turning off your phone when in fact you're out dancing with friends; maybe you say you're working late when in fact the only thing you're doing with your colleagues from the office is sitting at a bar drinking. That's not playing square and it hardly builds trust. But particularly for younger, twenty-something couples, opening up a little breathing room and getting to spend a night as a single person—without any sexual hookups—can be benign in the long run and perhaps even beneficial if it helps you get something out of your system and maybe even appreciate more why you find your relationship more fulfilling.

But narcissists lie for a number of other reasons—none of them good. For starters, they do it to self-enhance: You see it in the man who tells you he's earning a seven-figure salary when in fact he's earning in the low sixes, but since he's convinced himself he's worth far more and will soon be paid accordingly, why not just act as if that's already the case? It's the woman who tells you she graduated with honors from Stanford when in fact she got by with a low-B average from Texas A&M, but hey, she deserved the Ivy League, didn't she?

"Narcissists will do things to self-enhance, and you just can't believe they'd do it," says Pincus. "They just deny aspects of reality that don't confirm the grandiose vision. This need for being adored and admired just creates a myopia."

That shortsightedness is oddly self-defeating, because in many cases it's inevitable that the narcissist will get caught. At some point, a girlfriend's college chum will spill where she really went to school, a colleague who's had too much to drink at a party will let slip what a boyfriend really earns. But narcissists aren't thinking down the line when they lie—partly because the immediate self-enhancement need is so great, partly because they just don't plan to be around that long.

The much bigger and more destructive reason narcissists lie is so they can cheat. Those lies may at first be the same benign type non-narcissists tell—the fib about working, rather than drinking, with colleagues. But to narcissists they also serve as a way to open a breach. They never felt terribly constrained by the importance of telling the truth to begin with, but in the early stages of the relationship they had no reason not to. Now that they've started getting restless, an evening out might be a nice way to remind themselves of the allure of being free, and the very act of lying feeds that feeling of liberation. What's more, unlike the non-narcissist, who really and truly does want just to drink, talk and go home, the narcissist is—or soon will be—on the make, either with someone in that bar that night, or another one very soon.

Cheating is to a relationship with a narcissist what a stock sell-off is to a real estate or tech bubble: something that everyone knows is coming but no one wants to admit. Not only is jumping into bed with someone else the ultimate expression of the freedom the narcissist is seeking, it also carries the high risk of getting caught, in which case the betrayal may sink the relationship entirely—merely accelerating the desired ending. Equally important, cheating plays straight to a narcissist's characteristic sense of entitlement, behind which is often an unacknowledged sense of grievance. You work hard; if you're married, you take care of your spouse and family. But you're still a hot sexual property, so don't you deserve a little reward? Indeed, isn't there a different kind of injustice being done if you don't get one? Men might cheat more than women, but when cheating-inclined narcissists of either sex walk into a bar, both do it limned in a sense of justification and expectation.

"We've developed an entitlement scale to test narcissists," says Brad Bushman, professor of communications and psychology at Ohio State University. "One of the statements we ask people to agree or disagree with is 'If I were on the *Titanic*, I would deserve to be in the life raft.' The honest answer for a lot of narcissists who take the test is yes, they would." Once you're OK tossing women and children overboard so that you can snag a seat, cheating is little more than a misdemeanor.

Finally, terribly, may come physical abuse, which is hardly unheard of in relationships with narcissists. This, too, is characteristic of both sexes, though of course it is men who are vastly more likely to abuse than women. Chronic batterers, or, in the worst case, killers like O. J. Simpson, are surely playing out multiple pathologies, with narcissism merely an accelerant feeding an already bad blaze. But there is no denying that anyone involved with even an ordinary narcissist is at higher risk of being abused than other people are. An old but highly regarded 1990 study of a population of men who had either been ordered by a court to enter treatment for partner abuse or had volunteered to participate found that one of the best ways to predict which men would re-offend was to administer the NPI while they were in treatment. The ones who scored highest on the test were the ones likeliest to be back before long. The *Diagnostic and Statistical Manual (DSM)* does not make a direct link between narcissism and partner abuse, but it does define the three traits most abusers share with narcissists: exploitativeness, lack of empathy and entitlement—three of the crown jewels of the narcissistic personality.

The narcissist's need to maintain a positive self-image at all costs also means that a partner's behavior must be carefully regulated so that the necessary submission and admiration keep coming. That often means controlling the couple's finances, social calendar and even conversations, especially when they are in public and there is an audience at hand. Even when narcissistic abuse never rises to the level of the physical, this kind of demanding, suffocating, all-about-me totalitarianism becomes a sort of proxy battering, and any partner worn down by years of such treatment will confess to feeling awfully beaten up by the time it's all over.

Getting to that exit point is vital, but it should be handled carefully whenever the threat of abuse is looming. Having a third person close at hand when the break is made is one good way to ensure that things won't turn explosive. "A lot of people get hostile when they get rejected, but it's worse with narcissists," says psychologist Jennifer Crocker of Ohio State University. "Their anger and hostility reflect a sense of injustice." Restraining orders, safe houses, criminal prosecutions and all of the other legal measures necessary in the worst cases may come later, but the first and most important step is getting the partner out of harm's way—which means anywhere else but in the company of the narcissist.

FOR ALL OF THE OBSTACLES, not every single relationship with a narcissist comes to an end. Some linger on, often miserably, for years, with the victim typically hoping for something better and the narcissist continually promising it—and never delivering. Others, improbably, survive in a not entirely awful way. The very need for praise and reinforcement that defines the narcissist's personality gives the partner, who is the one doling out those goodies, a bit of leverage. If the partner is willing to babysit the narcissist's special brand of neediness— and ultimately, most aren't—some narcissists are willing to make at least some of the behavioral changes that will keep the relationship

THE BEAST IN YOUR BED

together and keep the reassurance coming, particularly if individual or couples therapy is involved.

It helps, too, if the non-narcissistic partner is emotionally self-sufficient and not terribly in need of the kinds of attention the narcissist demands—a rare breed of selfless person, admittedly, but a few of them do exist. A healthy extended family may play a curative role, too, providing a circle of people beyond the partner who can help fill the psychic hole that drives narcissism in the first place. And the more deeply even narcissists become involved in the complex weave of a larger family, the less inclined they'll be to do the rending and tearing that would be required to set themselves free. "If you can elicit some communal feeling from the narcissist, that can make a difference," says Campbell. "That tends to make things more satisfying for everybody. You do occasionally find people who marry narcissists and report that the relationship works because those kinds of extended bonds have formed."

Finally, of course, there can be a perverse kind of compatibility that occurs when two narcissists drift together. By definition, they're a rare pair, since a person who needs constant care, watering, praise and attention is not likely to get it from someone who requires the same thing. Still, in some ways, the personalities of twin narcissists harmonize perfectly. Narcissists, for one thing, are exhibitionists, and a sexy, attractive individual doesn't draw half the gawking and attention that a sexy, attractive couple does. What's more, neither partner is terribly interested in a deep emotional connection, and what you don't need you also don't demand from a partner who can't give it in the first place.

In one of the more memorable scenes in the movie *Annie Hall*, the lead character, played by Woody Allen, stops a beautiful, seemingly happy couple on the street and asks them how they account for the apparent success of their relationship. "Uh, I'm very shallow and empty and I have no ideas and nothing interesting to say," answers the woman.

"And I'm exactly the same way," agrees the man.

"I see. Wow. So you've managed to work out something," says the Allen character.

And so the beautiful couple has. But how long such a love match will last is another thing entirely. "It makes a kind of sense," says Campbell. "Imagine two shallow, fun-loving, self-centered people—the Ken and Barbie model. I haven't seen that exhibited much in marriages. But in the short term, there can be a weird kind of shallow intimacy."

Over time, the charm of even the most dazzling narcissist fades, and nothing does it quite like age. It's unlikely Warren Beatty really bedded 12,755 women, but he did have his share. Yet by 1991, when he was fifty-four and romantically involved with Madonna, who was only thirty-three, the wear had begun to show—and so, too, had a certain ironic wisdom. In the Madonna documentary *Truth or Dare*, Beatty is seen for the first time as a less radiant body in somebody else's orbit and seems not quite to know what to do with himself. In one bit of footage shot in a hotel room, Madonna is seen having her throat examined by her doctor. The doctor wants to continue the examination with the camera turned off, but she refuses.

"She doesn't want to live off-camera, much less talk," says Beatty. "There's nothing to say off-camera. Why would you say something if it's off-camera? What point is there existing?"

Maybe there was a certain disingenuousness in that, coming as it did from Beatty, who had lived much of his life the same way. But there seemed to be some enlightenment in it, too. In 1991, he met actress Annette Bening on the set of the movie *Bugsy*. The following year they married, and they have since had four children. The man who himself could not seem to live without a camera or a bedmate has been a husband for more than twenty years, has not appeared in a movie since 2001, and has done nothing to contradict the idea that he is comfortable with that quiet life.

Still, most narcissists don't come to such a self-aware pass. Madonna, in her fifties, has taken a fair bit of derisive heat for the amount of flesh-flashing that is still featured in her live performances—a sign of a healthily confident person surely, but an equally likely sign of "Look at me" urgency. Ultimately, many less celebrated narcissists simply end up alone—having exhausted the patience of every mate they've ever had. Some never quit the game—especially men, who tend to predecease women, meaning that the ones who are left become sought-after prizes in their dwindling community of contemporaries. Simple actuarial probabilities mean that that's true for a lot of non-narcissistic men too, but for narcissists it's of a piece with their entire lives. "If you're a man you can move to a senior home and still have a lot of relationships," says Campbell. "These guys just keep it rolling."

There's a tragicomic charm in that—but tragicomedy is hardly what narcissists imagine for themselves, and it's certainly not how they see themselves when they've still got their flash and they're still drawing stares and they're still the hottest romantic property in any group. The seeds of that sad end, however, are being sown even then. The narcissist's victims recognize that eventually—but only after hardship and pain. The narcissists themselves often never do.

CHAPTER SIX

The Bastard
in the Corner Office

It should have been hard not to like Steve Jobs. He was charismatic, brilliant, good-looking, visionary, and if he was fantastically rich, he was at least unflashily so. His outfit of choice, the black turtleneck and the well-worn jeans, may have been less a badge of humility than a mark of affectation, but there are other affectations—Lamborghinis, private jets, Malibu mansions. At least he picked one we can all afford.

Jobs's backstory made him irresistible as well: the adoptive parents, the vagabond young adulthood, the geeky interests and the geeky friends. Then, of course, there was the little computer company he cofounded in 1976 that he aimed to make a very big company, taking on leviathans like Univac, Honeywell, NCR and, of course, IBM, and doing so with a machine named unprepossessingly after a piece of fruit. The scrappy underdog role worked out splendidly for a while, as Apple Computer fought the big boys to a surprising draw. But the dramatic arc was not remotely complete. There would still be the theatrical crash and burn in the mid-1980s, when the company lost its way and Jobs was booted from his own boardroom. That public humbling was followed by the decade he spent in the wilderness trying to become once again the sensation he had been—a goal he achieved in

1996 when he made his celebrated return to the company he had started, righted the ship that had foundered without him and turned it into the most valuable company in the world. A story like that is irresistible, with a cinematic sweetness that was evident long before the Jobs biography was written and the actual movie was made.

But it was more than Jobs's native smarts and corporate success that made him special. Bill Gates, Henry Ford and Thomas Edison became American icons too, but there have never been any cults of personality around them. And while neither Ford nor Edison died as publicly or as young as Jobs, it's unlikely the passing of either one of them would ever have been met with the outpourings of grief or mounds of flowers with which Jobs's death was met, with Apple stores becoming impromptu gathering places for the stricken masses.

The reason—the thing that distinguished Jobs from the other greats—was that he understood something, and that something was the people around him. His very first Apple products may have followed the beige box model that was the computer standard at the time, but there was something primally appealing about them, too. There was the little rainbow apple that was the company's logo—a tiny icon that didn't invite you to work with the machine as much as play with it. The beige box soon gave way to a white box—a small, streamlined thing that you wanted to look at, to display, not just use. When the first little Macintosh came along—just a year before Jobs left the company—the central image in all of the ads was the computer itself with the loopy, cursive word "Hello" written on the screen. It was a new friend, a cute friend, and one that was excited to meet you.

Upon Jobs's return to the company in 1996, that same human sensibility returned with him. In the years he was gone, Apple had reverted to the beige-box model, and the computing guts of those boxes weren't terribly good. His first act was to blow up the entire dreary product line and replace it with the cuddliest, most people-smart computer to date—the bulbous, baby-shaped, multicolored iMac. "Hello again," the ads said this time. In a publicity photo, Jobs posed cross-legged on the floor, holding one of the huggable machines in his lap—and that's precisely the impulse users had. Actually, the impulse went beyond just cuddling the computer; since Jobs took the pains to visit a jelly bean factory before selecting the colors for the machines, you practically wanted to eat the things. You wouldn't admit to such an odd impulse, of course, but you didn't have to. What may have been the iMac's cleverest print ad of the era showed five of the computers in a circle, each in one of the available colors—blue, purple, orange, green and red (or, as they were marketed, blueberry, grape, orange, lime and strawberry). The single word below the image: *Yum.*

The same innate sense of what consumers like and want soon produced the later-generation iMacs, not to mention iPods, iPhones and iPads, with their user-friendly features and, in the case of the iPad, the brilliantly reassuring slogan "You already know how to use it." Jobs, clearly, was a man who *got* other people, who must have truly liked other people. How else could he be so good at understanding their needs? And yet there was another side to him.

"Fucking dickless assholes!" the ostensible people-person once screamed at a subcontractor who had disappointed him, according to Walter Isaacson's bestselling book *Steve Jobs*. "You guys don't know what you're doing."

"Your commercials suck," he told one of his iPad ad directors flatly. "The iPad is revolutionizing the world, and we need something big. You've given me small shit."

"Shit," actually, was a go-to word for Jobs: "This is shit!" he declared loudly, storming into the cubicle of someone who worked on the staff of one of his chief designers. "You've baked a really lovely cake, but then you've used dog shit for frosting" was how he critiqued the work of one of his employees at NeXT, the computer company he founded during his decade away from Apple. "Everything you've done in your life is shit, so why don't you come work for me?" was his come-hither pitch to a Xerox designer he was recruiting.

Jobs's misbehavior went beyond the abusive language that could be excused—almost—as simply the outbursts of a wildly creative man. He bore grudges (one of the only complaints about the original iPad was that it wouldn't run Adobe Flash Player, a senseless omission, except that Jobs resented Adobe for once refusing to write software for the iMac); he behaved pettily, once storming out of a five-star hotel in London, calling close friend and Apple designer Jony Ive, who was staying in the hotel, too, and had gone to pains to make the booking, with the petulant announcement "I hate my room. It's a piece of shit, let's go." He even exhibited a sadistic streak, once asking a job candidate, "How old were you when you lost your virginity? How many times have you taken LSD?" When the understandably flustered applicant went on too long in one of his answers, Jobs mocked him. "Gobble, gobble, gobble," he said.

But it was an undeniable fact that Jobs was a genius—the genuine article, even if he was also a genuine bastard. As Robert Sutton, author of the business book *The No Asshole Rule*, told *The Atlantic*: "Even people who worked with Jobs told me that they'd seen him make people cry many times, but that 80 percent of the time he was right. It's troubling that there's this notion in our culture that if you're a winner, it's OK to be an asshole."

Actually, it turns out to be OK even if you're not a winner—as long as you've got the power. In the long, high-stakes history of the business world, there have been no shortage of corner-office horror stories—self-interested and self-adoring bosses who get very rich and accumulate great power, in part by making the lives of the people around them unbearable, often taking the entire company down in the process.

The late Marge Schott, onetime owner of the Cincinnati Reds, was infamous for her ignorance of the game, her shortsighted stinginess (she once refused to display the results from other games on the home stadium scoreboard because the service cost $350 per month), and her blindness to anyone's needs but her own. During one opening day, weather threatened to delay the game, and after play finally did get under way, umpire John McSherry collapsed at home plate and died of a heart attack. "I don't believe it," Schott griped. "First it snows, and now this."

Worst of all, there was her bigotry. "Only fruits wear earrings," she observed, explaining her preference that her players eschew them. "Dave is my million-dollar ni**er," she said of African American outfielder Dave Parker. "Everybody knows [Hitler] was good at the beginning, he just went too far" was her take on the onetime German chancellor.

Al Dunlap, the famed and loathed turnaround artist who headed multiple companies, including Scott Paper and Sunbeam-Oster, was even worse than Schott, simply because he was much more powerful. He was renowned mostly for his blood-on-the-floor layoffs—at one point in 1996, firing half of Sunbeam's 12,000 employees—and the joy he seemed to take in such mass executions, writing a column for *Newsweek* touting the tough-love wisdom of wiping out people's livelihoods, and titling his self-celebratory autobiography *Mean Business*. He once threw a chair at his human-resources director, he skipped his own parents' funerals, he refused to pay for his son's college education, and, almost unimaginably, he would not offer financial help to his twenty-year-old niece when she contracted leukemia, according to various often cited accounts. Over the long term, his strip-the-workforce and boost-the-stock-price strategy didn't even work. Sunbeam ultimately filed for bankruptcy, but not before Dunlap was forced out after playing loose with bookkeeping rules to improve quarterly sales reports.

Jimmy Cayne, ex-head of the now defunct Bear Stearns, similarly helped wreck his own company, and was similarly guilty of exceeding conceit and an even more exceeding nastiness. When the chief of an investment firm introduced her eleven-year-old son to Cayne, he shook the boy's hand and told the mother, "That kid's got a rotten handshake. He's going nowhere in life." During one of the lawsuits that arose from the Bear collapse, Cayne described an opposing lawyer as "a 300-lb. fag from Long Island," and boasted of following him to the men's room. "I said to him, 'Today you're going to get your ass kicked big.'" He described a female reporter for *The Wall Street Journal* as "a cunt whose capability is zero."

Even before he assumed the reins at Bear, Cayne considered himself larger, grander, more gifted than the people around him. He excelled at bridge, a game that indeed takes a keen and tactical mind, and he didn't mind who knew it. "If you study bridge for the rest of your life, if you play with the best partners and achieve your potential, you will never play bridge like I play bridge," a young Jimmy Cayne once said to Bear Stearns manager Alan Greenberg. And that was during his job interview.

Carly Fiorina, whose six-year tenure at Hewlett-Packard ended in 2005 after she was pushed out by her board (but not before she was given $21 million in go-away money), was widely blamed for the failed merger between Compaq computer and HP's own computer division. Neither operation was doing well and few people believed that the two underperforming brands would somehow create one overperforming one—and they didn't. The merger tanked and HP stock lost half its value under her stewardship. In the process, she laid off tens of thousands of employees and apologized to no one for it. "The merger was such a great idea," she said in a 2006 interview. "We could decrease the cost structure by billions and billions of dollars. In the course of my time there, we laid off over 30,000 people."

No surprise that during Fiorina's failed run for the U.S. Senate from California in 2010, former HP employees piled on, speaking out furiously against her and launching a website opposing her candidacy. "The founders of HP were deeply concerned with their employees," wrote one. "Carly Fiorina is opposite of that. She is a complete narcissist. She is only concerned with herself and has no regard for people."

There again and always was that defining word. Certainly, not all louts and bastards in corporate suites are narcissists, but in the Venn diagram that maps those traits, there is an awful lot of overlap. You don't call someone dickless if you care a whit for how he might feel about such a description. You don't boast about your five-figure staff cuts if you don't also get a grandiose thrill from exercising that kind of power. And you certainly don't equate an umpire's death with a weather delay if you have the capacity to consider that the man had a family and that that family was grieving. Jobs, more than most, captured both the inspirational greatness and the institutional horror a narcissistic boss can represent. Said Tina Redse, a computer consultant and a onetime romantic partner of Jobs, in an interview with Isaacson: "Expecting [Jobs] to be nicer or less self-centered was like expecting a blind man to see." But while Jobs may have been the greatest, most florid narcissist in any corner office anywhere, he was hardly the only one.

The recent narcissism pandemic is a late-twentieth- and early-twenty-first-century phenomenon, but corporate bosses were leading indicators of the trend long before it fully showed itself—perhaps because, as with politics and show business, there are few fields that so perfectly meld and reward the combination of greed, ambition, lack of empathy and overwhelming ego that define the condition. In the nineteenth century, railroad magnate George Pullman built an entire town south of Chicago for his workers to live in, but charged them for basics like water and gas and would not adjust their rent even when he cut their wages. John Patterson, the head of National Cash Register, toyed with his senior employees like a cat with a yarn ball, firing top executives and then rehiring them, simply to break their spirits. Clothing makers Max Blanck and Isaac Harris were so concerned with cut-

ting losses at their sweatshop on the upper floors of a building near
Washington Square Park in Manhattan that they locked the doors
from the outside to prevent their workers—mostly young women and
girls—from making off with the merchandise. The company was the
Triangle Shirtwaist Factory, and when a fire broke out there on March
25, 1911, many of the trapped girls had no choice but to jump to their
deaths on the sidewalk below. Ultimately, 146 of them perished.

The workplace has never been a democracy, and it wasn't designed
to be. Companies without a clear organizational chart and well-defined
lines of power sound wonderfully collaborative, except for the fact that
they almost always fail. An office needs a boss, and a boss, like it or
not, is a monarch. As with monarchs, too, bosses come in all varieties—
kind, benign, malign, monsters. There is little way of knowing which
one you'll get when the two of you shake hands and you accept a new
job. But you'll learn quickly—and if your boss is a narcissist, you'll
learn terribly, too.

THERE ARE a lot of ways bosses get where they are—ability, experience, education, connections and often nothing more than a bit of
right-place-at-the-right-time luck. But the source of their power goes
a lot deeper, too.

Among nearly all social animals, the first and most direct route
to power is dominance. The chimp that achieves alpha status is the
one that's simply the biggest, toughest and scariest of the males. Possessing those qualities—and the temperament to use them—earns
him authority over the rest of the troop and, not insignificantly, his
pick of the females. The alpha lion in any pride similarly does not
achieve his high rank by his good works or his listening skills, but by
intimidating and even chasing off other males—sometimes in a new
pride he simply approaches and attacks. One of his first acts in his new
leadership role will often be to kill any cubs the other males fathered.

This brings the females back into estrus, making them available for breeding—a job he happily performs all by himself.

Humans, throughout history, have operated by similar if usually less murderous rules. Sand kicking on beaches, bullying in school-yards, angry shoving in bars and at sporting events are all about prov-ing who's the biggest, who's the strongest and who'd better watch his step. The implication is also that the bullyboys would be better breed-ers, providers and protectors of young, though that's hardly in the conscious mind of a bar brawler when punches are being thrown. Still, in both primitive and contemporary human cultures, physical size and the willingness to intimidate have long been directly correlated to power.

"It can seem counterintuitive," says social psychologist Jessica Tracy, who teaches at the University of British Columbia. "You'd think that bullying and terrorizing would not be a way to earn social favor. But we've always accorded high status to people who can force us to do their will through simple intimidation. Those strategies work and they've thus endured."

Fortunately for the peace and safety of the tribe, intimidation does not always have to be directed at competing members of the community—it can be directed at outside enemies, too. Protecting the group from an external threat is actually a one-two way to win favor: Not only does the community owe you one for putting your safety and even life on the line to protect them, you've also reminded the few members who might oppose you that you could just as easily turn your strength and power against them. There's a reason successful warriors so often come home to good jobs, the adoration of females, and civilian males who never let them buy their own drinks. There's a reason, too, that Generals Washington, Grant and Eisenhower eventually became Presidents Washington, Grant and Eisenhower. Something similar is true in the more kabuki world of sports. It's the alpha athletes who hoist the trophies and date the supermodels, while the beta males become part of their posses and accompany them to clubs and bars. Athletes may even follow warriors into high public office—as ex-congressman Heath Shuler, who was previously NFL quarterback Heath Shuler; ex-senator Jim Bunning, who was once Major League pitcher Jim Bunning; and Detroit mayor David Bing, who first won fame as NBA star Dave Bing, have proven.

But raw power and the threat it implies are not the only ways to achieve dominance. So is control of essential resources—the stuff everyone else in a community needs and can't survive without. Successful hunters—adept at stealth and speed and aim—become very prestigious figures in any tribe, even if they are small or slight. They may not have much weight to throw around, but they don't have to, since the message they can telegraph to the rest of the group is a simple one: Submit or starve. This is true, too, of the person with the greatest control of arable land or fishable streams or, in smaller cultures without a lot of mating options for young males, marriage-age daughters.

"People who control resources have something to offer the group," says Tracy. "But the implication of that is that they also have something to withhold from the group. Even without physical size or strength, they can thus create fear in the entire community. Other individuals submit by complying with their demands and rules."

In modern cultures, in which we all acquire our own food and own mates, we still find ways to reward resource control richly. Real estate magnates grow wealthy by owning land, and then use that wealth to accumulate still more—buying up whole strips of beachfront property or whole blocks of downtown lots. Want to build a retirement community or an office building? Talk to them. You get rich, too, if oil is found on your land—and richer still if you buy more land and more wells. Even comparatively benign figures like the fiscal wiseman and Berkshire Hathaway CEO Warren Buffett implicitly threaten people, whether they realize they're doing it or not. Every company Buffett buys up represents thousands more jobs and thousands more lives he quietly controls. When he acquired H.J. Heinz in 2013, that one deal represented 34,800 employees whose livelihoods depend on his stewardship of their company. Would you want to be the one to cross him?

The third—and easily the most civilized—type of authority flows not from control of tribal resources or the simple business of scaring the daylights out of everyone else. It comes, instead, from the gentle quality of possessing cultural information or values that benefit the rest of the community.

Across all human societies, poets, painters, surgeons, philosophers, jurists, architects, astronomers and more rise to positions of enormous influence and respect because they are the custodians of skills, talents and ideas they pass on to the rest of us. This has so little to do with what we typically think of as power that the influence that comes from prestige is often accorded to people who in other contexts would be thought of as utterly powerless. Ruth Bader Ginsburg, an increasingly frail-looking octogenarian, is in a position to wield more influence with a single utterance from the Supreme Court bench than most people ever will in a lifetime. Stephen Hawking is physically incapable of doing anything at all without assistance, yet when he speaks or writes—always with the aid of a machine—the world listens and reads. His power comes from the mind that resides in a broken body. For all of our species' more primitive tendencies, this submission to wisdom speaks very well of us.

"We are the only one of the great apes who use prestige," says Tracy. "All of the other great apes use dominance alone. That's partly because they simply have less cultural information to pass on, but it's also because to the extent that they do, they don't show the same deference to the individuals in possession of it."

All the same, prestige in the hands of a human being is not a guaranteed route to power or influence. It's not just that we have more

cultural information to share than apes do, we also have expectations about how that sharing should work. We value humility and generosity in a gifted person—indeed, it helps us get past our natural if
unadmirable envy that we don't necessarily have the same talents.
The Oscar-winning movie star who thanks her agent and her director
and screenwriter may seem like a simple Hollywood trope, but it
acknowledges the collaborative nature of the work and parcels credit
appropriately.

The late Bum Phillips, the wonderfully frank-speaking coach of the
Houston Oilers and later the New Orleans Saints, once paid the legendary Don Shula—Super Bowl–winning coach of the Miami Dol-
phins and Baltimore Colts—an exquisitely apt compliment: "He can
take his'n and beat your'n; then he can take your'n and beat his'n." It
was Shula's talent, in other words, even more so than that of his team,
that spelled victory. Phillips distinguished himself by offering such
high praise to a rival, and Shula equally distinguished himself by never
saying any such thing about himself—even if it was demonstrably
true. The person who is gifted but is also a braggart might win trophies, but loses friends and admirers.

"Achieving prestige takes a number of things—smarts, achievement," says Tracy. "You also have to be a nice person. A talented jerk
is more ambiguous."

Indeed, all three human routes to power can be both benign and
fraught. Dominance in the traditional sense of physical menace or violence is no longer an acceptable avenue to leadership, but physical size
and a strong, even intimidating personality are. In the twenty-nine
presidential elections since 1900, the taller candidates have won eighteen times and lost only nine. (In two cases, the candidates were the
same height.) Twenty-nine of the forty-three men who have been
president were five-feet-ten or taller, and eighteen of them exceeded
six feet. Compare that with the current average height of the Ameri-

can male, which is 5 feet, 9½ inches. Lyndon Johnson, who ties Abraham Lincoln as the tallest American president at six-four, was famous for using both strong-arm persuasion and his physical size to cow political opponents.

"I never trust a man unless I've got his pecker in my pocket," the great statesman once said. During conversations, Johnson was famous for grabbing the arms, knees and even lapels of other people and leaning toward them with an intrusiveness that went beyond merely invading their personal space, to conquering and occupying it. A famous four-photo series of then Senator Johnson shows him literally talking down to the older, shorter Rhode Island senator Theodore Green, leaning closer and closer to him so that by the last frame poor Green is bent half backward, holding on to a desk just to stay upright. And Green was an ally, a Democrat like Johnson. There's a thin line between strength and bullying—and it's a line Johnson routinely crossed.

Resource control can similarly be used both gently and crudely. Petro-dictators who rule tiny, otherwise inconsequential countries are some of the most powerful men in the world, simply because they have much of the planet's oil supply in their hands. African despots in mineral-rich countries may live petted, privileged lives while everyone else suffers poverty. Even in North Korea, which has virtually no natural resources or products the world can't get elsewhere, the same wealth divide exists—with the rulers drinking cognac and driving luxury cars while most of the 24 million citizens starve.

In the workplace, all three kinds of power are at work. Your boss has single-spigot resource control over some of the most important aspects of your life—the money in your pocket, the food on your table, the health care you either will or won't receive. A boss who likes you can turn that knob one way and you get an even bigger rush of rewards; a turn in the other direction and it all goes away. George Steinbrenner, perhaps the most successful owner in the history of baseball, was known for his capricious firings and rehirings of managers, spinning Gene Michael, Bob Lemon, Billy Martin and others through his revolving door of employment and unemployment repeatedly. He signed the contracts, he cut the checks and if those men wanted a job in baseball, Steinbrenner seemed like their best shot. So they bit their tongues and took what he gave them.

Intimidation and power displays are common too. Bad bosses pound desks, shout at subordinates and throw tantrums. It would be a criminal act, of course, to strike an employee, and in nearly all workplaces that simply doesn't happen, but we're nonetheless wired to react to nearly any expression of aggression as if we are indeed in danger of being hit. Long ago, I was in a one-on-one meeting with a hotheaded boss who thought nothing of losing his temper if he felt the need. During the course of the conversation, he got angry and punctuated the point he was making by throwing a golf ball–sized eyepiece used for viewing slides across the room. It was not aimed at me but if it had been it could have done me real harm. The message sent from the primitive region of his brain to the primitive region of mine was unmistakable: He had the power to hurt me and would not hesitate to use it.

The boss whose power comes from prestige may show the gentle wisdom of a Ginsburg or Hawking—but may not too. Jobs, after all, possessed a type of knowledge and intelligence that transformed the modern world, but his behavior hardly matched his creative gift. Henry Ford achieved a similar transformation a century before Jobs, yet he was a virulent anti-unionist and a flagrant anti-Semite. Even Bill Gates, whose Microsoft operating system and later, greater philanthropy have provided the world resources of almost incalculable value, could be every bit the bully and bastard Jobs was. "That's the stupidest fucking thing I've ever heard," he would tell subordinates if he didn't like an idea, according to a 2011 memoir by Microsoft cofounder Paul Allen. "I could code that in a weekend," he'd say to an employee whose programming skills he didn't admire. Genius, clearly, is not the same as goodness, prestige is not the same as integrity, and the possession of power is no guarantee that it will be used with restraint—especially when narcissism is stirred into the mix, which it is with disturbing frequency.

Narcissistic black hats don't outnumber good-boss white hats in corner offices, but they're nonetheless disproportionately represented— far exceeding their percentages in the overall population. That's because, as with narcissistic coworkers, the playing field is tilted in their direction—rewarding energy, cockiness and barely contained arrogance, and ignoring or even penalizing quieter qualities. The boss who startled me with the hurled viewing lens got his job in the first place by approaching a major magazine publisher and arguing that a small, digest-sized periodical the company owned should be upgraded into a glossy, full-sized, mainstream monthly. That would require spending a lot of money to expand the print run, widen the distribution chain and sign quality writers and photographers. Before the corporate bosses did any of that, he added, they should hire him to run the whole operation. And they did. He did not sink a half-court shot like that by being modest.

"Narcissists seem brave, they radiate charismatic energy and they self-promote like mad," says psychologist Robert Hogan, a former professor at Johns Hopkins University and the founder of Hogan Assessment Systems, which provides personality tests to industry. "The big thing for narcissists is that they interview very well. Search committees just can't get enough of these guys."

The problem is that the honeymoon that follows that courtship doesn't last. The first phase of any relationship with a narcissist is known as the emergent zone, and it can be a real, if transient, pleasure. There's something irresistible about a narcissist's wit and energy, whether you're in a bar, at a party or sitting across a boardroom table, and a person in possession of those qualities is someone you want to spend more time with. This is the same dynamic that occurs with a narcissistic coworker, but with a boss—someone who's running the show—things are that much more thrilling and you're only too happy to fall in line. It's only in the later phase, what's known as the enduring zone, that the egotism, self-absorption and insensitivity of the narcissist emerge.

Psychologist Delroy Paulhus of the University of British Columbia conducted a longitudinal study in which he set narcissists—or, as he decorously called them, "trait self-enhancers"—to work on a project with non-narcissists, had them meet at regular intervals and followed them from the time they met to the time they got to know one another and finally to the time the working relationships inevitably fell apart. Typically, this boom-and-bust cycle played out over a period of just weeks. All of the subjects filled out questionnaires at various intervals rating their impressions of the other group members, and while the non-narcissists' scores stayed relatively stable, the narcissists' started high and then cratered.

"At the first meeting, self-enhancers made positive impressions," Paulhus wrote. "They were seen as agreeable, well adjusted, and competent. After 7 weeks, however, they were rated negatively. . . . If the bulk of their social interactions [were] short-term, then self-enhancers could lead rewarding and productive lives."

Keith Campbell echoed this idea in a 2009 paper, paraphrasing the dictum of the play *Glengarry Glen Ross*, in which the salesmen in a fictional real estate office are taught "Always be closing"—in other words, approach every sale as if it's a done deal and you're just moving toward the inevitable signing. In the case of narcissists, Campbell believes, the rule should be: Always be emerging.

That's possible, of course, only with quick-hit relationships that can end before they turn toxic. In the workplace, the onset of toxicity is just the first part of what can be a very long and very ugly journey. The

biggest thing that causes the pleasure of the emergent phase to collapse into the horror of the enduring phase so quickly is the narcissistic boss's brittleness of ego and paradoxical lack of self-esteem. In
many ways, high self-esteem is synonymous with pride, and we can
often tell the real thing simply by looking at it. Across nearly all
cultures, Tracy reports, humans exhibit pride in the same way: a slight
tilting back of the head (not too much—typically fifteen degrees); a
small smile (not too big, otherwise pride is mistaken for general happiness); and arms held out from the body—either with hands on the
hips or, in the most demonstrative examples, thrust above the head in
fists. Young athletes may learn such self-celebratory posing and fist-
pumping by watching pros do it on TV, but it comes to all of us from
a deeper and much more primal place.

We assume the pride pose for major accomplishments—the Super
Bowl–winning kick, the admission to Harvard, the phone call telling
you that you just landed a seven-figure deal. But we do it for small suc-
cesses, too—standing back from the kitchen counter and admiring a
cake we just made, say. We do it even for proxy accomplishments—
watching from the sidelines as a daughter plays soccer, our stance
opening and broadening in almost direct proportion to how well she's
doing. Even in isolated populations on the island of Fiji, investigators
have observed the same suite of gestures we display. There, as elsewhere, they seem to serve an important purpose.

"Pride displays send a rapid and automatically perceived message of
high status to other group members," says Tracy. "It signals who you
are and what your position is. The emotion associated with the display
has a different but equally important purpose for the person doing the
signaling: It's both a reward for achievement and a motivator to ac-
complish more. You try to replicate the feeling."

In many situations, of course, we have to temper our social signaling. It would hardly do to rise from your seat at a business meeting and

stand arms akimbo in front of your colleagues every time you make a good suggestion. But easing back in your chair and exhibiting that tiny smile? You've probably done it a thousand times.

Alpha characters, especially alpha narcissists, are more explicit about things, and often they've got reason for pride, a fact that is conspicuously evident in American presidential politics—a true hothouse for narcissists. Men like Barack Obama and Ronald Reagan stand onstage at their national conventions holding the hand of their running mates aloft, and they look loose and comfortable and genuinely at ease. They had that poise before they assumed office, and they retained it once they were in power. The same was true of John Kennedy and Teddy Roosevelt and even Franklin Roosevelt, who projected a jaunty self-assuredness without even the ability to rise from his chair. People of different political stripes may disagree about the quality of the men's legacies, but nobody denies their natural talents or their ability to press their agendas effectively, in part due to their ease with themselves and their certainty about their ideas.

Compare them with the physical signaling of other alpha men who didn't fare so well. Benito Mussolini favored triumphal poses, but he was a bumbler, a fool and a despot—and he looked comical on a dais. Richard Nixon shrank from people and lived in an emotional and sometimes literal hunch. Even his signature arms-up, V-for-victory pose was a painful thing to witness—his suit jacket always awkwardly buttoned, his smile more rictus than real. Al Gore was nothing short of a plank of living wood, a fact no lip-locks with Tipper or self-effacing jokes about his lack of charm could fix. He and Nixon made people uneasy largely because they seemed uneasy themselves, never mind the fact that they still had the narcissistic temperaments necessary to pursue the presidency. Nixon turned out to be a disaster of historic proportions and Gore never even got his shot. Yes, he won the popular vote by a slim margin, but just a little more ease and charm might have been all it would have taken to flip Florida or one of the states he lost by razor-thin margins into his column, giving him the presidency outright.

In the workplace, it can be hard to distinguish whether your narcissistic boss is an awkward Gore or an easy Reagan, because the stage on which they perform is smaller and the gesturing is thus subtler. But there are clues—and one is in the smile. Nineteenth-century French physician Guillaume Duchenne was the first to parse the facial mechanics of a smile, observing that two major muscle groups are involved: the zygomaticus major, which controls the corners of the mouth; and the orbicularis oculi, which lifts the cheeks and crinkles the eye. This combination is as pleasing to see as it sounds, and is generally perceived as an indication of genuine positive emotion. Phony smiles—the cocktail-party smile or the "Someone else got the job I was up for but I have to look like a good sport" smile—activate only the mouth muscles. Picture Nixon's smile. Now picture FDR's. Which man would you rather have for a boss? Both may be narcissists, but they're coming at the condition from different directions.

The eyes can be a clue as well. Real pride and real self-esteem, even if they're narcissistically rooted, are much more an inward than outward experience. They thus require no eye contact with others; indeed, truly feeling the feelings may even require looking away— a signal of humility tempering the pride. Mask-model narcissists are likely to make the opposite choice—looking directly at other people, even scanning from person to person in the room. They've told a joke, made a sale, scored an argumentative point, and their insecurity is such that they have to amplify and confirm the experience eyeball to eyeball. "A direct eye gaze conveys dominance," says Tracy. "It can be an attempt at reinforcing social standing." When you're an insecure narcissist, that attempt is pretty much a full-time job, and when you outrank everyone else in the room, you can guarantee that that lofty standing will always be acknowledged.

Some of us are better at reading such physical signaling than others, but even people who are body-language illiterates quickly learn in other ways if they've drawn the short straw of a narcissistic boss. That's because of one of the other great signs of the fragile ego: anger, bullying, even rage, which follow the bright, emerging phase of your relationship with a narcissist as surely as the roar of thunder follows the dazzle of lightning.

According to one 2007 study conducted by Zogby International and others, 37 percent of all workers have at some point in their careers been bullied on the job. That mistreatment includes verbal or even physical abuse, intimidation, humiliation—openly derogating the employee in front of others—or sabotaging the employee's efforts to complete a job or project and then punishing the inevitable failure. That may be a decided minority, but 37 percent nonetheless factors out to a whopping 54 million people who have known the experience of getting up in the morning and dreading going to work. Among epidemiologists, that would be known as an epidemic.

Nathanael Fast, professor of management and organizational behavior at the University of Southern California, explored how a boss's fragile, narcissistic ego may contribute to this kind of abuse, in a 2009 study straightforwardly titled: "When the Boss Feels Inadequate: Power, Incompetence and Aggression." Fast first recruited a sample group of ninety people employed in various professions at various levels and had them rate the degree to which their jobs offer them a sense of power and authority—from a score of one, for not at all, to seven, for a great deal. He then administered them a version of the Fear of Negative Evaluation (FNE) test, which, as its name suggests, measures how comfortable or anxious people are with the idea of being criticized or found wanting. A high FNE score is a proxy for low self-esteem, since if you really do feel good about yourself, you don't give a fig for what other people think about you.

Finally, Fast had the subjects fill out a questionnaire that measures aggression. The survey asked them to agree or disagree on a scale of one to five with statements that included "I can't help getting into arguments when people disagree with me" and "Given enough provocation I may hit another person." A score of one means "extremely uncharacteristic of me"; a five means "extremely characteristic of me."

Aggression in the workplace, Fast found, flows from a particular balance of power and self-esteem. Low power and low self-perceived competence do not lead to much lashing out, because subjects in subordinate jobs who, deservedly or not, feel that they belong there have less to prove and fewer ways to be seen as inadequate. Low power and high self-perceived competence lead to more aggression, in this case because subjects see themselves both as talented and as underutilized, which fosters resentment and frustration (think of surly clerks at the Department of Motor Vehicles or the post office, who may have all manner of gifts that people elsewhere in their lives recognize, but who spend their days in jobs that offer them little reward and almost no real power or prestige). Among high-power individuals, a healthy sense of confidence actually reduces aggression, since their skills and their position were well-matched and they know it. The only truly dangerous combination Fast identified was high power and low self-perceived competence—with a constant pressure to achieve forever in tension with a constant worry that you'll come up wanting. This is particularly fraught, because far from being underutilized, such people often find themselves with too much on their plates—the result of seizing any opportunity to exhibit their surpassing talents, even if those talents aren't all they believe them to be. That can be the case with any insecure leader, but when a leader suffers from a true case of mask-model narcissism, with its bottomless feelings of unworth, things only get worse.

"When you have power you also feel this increased demand that you keep showing other people how good you are," Fast says. "This can map directly on the larger idea of narcissism if you in fact don't feel competent. A narcissist wouldn't necessarily be aggressive all the time, only if they feel insecure. It's their go-to thing."

That go-to thing is also dangerously a zero-sum thing. The definition of narcissistic insecurity is that there's never enough praise or success to fill the emotional vacuum behind the disorder; the next step is thus to diminish other people so that at least you rise by comparison. When you're standing on a pedestal that can't get any taller, the only thing left is to make other people stand in a hole. "There's power in demeaning the people around you," says Hochwarter. "It's a perverse kind of power, but for the insecure narcissist it doesn't matter. It's all necessary to keep the ego fed."

The workplace in which this kind of abuse takes place does not have to be an office, of course. It can be a warehouse, a factory floor, a military unit or even a setting in which the workers aren't technically employees at all and the job they're doing is seen by most people as fun and even glamorous. In the spring of 2013, Rutgers University basketball coach Mike Rice was summarily sacked when a video was released showing him physically and verbally abusing his players. He shoved them, threw basketballs at them and cursed them in the ugliest imaginable ways.

"You fucking fairy!" he screamed at a player in a particularly appalling piece of footage. "You're a fucking faggot!"

Drill sergeants, certainly, have regularly trafficked in this kind of smack-talk, but Rutgers ain't the Marine Corps, and the whole point of such abuse in the military is to build toughness and annihilate egos before building them back up in the Corps' image. Wise or not, humane or not, it works. Among sports coaches, at least in the pros, some of the same might once have been tolerable. Vince Lombardi could likely get away with things a modern NFL coach, to say nothing of a college coach, could not. But times have changed and this kind of behavior is not remotely tolerated anymore—particularly when it includes ethnic or sexual slurs. The fact that Rice considered himself an exception to that new norm said a good deal about his narcissistic pathology.

Gil Biruta, a Rutgers player who later transferred to the University of Rhode Island, was born in Lithuania and became a favored target of his coach's abuse. Rice routinely addressed Biruta as a "Lithuanian bitch," according to Eric Murdock, a former NBA star who worked as director of player development under Rice from 2010 to 2012. Worse— exponentially so—was Rice's behavior at a youth basketball camp he coached. When three young boys showed up late one day, Rice verbally abused them in front of the other boys, including in his dressing-down a comment on the fact that the boys were wearing flip-flops. "Flip-flops are for faggots," he declared.

As far as anyone outside of Rice's family knows, he has never been formally diagnosed as an insecure narcissist. Maybe he was just a son of a bitch with an anger problem, but a lot of factors point the narcissism way. For starters, he was in an exceedingly public job. You don't fight your way up the fiercely competitive college-coaching ladder in the first place if you don't crave a position that offers you plenty of opportunities to be seen and be known. More important, after he arrived at Rutgers he quickly found himself in a very unenviable spot: He was a successful professional who all at once was not succeeding. From 2007 to 2010 he had been head coach at Robert Morris University near Pittsburgh, finishing first in his division and taking his team into the postseason all three years. That helped land him his job at Rutgers, where in the same number of seasons he finished 13th, 11th and 12th and amassed a cumulative record of 44 wins and 51 losses. When your inadequacy is not just self-perceived, but can be crunched down to multiple decimal places and publicized to the world, that can be awfully hard to take.

More important was the specific nature of his rage. The act of singling out designated targets for abuse and making sure other subordinates see it is a particular part of the narcissistic manager's toolbox too. "Abusing one player or one person at a time sends a very distinct message to the others," Hochwarter says. "It infuses them with a feeling of uncertainty, creating the sense that they might be the next target. At the same time, it elevates the boss's feelings of power."

That isn't to say that any boss who seeks to make an example of a malingerer or underperformer is abusive; indeed, that can be a valuable if painful management tool. But most don't take it too far. A healthy, non-narcissistic boss feels the target's pain, something that an empathically numb narcissist doesn't. What's more, non-narcissists don't lose sight of what is supposed to be their larger goal, which is to improve the performance of the entire organization—something that doesn't happen when you crush the confidence of people who could be making a valuable contribution. When Biruta left Rutgers, the school lost the only player on the team who had started every game of the 2011 season, one who, not incidentally, carried a 3.57 grade point average during his freshman year. Shedding players who are both athletic and academic stars is not how a team moves out of thirteenth place—but that was something Rice had apparently lost sight of, to his team's and his own misfortune.

The next steps in the steep slide of the narcissistic boss are the twinned habits of laying blame and denying responsibility, and it's almost inevitable that both will surface. An organization suffering under the whip of an abusive or egomaniacal leader is hardly an organization functioning at its best, after all, and that means mistakes are likely to start getting made. Behind nearly every mistake will be the person or people who made it, and bosses can and do make their share. Like narcissistic coworkers, however, they are often utterly incapable of admitting as much. Tracy equates the narcissistic ego to a pot of water that is always just below boiling temperature. Keeping it from bubbling over requires minimizing any experiences of shame, maximizing displays of pride and hubris and resisting or attacking anyone who tries to upset the balance. That kind of fragile equilibrium leaves no room for a candid admission of fault.

Just as with Rice, it's hard to say with certainty if George W. Bush is a narcissist—or at least exceeds the baseline level of narcissism for anyone who seeks or wins the presidency. The most common description of him was always that he is someone who's comfortable in his own skin, and the overuse of that trope doesn't make it any less true. He was clearly less experienced in governance and less well-informed about policy than Gore, but he projected a genial lack of pretension that made it easy for people to imagine being his friend—and easy for them to suspect they'd enjoy that experience. This is the famous who-would-you-rather-have-a-beer-with test, and Bush won it in a landslide. That same winking unseriousness infuriated his detractors, but it might have been a genuine sign of someone who could stand back from the job he held and never be too wowed with himself for holding it—certainly not the way a true narcissist would be.

On the other hand, there was Bush's seeming blindness to his manifold shortcomings and those of his administration. In the summer of 2004, even as deficits were exploding, the Iraq war was spinning out of control and the Afghanistan war was settling into just the bloody stalemate critics had warned about, Bush famously drew a blank when asked by a White House reporter if he could think of a single mistake he'd made in his first term.

"I wish you'd have given me this written question ahead of time so I could plan for it," he joked—sort of—as he bought time. "I hope—I don't want to sound like I have made no mistakes. I'm confident I have. I just haven't—you just put me under the spot here, and maybe I'm not as quick on my feet as I should be in coming up with one."

In a follow-up question, another reporter asked him if he felt he had failed in any way to explain the justification for the Iraq war to American voters—a softball question that actually offered him an escape route for the tough grilling he was getting on the war, since it would have allowed him the politician's familiar dodge of arguing that the policies are sound, they just have to be explained to people better. That's an admission that even would have contained a tiny, surely tolerable *mea culpa*, since Bush could have taken the minor blame for poor messaging and avoided the major blame for massive military bungling. But even that much of a concession seemed anathema to him.

"That's the kind of thing the voters will decide next November," he answered. "That's what elections are about. They'll take a look at me and my opponent and say, let's see, which one of them can better win the war on terror? Who best can see to it that Iraq emerges a free society?" It was a deft flipping from defense to offense, one that conceded not an inch of ground. In this case, Bush did fit the profile of the fragile narcissist perfectly—insensible to the multiple advantages of manning up to a mistake, not just because it earns you respect for your candor, but because it might help you avoid committing the same blunder again.

"There's a reason narcissists don't learn from mistakes," says Hogan, "and that's because they never get past the first step, which is admitting that they've made one. It's always an assistant's fault, an adviser's fault, a lawyer's fault. Ask them to account for a mistake any other way and they'll say, 'What mistake?'"

That can pay short-term dividends—at least to the narcissist—but it has long-term consequences. Ben Dattner, a professor of organizational psychology at New York University and the author of the book *The Blame Game*, believes that one of the best possible indicators of the level of narcissism in a CEO and a board of directors is the corporate annual report. As a general rule, if it's been a good year, CEOs will attribute everything to their visionary leadership; if it's been a bad year, they'll point to larger, uncontrollable forces that were not their fault. Dattner has actually crunched the numbers and found that

CEOs and management teams are three times likelier to take credit for results when the share price has gone up significantly than when it's remained relatively flat, and three times likelier to blame outside circumstances when the price has gone down.

"The winners will point to their long-term growth strategy and their good execution," he says. "The others will talk about the euro crisis or the Japanese tsunami and escalating fuel prices, all of which were out of their control and all of which also explain the problems." When Carly Fiorina was once asked by *Fortune* magazine to explain why the HP–Compaq merger failed so badly, there was not a shred of self-awareness or accountability in her answer. The problems were all due to an extended downturn in corporate IT spending. That was it. Nothing to see here, so move on.

But that turns out to be exactly the wrong strategy. Companies and company executives that take responsibility when things go wrong not only earn the respect of their shareholders for being truthful, they also convey the sense that they're in control of things. "Their message is: 'This is what we did wrong, and this is how we'll fix it,'" Dattner says. Blaming outside circumstances suggests you'll always be buffeted by random events. Not every company has a bad year after a natural disaster or a currency emergency, and one of the greatest signs of a good management team is if they stay upright when other companies are being turned upside down by events.

Admitting mistakes is good for the bottom line too. Studying long-term performance analyses, Dattner has found that as a rule, companies that make a habit of shouldering responsibility for problems outperform the stock market year to year. Those that adopt the "Who, me?" strategy tend to fall short. "If you claim that things were out of your hands," he warns, "shareholders start to ask, 'Why don't I just pull my money out and take it to Vegas?'"

A related 2007 study by a pair of Penn State University business professors came at this idea of executive-suite ego and long-term profitability another way. The researchers graded 111 unnamed CEOs in the computer and software industries on their likely level of narcissism, using a number of admittedly inferential methods—how many times they used first-person pronouns in interviews, say, or how large their picture is in the company's annual report. When they looked at the performance of those bosses' companies over the course of years, they found greater volatility—both positive and negative— among the ones led by presumed narcissists. The companies of those with more modest temperaments did better and remained more stable over the long term.

The third part of the narcissistic boss's toxic triptych—after denying blame and abusing subordinates—is stealing credit. Here the case is not always as easy to make as it is when a coworker wrongly claims ownership of a colleague's idea or efforts. The fact is, most bosses hear a thousand suggestions and read a thousand reports or proposals a week, and it's their job to synthesize them all and make decisions based on them. If you're the one who assembles all of these components into a coherent business plan, well, who else but you should get the bulk of the credit?

Still, there are limits beyond which no bosses ought to go. And yet they do. "You want to talk about being thrown under the bus?" writes one of the respondents in Hochwarter's voluminous collection of employee surveys. "I worked on a report for a month straight—Saturdays and Sundays, late into the evenings. Then my boss took my name off of the cover and put her name on it (in bigger print, no less). During the presentation in front of her superiors, she was asked a question about something that she knew absolutely nothing about. You got it, she blamed me by name."

"My boss wasn't even considered for a promotion until he started taking credit for my work and ideas," wrote another. "One of his new colleagues sent me an e-mail asking if he made this behavior a habit, and I responded with an unequivocal . . . YES!"

Galling as this kind of thievery is, it's an exceedingly common part of the narcissist's behavioral template. "You really are just an instrument to the narcissistic boss," says Michael Maccoby, associate fellow at the Saïd School of Business at Oxford University and author of *Narcissistic Leaders*. "They're very unaware of other people and they're completely unaware of their own behavior. If you give them an idea, it's their idea and they don't see anything wrong with that. Indeed, if you don't really care about credit and you want to get an idea across, make the boss think he or she came up with it."

Smart narcissists—and most of them who have climbed to the boss's suite aren't dumb—are usually less obvious about things. Sometimes they simply fold a portion of the work they should be doing into the job responsibilities of a subordinate and then take credit for the results. This is common among politicians who know not a whit about, say, the local watershed but go into a debate sounding well-informed thanks to the talking points provided by a junior researcher.

Depending on where the boss falls along the narcissistic spectrum, employees who work for a flagrant credit-grabber aren't completely without recourse. There are low roads they can take: Hochwarter has seen bad subordinates sabotage a narcissistic boss by, say, leaving a key page out of a report or saying a meeting starts at three when in fact it starts at two.

"The mentality is 'I'm not going to make that asshole look good,'" Hochwarter says. That's a tricky game to play, of course. "It seems appealing to fight fire with fire, but in the organizational reality, in which one person controls all the resources, it's going to be a short fight." Not only can the sabotage strategy get you sacked, it also does nothing at all to achieve your ostensibly larger goal, which is to stay on the job and simply be well treated and receive proper credit for the work you do.

A better, more effective approach is to share an idea with trusted colleagues as widely as possible before you set to work on it. That indelibly brands it as your own and makes it impossible—or at least uncomfortable—for the boss to try to grab it. Actually approaching the boss—carefully, diplomatically, unaccusingly—and raising the issue may sometimes help. A mild narcissist may still have some shame capacity. But one with a feverish, full-blown case of the condition? Don't even try it.

THE ENDURING DREAM of every employee working for a narcissist is that a great moment of score-settling will finally arrive. The boss will steal one too many ideas, abuse one too many employees, fly into a rage at precisely the wrong moment in front of precisely the wrong person and that will be that. You don't have to be a Rutgers player to know that there were probably a lot of high fives and backslaps the day Mike Rice was marched off campus forever. You didn't have to be a Cincinnati Reds fan to be happy when Marge Schott was banned by Major League Baseball from running her team and not long after that sold her controlling interest.

The problem is, those kinds of public shamings come too rarely. Most narcissists manage their dysfunction well enough to stay just on the safe side of plausible deniability—what looked like verbal abuse was merely a needed employee reprimand; what the disgruntled subordinate claims was a stolen idea was actually one of many things the boss had been considering for a while. "Narcissistic bosses usually don't crash and burn," says Hochwarter. "At best, they just crash and smolder." That takes a long time to happen, however, and consumes a lot of years in a lot of employees' lives.

The most decisive—and certainly most delicious—option for an aggrieved worker in a narcissist's office is simply quitting. Slamming your resignation letter on the boss's desk and striding out to take a better job somewhere else is satisfying in both its finality and its totality. Instantly, the feared figure is stripped of all power, reduced to a person of utter inconsequence in your life. Not only does this spell immediate freedom for the exiting employee, it can also contribute to the long-term decline of the boss. When an organization starts hemorrhaging talent, CEOs and boards of directors want to know why. If the boss gets blamed for the brain drain and is ultimately removed, it means relief for the employees still there and ex post facto vengeance for the former ones.

Those fantasies of just punishment, of public exposure, of the narcissistic boss brought low, fill the workdays of too many employees, for whom the job holds few other pleasures. One of the most overworked themes of any corporate retreat or sales conference is that the company is actually a sort of family—we all belong to it and we all must do our part to make it work. There's actually a lot of truth in the idea, especially considering that you spend so many of your waking hours in the total-immersion company of the people who work beside you. But the dark side is that the company can be dysfunctional and damaging like a family, too—especially when a bad boss, like a bad parent, reigns. Both children and employees don't always have many alternatives except to keep their heads down, pull together and do their best to manage the person who is supposed to be managing them. Kids, of course, grow up eventually, and for employees, other jobs do come along. Emancipation, in both cases, is a real and enduring thing. For many employees, it can't come too soon.

CHAPTER SEVEN

The Peacock
in the Oval Office

Here's betting you don't want to think about Lyndon Johnson's penis. I'm not sure even Lady Bird wanted to think about Lyndon Johnson's penis, but at least she signed on for the job. The rest of America? Not so much.

Plenty of people did have to deal with the Johnson johnson, however, especially during the five-plus years he was president. By a lot of measures Johnson was—not to put too fine a point on it—crazy. It wasn't so much his fierce ambition—extreme even by the standards of the narcissist, though driven at least in part by the fact that he came from a family of men who had died young of heart disease and he lived with a sense that he was always racing the clock. It wasn't just his animus toward his political enemies—particularly the Kennedys and most particularly Robert; that was just the way he played the extreme contact sport that was 1960s American politics. And it wasn't merely his relentless, bloody micromanagement of the Vietnam War. It was a hideous and murderous exercise, but it was as much the result of floundering, fearful, willful blindness as anything else. What made Johnson nuts was the side most Americans never saw of him.

It ought not to have come as too much of a surprise that a man who affected a certain rough-hewn, country courtliness in the public eye might, in private, be foulmouthed, boorish and an often-hard drinker. The halls of government are filled with such two-faced figures. It might not have come as a surprise, either, that he was a serial philanderer, regularly helping himself to women both on the White House staff and in his and Lady Bird's social circle. Lady Bird knew, and made a dignified, First Lady's peace with it.

"You have to understand, my husband loved people. All people," she said in a 1982 TV interview. "And half the people in the world were women. You don't think I could have kept my husband away from half the people?"

Maybe not, and Lady Bird certainly would not be the first First Lady to have to reckon with a sense of sexual entitlement in the occupant of the Oval Office—as Hillary Clinton, Jackie Kennedy, Eleanor Roosevelt and Florence Harding could attest. But as far as we know, she was surely the first—and, mercifully, the only one—who had to deal with the problem of flagrant presidential flashing.

Johnson's appalling habit of conducting meetings and even press conferences while on the toilet is well documented and oft repeated, though it's no less jaw-dropping for its relative familiarity. It's not easy to peel back all of the layers of pathology behind this most primal kind of exhibitionism: something proudly infantile, perhaps; some sort of animal turf-marking; some statement of dominance, surely (you can hardly make other people stand still to witness such a disagreeable exercise unless you truly are the alpha male).

The full-frontal displays, however, were something else. Some of the most alarming examples of LBJ's behavior were described in the 2009 book *In the President's Secret Service*, by former *Washington Post* and *Wall Street Journal* reporter Ronald Kessler, who gained extensive access to agents who protected multiple presidents across multiple decades. According to Kessler's reporting, Johnson would no sooner board *Air Force One* than he would drop his public persona and replace it with the real, ranch-bred deal.

"You dumb sons of bitches, I piss on all of you," he'd say in the direction of the crowd of people and press outside the plane as soon as the door was closed. He would then retreat to his stateroom and begin getting undressed, stripping down first to just his socks and shorts and often to nothing at all, sometimes while the door was open and staff members (many of them women) or immediate family members (all of them women) came and went. During an outdoor press conference at the Johnson ranch, he once turned to the side, unzipped and began peeing freely into nature, at the same time keeping his face turned to the reporters and continuing the colloquy. One morning at six a.m., a Secret Service agent spotted the President similarly relieving himself off the back porch of the ranch house, greeting the dawn in his own particular way.

Robert Caro, Johnson's tireless biographer, who has devoted three lengthy volumes—so far—to the late President's life, tells similar stories: Johnson's nickname for his favorite part of his personal anatomy ("Jumbo," of course) and the time, when he was serving in Congress, that he brandished it for another legislator who walked into the bathroom while he was relieving himself, and asked, "Have you ever seen anything as big as this?" There is nothing in any of the literature that suggests this behavior was considered acceptable, even if it was reluctantly accepted, or that it was appreciated, even if people were willing to tolerate it.

This kind of exhibitionism needs no help from narcissism to make it into the medical texts. In the *Diagnostic and Statistical Manual* it is its own, freestanding condition, at least if it interferes with daily functioning (which getting naked in public has a fair chance of doing). But exhibitionism can also be an expression of narcissism, particularly in a person who has chosen a "Look at me" career like politics and who, like Johnson, also exhibited so many of the grandiose, destructive contemptuous-of-others symptoms of the full-blown narcissist. In his case, it was all enough to cause real concern among those closest to him about the stability of the man running the most powerful nation on earth.

"If Johnson weren't president," said retired agent Richard Roth, according to Kessler's book, "he'd be in an insane asylum."

That might be so—but it might well be an asylum that served as home to a lot of other presidents and heads of state. A little narcissism can be a good thing in many jobs; a lot of narcissism is a bad thing in almost all jobs. But it's perhaps only in the presidency that a big, roaring case of it not only doesn't hurt, but is actually a threshold requirement—the temperamental entry fee that qualifies you to participate in the game in the first place.

Aspiring to lead even a small nation requires a level of vanity that seems to border on madness. It is a kinetic, public, killingly overscheduled life, one that feeds the occupant of the throne room a steady dose of the drug of power, but exacts a physical and emotional payment no wholly sane person would want to endure. The walk-and-talk glibness of dramatizations like *The West Wing* or *The American President* is fun but fantastical—a flip, Hollywood notion of what the relentless, airless bubble in which a head of state really lives is like. It's more than the studying of briefing books, droning of policy meetings, negotiations and strategy sessions—closed-door gatherings in which you can at least act cranky if you feel cranky and look bored if you are bored. It's also the ribbon cuttings and glad-handing and summit meetings and press availabilities and the total-immersion, eighteen-hour-a-day grind of a campaign that begins two years before an election is actually held and can involve making the same speech over and over again on half a dozen tarmacs in a single day. And in every single one of those venues you have to keep the mask up and the smile fixed, lest a stray camera catch you being what you undeniably are, which is just plain human.

And all that performing concerns mostly the theater of being president. What about the substance of the job—and the heat you'll take if people decide you're making a hash of it? Unemployment ticks up? Your fault. Markets dip? Ditto. Oil prices rise? It's on your watch, isn't it? Five minutes before you first set foot in the Oval Office the whole mess was the other guy's doing; five minutes after, it's all yours.

"Being president is like being a jackass in a hailstorm," said Johnson in an admirably candid moment. "There's nothing to do but stand there and take it."

"As to the presidency," a retired Martin Van Buren confided, "the two happiest days of my life were those of my entrance upon the office and my surrender of it."

"I am heartily rejoiced that my term is so near its close," said James Polk, who did not stand for reelection after four successful years in office. "I will soon cease to be a servant and will become a sovereign."

Finally, there are the private agonies, the staring-at-the-ceiling-in-the-dark-of-night moments all presidents describe. George W. Bush was roundly criticized for not responding before September 11 to intelligence warnings that Osama bin Laden was planning to strike inside the United States; Franklin Roosevelt was similarly slammed for allegedly being asleep at the switch in the run-up to Pearl Harbor. Maybe they were both guilty as charged and maybe they weren't, but no one doubts that both men agonized about the thousands of people who had died—perhaps avoidably—while they had the conn.

And yet men and, increasingly, women still seek the office, lust for it, really, and pursue it with a mad-dog hunger, firmly convinced that not only are they equipped to lead, they are better equipped than any other person who might harbor similar aspirations. In a single four-year cycle, there can be a dozen or so people who actually set about running for president, but on the benches and in the political farm clubs around the nation there are likely thousands more who are thinking about making a bid someday. Back in 2006, when there was still a constituency in the Democratic Party stinging from the electoral sleight of hand that had denied Al Gore the presidency in 2000 and hoping he'd make one more run, I saw him at a public event and asked him if he wouldn't feel almost obliged to jump into the race if he truly, soberly came to believe that he was the best person for the job, particularly when it came to issues like climate change, about which he feels so passionately.

"But that's what everyone decides when they run for president," he answered with a small laugh. "You don't become a candidate in the first place if you haven't first reached that conclusion."

People come to the presidency in a lot of ways. There are princeling presidents—FDR, the younger Bush, John Kennedy, scions helped along by bloodlines and money to an office that most people consider out of reach. There are scrapper presidents, people with humble—sometimes almost tragic—backgrounds who fight their way to the presidency and arrive there ebulliently (Bill Clinton), self-importantly (Jimmy Carter), eccentrically (LBJ), bitterly (Richard Nixon), but grab the prize all the same. There are happy presidents like Ronald Reagan; genial if awkward presidents like George H. W. Bush; war hero presidents like Andrew Jackson, Ulysses S. Grant, Teddy Roosevelt and Dwight Eisenhower, men who have already been commanders once and decide that they enjoyed the experience so much they'd like to go right on running things, even if they have to do it in the drabber colors of civilian clothes. But not a single one of them didn't at some point reach the cocky, self-adoring conclusion that, yes, he was the one person out of hundreds of millions who most deserved to lead the nation.

Diffident people don't get to the White House. Humble people don't get to the White House. As surely as you have to be a natural-born citizen and at least thirty-five years old to seek the presidency at all, so too do you have to be a shameless, chest-thumping, unapologetic narcissist—however discreetly you might try to conceal that fact. That, history has shown, can be either a very good thing or a very bad thing, but it is, for better or worse, an unavoidable thing.

ONE OF the most direct reasons narcissists are overrepresented in the ranks of U.S. presidents is that they're so bloody good at running for the office in the first place. A presidential campaign is, after all, nothing so much as a two-year, marathon job interview, and the same skills that make job candidates such a hit in the human resources office—enthusiasm, charm, energy, ideas—work equally well on the campaign trail. In both cases, narcissists do more than simply perform well—they have a lot of fun doing it.

There are, certainly, plenty of exceptions to the Happy Warrior rule. Nixon was no one's idea of a social creature. He appeared sublimely uncomfortable in his own skin and made other people uncomfortable when they were around him. His manifest success—he was his party's presidential or vice presidential nominee in five out of six elections from 1952 to 1972, and in that final run scored a then-unprecedented forty-nine-state landslide—was due more to doggedness, guile and native tactical skills than to personality. George H. W. Bush, a vastly more appealing man than Nixon, nonetheless famously glanced at his watch during a 1992 town hall–style debate with Bill Clinton and was pilloried for appearing as if he didn't want to be there in the first place. Later, after he had lost the election and was free to speak more candidly about it, he acknowledged that that was entirely true, but not because he didn't care about the issues being debated or the people who were affected by them. Rather, it was because he disliked the game-show feel of the entire exercise and felt the time could be better spent actually governing. That's a perfectly reasonable sentiment, but since debates are a fixture of modern campaigns, it pays to enjoy them as Clinton manifestly did, or at least be able to fake it believably.

Clinton, of course, is a wholly sui generis character, someone who is to other great campaigners like Reagan, Kennedy and FDR what Cy Young was to Tom Seaver, Nolan Ryan and Bob Gibson—the greatest of the greats, even among a crowd of Hall of Famers. During both of Clinton's presidential campaigns, rallies and other events chronically ran late, not just because his volubility could keep him talking long past the planned length of his stump speech, but because he could not resist the lure of the rope line. As long as there were hands outstretched, he wanted to shake them. Obama, no slouch on the campaign trail, always did better in big arenas than in the more intimate dynamic of the one-on-one. Reagan, who did excel at the face-to-face, also ad-hered to a clock—enforced by his handlers—and ducked out after a prescribed time. Clinton never had enough.

"I like the job. That's what I'll miss the most," he said somewhat poignantly near the end of his presidency. "I'm not sure anybody ever liked this as much as I've liked it."

Part of Clinton's joy, of course, came from the fact that every hand he touched was touching his back and every vote he won was like a kiss—a validation, a sign that one more person had not only chosen him but liked him. More than a decade after Clinton's presidency ended—when he remained a globally incandescent presence with his foundation and speaking tours and work on both his wife's 2008 pres-idential campaign and Obama's two campaigns—*Time* magazine's Joe Klein was asked what Clinton's long game is, why he keeps working so hard. "Clinton's long game is the same as it's always been," Klein answered. "To be loved by every one of the seven billion people on the planet."

That combination of hunger and charm did not always serve Clin-ton well, as his reckless, 1998 sex scandal illustrated. Part of that was surely nothing more than adolescent appetite—he liked sex, he wanted sex, and he was surely in a position to get sex. Such impulses and opportunities hardly make him special among presidents, but most of them also have an internal policeman, a piece of the self that can hold up a hand and ask, *You know this isn't a good idea, right?* Clinton's cop was on the take. The part of him paying that behavioral bribe money was the part that needed not just the metaphorical kiss of a vote, but the real kiss—and more—of a person who could validate him in the most primal way possible, tell him he was good enough not just to send to the White House, but to take to bed.

Whatever the price to the nation and to Clinton's own presidency that his ravenous needs exacted, his craving to be loved is wholly of a piece with the mask model of narcissism, the endless attention-seeking that compensates for a bottomless emotional hole of some kind. Nobody can really psychoanalyze someone else from a distance, and even a psychologist would not pretend to try without meeting and treating the person. But Clinton's upbringing is a matter of historical record—his biological father died in a car accident three months before he was born; his stepfather was an abusive alcoholic; he was something of a misfit at school, describing himself as "the fat kid in the band." There are few psychologists who wouldn't trace a pretty direct line from that kind of background to a deep need to seek and feel love.

Clinton was very, very good at achieving that goal, something that I got to experience at close proximity one day when I improbably found myself in the Oval Office. It was July 1995, several months after my first book, *Apollo 13*, had been published and just one month after the release of the movie that was based on it. I was invited to the White House to be present when Clinton awarded Apollo 13 commander Jim Lovell—with whom I had collaborated on the book—the Congressional Space Medal of Honor. It was a tribute that many historians had long agreed Lovell had earned, but since NASA had always preferred to forget about its one lunar landing mission that didn't actually land,

Lovell had been denied. It would be up to a sitting president—who actually chooses the recipients, despite the congressional reference in the name of the award—to choose Lovell. And that month Clinton did.

A small circle of other people involved in either the movie or the space program, including Tom Hanks, who played Lovell, and Pete Conrad, the third man on the moon, were in attendance as well, but our little group was dwarfed by the staffers and the press scrum, who were there to cover the award presentation and also to question Clinton afterward about that day's most pressing news, which was how the United States planned to respond to that month's mass killings of civilians in Bosnia. When both the presentation and the press availability were done, Clinton came over to our group to shake hands. I scanned the four people in line who preceded me, realized that I was the only one he had never met before and reckoned I'd better introduce myself. I began to do so, but I had barely gotten out my name, much less what business I had being there, before he waved me off.

"I know," he said. "I know who y'are." There was a nonchalance to it, a matter-of-factness that implied of *course* he knew who I was. How could anyone not know who I was? Every rational brain cell I had told me that this was the Clinton charm I'd heard about, the make-you-feel-like-the-most-important-person-in-the-room-for-five-seconds magic that so many other people had described. I recognized it for exactly what it was—and fell for it all the same.

That experience might be common to anyone who's ever shaken Clinton's hand, but a few minutes later there was a tiny, silent moment that I like to think was more particular to the circumstance. The room had broken up into two small conversational clusters by that time, with Hanks, Conrad and a couple of others to my left, and Lovell and Clinton to my right. The dynamic between those two fascinated me: Lovell was the Eagle Scout, astronaut and Naval Academy officer, a man who had been married to the same woman for more than forty years and served his country for most of his adult life. Clinton was the philanderer, the bad boy, the too-cute-by-half pol who may never have technically dodged the draft but had done a nifty job of tap-dancing around it. And yet he was also Lovell's commander in chief—which means a lot to a career naval officer—not to mention the man who'd accorded him the space honor others had wrongly denied him. I had come to know Lovell well and care about him and his family quite a bit—and still do, for that matter—and wanted to stand alone and watch that moment play out.

There by myself in the middle of the Oval Office rug, however, I must have looked like the social misfit—the fat kid from the band at this particular party. Clinton, who never took his eyes off Lovell, spotted me peripherally, touched Lovell's arm, steered both of them three or four steps my way and gathered me into their conversation. It was a very small gesture—something I've done a thousand times for other people at parties and other people have done for me. But this was the President of the United States doing me that little kindness, and to the extent that it would ever matter to him, he'd won my support for as long as he remained a public figure. The man is that good—and if he weren't a love-hungry narcissist, he'd be less good.

IT TAKES MORE than mere neediness and charisma to be a true narcissist—and it takes more than mere narcissism to make it to the White House. In America's short history, forty-three men have already been president (never mind the fact that Barack Obama is technically called the forty-fourth president; Grover Cleveland, who served two nonconsecutive terms, is counted as both the twenty-second and twenty-fourth presidents—a bit of historical ridiculousness that has, unfortunately, stuck). That's a great many, very different people with a great many different personalities.

Taking the psychological measure of even a living president in an era in which every tic and twitch is captured on TV, every other staffer leaks personal details, and the presidents themselves eventually write memoirs is still not an easy thing. Nobody knows another person's psychic secrets, and some presidents seem uninterested in ever exploring their own. Bush the younger was explicit about the fact that he was not the kind of man who would spend much time reflecting on his actions or analyzing his motivations. Nixon was openly disdainful of both the science of psychology and of psychologists and psychiatrists themselves. But every word a president utters, every initiative he proposes or executive order he signs, is inevitably an indication of the mind behind the action, and it's hard not to come up with at least a good police sketch of the psychology driving the man.

Some of the earliest and still most impressive work involving these so-called historiometric measures of a president's personality was conducted in 1988 by psychologist Dean Simonton of the University of California, Davis. At the time Simonton did his work, Reagan was just completing his second term, which means that both Bushes, Clinton and Obama are not included in the study—a true loss, since the last three at least are deeply intriguing characters. Still, Simonton did manage to gather the other thirty-nine presidents into his sample group, which all by itself meant a lot of work.

The first step was to scour the historical record for biographical details on the presidents' lives, including education, birth order, family size, parental death, socioeconomic status and more. Simonton then added the men's record in office, including legislation signed, vetoes issued (and overridden), military adventurism, programs proposed, economic performance and number of terms served. Finally, and most trickily, he recruited a panel of evaluators who, using the same historical data, profiled the presidents on fourteen personality dimensions, such as wit, pettiness, poise, flexibility, moderation, friendliness and intellectual brilliance; and on eighty-two other qualities exhibited in office, such as the ability to delegate, the willingness to compromise, a tendency toward impatience or abruptness and an ease or unease with the press (a good test of interpersonal skills if ever there was one). All of this data was then crunched to produce five different presidential types, which Simonton labeled charismatic, interpersonal, deliberative, creative and neurotic. All of the presidents—like all people—exhibited a mix of these five traits; where they ranked on a sliding scale for each came together to form any one man's personality.

The numbers that Simonton and his team came up with were both surprising and unsurprising, depending on the president. For all five character types, a score of zero was considered average. The further a president moved above that line, the more of that quality he possessed; the further he moved below it, the less. In the twentieth century, the most charismatic president was FDR, with a way-above-the-mean score of 2.5. He was followed, unexpectedly, by Johnson—who at least in public could be folksy—at 1.5; Kennedy clocked in at 1.3; and Reagan and Teddy Roosevelt were tied at 1.2. Among the big losers on the charisma scale were the bibulous Grant, at –2.2, and James Madison, at –1.2, whom some twentieth-century historians have depicted as jealous, stubborn and even dishonest, claiming more credit for shaping the Constitution than he deserved.

Lyndon Johnson set the modern-era record for neuroticism, with a 1.5. He was eclipsed in history only by Grant, at 1.9, and by one-term-wonder Polk, at 2.5. (It was perhaps Polk's frenzied ambition that made his presidency so energetic and aggressive, with enormous land gains in the southwest, a restructuring of the U.S. Treasury, the settlement of a trade conflict with Great Britain, and a hard, effective hand with Congress.) The least neurotic, most equable president in American history? No surprise here: Reagan, at –1.8.

On other metrics, George Washington wins for deliberativeness, at 1.6—presumably, getting a new country plopped in your lap will bring out those qualities in a man. Grant comes in last, at –2.6: whiskey will do *that*. FDR and Nixon both score high on creativity, at 1.4 (hello New Deal, Social Security, Clean Air Act and the opening to China).

Harding, Coolidge and Taft are the twentieth-century losers on that score, at –1.4, –1.4 and –2.2, respectively. The least interpersonal presidents in history were the professorial Wilson and—no surprise here—Nixon, in a two-way crankiness tie at –2.3. The top honor in the interpersonal category is also a two-way tie, at 1.3, between Washington and dark horse Gerald Ford—who performed brilliantly in the simple business of making the White House and the president lovable again after the Constitutional atrocities of Watergate.

Certainly, not every score feels intuitively right. Johnson's 1.5 charisma ranking seems way too high, even if his drawl and jowls and southern ways endeared him to the just-folks crowd. Nixon's .9 neuroticism score is higher than most, but given what we now know about him—especially the foulmouthed racism, anti-Semitism and paranoia evident on so many of the White House tapes—he ought to have blown the doors off that particular scale. Still, the numbers overall seem pretty robust.

"The original personality descriptions were based on the president's whole life," says Simonton today. "And individual differences in most personality characteristics tend to be relatively stable over time." What the presidents were when they came into office, in other words, is fundamentally who they were throughout their terms, and the nation either paid for or benefited from those qualities, depending on the president.

In the years since, Simonton has extended his work to test both Bushes and Clinton, along with the original thirty-nine, on other scales, particularly openness to new ideas, IQ and, significantly, intellectual brilliance, a measure of your ability to do something creative with whatever raw intelligence number you've got. Our brainiest presidents, going by inferred IQ—as measured by vocabulary, academic record and more—were John Quincy Adams, at 165; Thomas Jefferson, at 145; JFK, at 138.9; Clinton, at 135.6; and Carter, at 130.2. The nincompoop presidents were Harding, at 107.8; James Monroe, at 109;

Grant and Andrew Jackson, tied at 110; and the younger Bush, at 111.1. Intellectual brilliance, the better measure of a president's contribution to history, often diverged sharply from raw intelligence. Carter's IQ availed him nothing, with his brilliance score a perfect 0.0—or exactly average. Adams's IQ might be 20 points higher than Jefferson's, but Jefferson's brilliance is more than twice that of Adams— 3.1 to 1.2. Wilson lived up to his 133 IQ with a 1.3 brilliance score; Monroe, similarly, lived down to his low IQ, clocking in at a −1.4 on brilliance.

In 1997, psychologist Ronald Deluga of Bryant University in Rhode Island used some of Simonton's data and some he gathered himself to take a more sharply focused approach to presidential character, looking specifically at charisma and narcissism. Deluga, like many historical psychologists, sees a lot of potential good in a narcissistic president. For one thing, he stresses, people following narcissistic leaders tend to work hard for them, often overperforming by beating deadlines, putting in longer hours and generally delivering more than they've been asked to deliver. This is especially important during presidential campaigns, in which the nonquantifiable enthusiasm factor can spell the difference between a victory and a loss. Obama outflanked Hillary Clinton during the Democratic primaries in 2008, mostly because of his superior ground game, a volunteer army staffed by young, excited, emotionally engaged volunteers. "Yes, we can" became less a slogan than a happy declaration.

Once in office, presidents put the same narcissistic energy to work motivating their staffs and herding the 535 cats in Congress. "Given the vast responsibilities of American presidents," Deluga writes, "effective and decisive leadership may require an individual demonstrating ample doses of narcissism."

To determine how the same thirty-nine presidents Simonton studied ranked on the narcissism scale, Deluga used similar historiometric data, and, more directly, also scored his thirty-nine subjects on the forty-question narcissistic personality inventory. That's an awfully presumptuous thing to do, since the NPI is supposed to be filled out by the subjects themselves, which can be hard when the overwhelming majority of your sample group is dead and the rest would be highly unlikely to sit still for the indignity of completing the questionnaire. So Deluga and his panel of raters completed the forms themselves, based on what the mound of historiometric information suggested that the presidents themselves would have answered. Yes, this was a highly imperfect alternative—but again, it produced results that feel intuitively right.

There is no such thing as a globally average NPI score, since self-esteem is subject to so many variables—age, income, education, culture and more. But 16 serves as a sort of clustering point, from which most people don't stray by more than a couple points either way. According to Deluga's work, America's most narcissistic president—weighing in at a self-adoring 35—was an apparent underdog: Chester A. Arthur. Hardly a presidential star, Arthur served just one forgettable term, from 1881 to 1885, dealing mostly with small-bore matters like civil service reform, rebuilding the Navy and striking trade deals. One of his most pressing policy challenges was how best to spend America's then-massive $145 million budget surplus—a problem modern presidents would surely love to have. But Arthur had more immediate things to do at home in the White House. There was the redecoration of the great mansion's staterooms to attend to—a job he would entrust only to the celebrated interior design genius Louis Comfort Tiffany. There were the twenty wagonloads of old furniture that did not please the President that had to be carted away and the more sumptuous replacements to be brought in. There was Arthur's extensive wardrobe—which included a reported eighty pairs of pants—and his habit of changing outfits two or three times a day, the better to display all that finery.

THE PEACOCK IN THE OVAL OFFICE

In his time, Arthur was variously nicknamed Elegant Arthur and The Gentleman Boss and, yes, even The Dude of the White House. One political cartoon from 1883 showed a nattily attired Arthur, with a caption that read: "According to your cloth you've cut your coat, O Dude of all White House residents; We trust that will help you with the vote, When next we go nominating Presidents."

Finishing a close second to Arthur in the NPI was FDR, at 33.33, just the kind of stratospheric narcissism score you'd expect from a man who had both the arrogance to think he deserved four full presidential terms and the charisma to go out and win them. The eccentric LBJ finishes just a point behind Roosevelt, at 32.33. Other high scorers were John Tyler, at 31.00, and his immediate predecessor William Henry Harrison, at 28.67 (a level of cockiness that may have contributed to his belief that he could deliver a ninety-minute inauguration speech in bitterly cold weather without wearing a topcoat, leading to a fatal case of pneumonia that ended his life and his presidency just one month later). The Founding Fathers, as a group, scored high, with John Adams at 28.33, George Washington at 27.67 and Thomas Jefferson at a surprisingly modest 17.33, which is still over the national mean, but not by much.

At the other end of the narcissism scale in Deluga's study was—no surprise here—Calvin Coolidge, at a rock-bottom 5.00. Popularly known as Silent Cal, he came by his reputation for reticence rightly, speaking and writing sparingly and showing particular reserve at cocktail parties and formal dinners, which most politicians find irresistible since it gives them an opportunity to hold forth. "I think the American people want a solemn ass as president and I think I will go along with them," he once said. Coolidge was not without wit. A popular story has it that a woman seated next to him at a dinner party once said, "Mr. President, I've made a bet against a fellow who said it was impossible to get more than two words out of you." Coolidge replied:

"You lose." That story may well be apocryphal, but there's a reason it has persisted so long in popular lore: It neatly captured the man Coolidge demonstrably was.

Other low scorers included William McKinley, at 6.67 (far, far behind the gaudy score of his vice president, Teddy Roosevelt, who came in at an unsurprising 29). The decidedly unflashy Harry Truman, Dwight Eisenhower and Jimmy Carter scored a modest 13.00, 14.33 and 16.00, respectively—unexpectedly low in the case of Carter, who despite his unpretentious ways was known for a stubbornness and arrogance that could infuriate his staff. JFK, for all his Camelot dazzle, came in at 22.67, two points behind Nixon at 24.67 and five behind Reagan at 27.67.

On the whole, the average score for all of the presidents is 19.53, a class curve dragged down a bit by some of the single-digit or low-teen stragglers, who are nonetheless outnumbered by the 20-plus high scorers, 21 to 9. But the nearly 20-point average is a not-inconsequential 4 points above the national mean, which in the narcissism sweepstakes may be a little like a pitcher adding just a few extra miles per hour to his fastball—enough to lift you above the rest of the crowd and into the elite.

A final ingredient in the narcissistic mix that makes a successful president is at least a small dollop of something unexpected: psychopathy. As a rule, we prefer not to have psychopaths in high office, and it's hard to argue with a policy like that. But psychopathy is not something we've ever fully understood. Some of the elements of the psychopathic personality include risk taking, fearlessness, social dominance and immunity to anxiety—all of which, exercised properly, can be indispensable when a president is, say, ordering troops into battle or taking a flyer on an ambitious and unprecedented social program like Social Security or Obama's health care reform. Even dishonesty, another element of psychopathy, can have an upside. FDR was notoriously cagey with his staff and with Congress, always seeming to agree with all of them and keeping his true positions a secret until he acted. Clinton was similarly inclined. Clinton's presidency was a solid if unspectacular success, and FDR's was legendary. "Narcissism and psychopathy are kind of kissing cousins," says Campbell.

Just how intimate that kiss is was explored in a 2012 study, in which a team of researchers at Emory University, the University of Georgia and elsewhere ranked all of the presidents with the exception of Obama on what's known as the Fearlessness Dominance dimension of psychopathy. Again using historiometric measures, and again using zero as the mean, they were able to place the presidents on a scale ranging from Teddy Roosevelt's 1.462 at the top to William Howard Taft's -1.579 at the bottom. Flanking either side of the mean were the cautious Carter, at .007, and Wilson, at -.032. Among the top ten finishers in fearlessness and dominance were just the presidents you'd suspect, including JFK, FDR, Reagan, Clinton, Andrew Jackson and George W. Bush. Among the bottom ten were Hoover, William McKinley, Coolidge and Andrew Johnson.

Here, too, there were some misses. Harry Truman's -.668 put him ninth from the bottom, yet he dropped the atom bombs on Japan, waded into Korea, fired General Douglas MacArthur and took control of the steel industry to prevent strikes from interrupting supply to the military. That's not the behavior of a timorous man. Martin Van Buren ranks eighth from the top for no discernible reason, after serving just a single bland term distinguished mostly by the economic panic of 1837. But on the whole, the public perception of most of the men seems in keeping with their Fearless Dominance scores, and as a general rule the nation benefited from having a bold figure in the White House.

"Boldness often associated with psychopathy may confer advantages across a host of occupations, vocations and social roles," the investigators wrote. "[It's] an important but heretofore neglected predictor of presidential performance."

FOR EVERY NARCISSIST who makes it to the White House, there are many who ache for the job just as much as the winner but nonetheless fall short. The losers are often more interesting and certainly more fun than the winners, since as messy as a presidential campaign is, it does do a pretty good job of winnowing out the flakes and eccentrics— with some key exceptions—and ensuring that mostly sober, serious people get to the Oval Office.

One of the longest-standing jokes on Capitol Hill is that the U.S. Senate is made up of 100 people who get up in the morning and see the next President of the United States staring back at them from the bathroom mirror. Surely there are exceptions to that rule, but given the list of senators and ex-senators who have sought the presidency in just the 2000s—Al Gore, Bill Bradley, John McCain, John Kerry, John Edwards, Joe Biden, Chris Dodd, Hillary Clinton, Barack Obama, Rick Santorum, Dan Quayle, Orrin Hatch, Elizabeth Dole, Joe Lieberman, Carol Moseley Braun, Bob Graham, Mike Gravel, Evan Bayh— it's hard to argue with the idea that the upper chamber is indeed the place for self-promoting dreamers. In many cases, they don't have a shot and even they may know it. But the "Look at me" drug just becomes intoxicating.

"Up through the 2008 cycle, the vanity run for president was typically an older statesman—Dodd, Biden—who, bored with his various committee chairmanships, decides to throw his hat in the ring," says Jay Newton-Small, *Time* magazine political reporter and White House correspondent during the George W. Bush administration. "He doesn't have a real possibility of winning, unless by chance everyone else in the field dies in a plane crash or is stricken by scandal and he's the only adult left in the room for the party to turn to. But he does it for the prestige and the name recognition and the narcissistic satisfaction of the adoring crowds. It's surprisingly easy to pack a room full of Chris Dodd fans in Iowa, even if they never vote for him."

Senators aren't the only showboats bothering the poor folks of Iowa and New Hampshire. There are also pizza magnates (Herman Cain), billionaire industrialists (Ross Perot) and former officeholders (ex–Arkansas governor Mike Huckabee and ex–House Speaker Newt Gingrich). Some of these lost-cause candidates are in it at least partly for the payday.

"In the last cycle, vanity runs have taken a decidedly materialistic bent," says Newton-Small, "running for president to get a Fox News contract or sell a book. Newt, of course, got all wrapped up in it and started believing his own hype."

Sometimes, too, the goal is smaller and almost poignantly meaningless—to have a voice in shaping the party's platform, say, an utterly pointless statement of principles on which a candidate ostensibly runs, but, in truth, rarely ever reads. There is the convention speaking slot, too—the chance to stand up and address the party, typically sometime between the speech by the party chairman and the one by the governor of the state hosting the convention, during an hour in which the only people watching are the C-SPAN junkies. Still, that was the "Look at me" payment the ex-candidate extracted from the party after losing three primaries and agreeing to pull out of the race so the people who had a real chance at the nomination could have a clear field.

Then, of course, there is Sarah Palin, who never ran for president but who is a figure entirely unignorable by both psychologists and political scientists. If narcissism knows no gender boundaries, politics is another matter entirely. In 2013, the American polity applauded itself for the fact that the number of women in the U.S. Senate had reached twenty for the first time in history—a modest accomplishment given that it still means that 51 percent of the population is represented by just 20 percent of the seats. In the House of Representatives, the seventy-eight female members represented an even smaller share of the total—just 17.9 percent. The ranks of women who have made credible runs for president are even thinner: Elizabeth Dole in the 2000 cycle and Hillary Clinton in 2008. Braun's 2004 bid was a quixotic and wholly hopeless thing, even if she didn't think so. Ditto then Congresswoman Shirley Chisholm in 1972 and then Senator Margaret Chase Smith in 1964. If men who consider themselves qualified to wield more power than any other human being on the planet are, by definition, narcissists, women must surely wear the same scarlet *N*, too. And yet, in American presidential politics they've tended to wear it lightly.

Clinton's biggest selling point has never been her flash or sizzle or ability to charm a room. During the 2008 campaign, then Senator Obama took deserved heat when, during a debate, Clinton made a self-effacing remark about her often-low likability numbers and he grumbled back, "You're likable enough, Hillary." But while the remark may have been unmannerly, it was not untrue. Clinton is merely likable enough, but the reason that's sufficient is that her other skills more than make up for her less-than-cuddly personality. People may or may not want to vote for her, but even her worst detractors can't deny that she knows her stuff. Dole's qualifications were hard to argue with, too: She was secretary of both the Labor and Transportation departments before her presidential run and a senator from North Carolina afterward. She was more of a people-pleaser than Hillary, working a room with a friendly ease leavened by southern approachability, even if her campaign never got nearly as far as Hillary's near-miss did.

But Palin? The ability of the ex–Alaska governor to electrify a crowd was undeniable—and the sheer delight she took in the campaign process was evident from the first moment she took the stage at the 2008 Republican National Convention as the GOP's vice presidential choice. Hillary Clinton can't light fires like that, and while Obama can, he doesn't seem to have nearly as much flat-out fun doing it as Palin does. But running is a means to an end, and that end is governing—which clearly appealed to Palin less.

Mark Halperin and John Heilemann's bestseller *Game Change* documented in squirm-inducing detail Palin's 2008 vice presidential run, which became the disaster it was in part because of her extreme narcissism—her odd preoccupation with her popularity polls at home in Alaska, her entitlement-driven outbursts at her staff and handlers, her six-figure wardrobe bills. Her permanent state of grievance toward what she dubbed "the lamestream media" was perfectly in keeping with the narcissist's inability to accept criticism and instead to assign blame for self-created problems. During their televised interviews with her, Katie Couric and Charles Gibson may indeed have asked Palin borderline condescending questions they would not have asked other candidates: What newspapers do you read? Do you know what the Bush Doctrine is? But they were legitimate questions given the office she was seeking and the lack of gravitas she projected—not to mention the fact that the Bush Doctrine question was prompted by the fact that she indeed did not seem to know what it was when it was brought up in a different context. It's nobody's fault but hers that the answers were beyond her reach. Palin's later decision to resign the governorship just two years into her sole four-year term in favor of pursuing TV and book deals also fits nicely with the narcissist's need to go where the lights are brightest.

"You could write whole chapters on Palin," says Newton-Small. "She parlayed her half-term stewardship of Alaska and flirtation with a 2012 presidential bid into two bestselling books, a Fox News contract, a reality TV show and [her daughter] Bristol appearing on *Dancing with the Stars*."

And what about that 2012 dalliance? Even as the serious GOP candidates were beginning to launch their campaigns, she embarked on a national tour that included three key primary and caucus states—South Carolina, New Hampshire and Iowa—in a bus wrapped in a picture of the Constitution. There is no evidence that she ever really planned to run, and her appearance in battleground state after battleground state just as the real candidates were showing up there for the first time began to look like the most infantile kind of attention grab, an inability to tolerate other people having the presidential toy, even if she didn't want to play with it herself.

As the idea that all Palin wanted was media attention became increasingly evident, her support among everyone but her most passionate believers began to calve away. No other politician had quite achieved the same mix of narcissism, high profile and low skill set that she had, and all but a hard core of an electorate that was once dazzled by her began to recoil at the very thought of her. If Palin did run in 2012, Republican strategist Mike Murphy told Newton-Small the year before, "there would be thunder from the grass roots, celebration in the [Obama] White House and despair among GOP leaders."

THERE IS, of course, no shame in failing to win the White House after actively seeking it or even just toying with the idea, whether you're a flaming narcissist or not. Cain, Gingrich and even Palin played by the rules and caused no real harm, except perhaps to the people who believed in them—and then the hurt was fleeting. The true peril comes from people who do attain power, impelled partly by their own narcissism, and bring their administration or party or even entire country down around them. That can happen through sloppiness and self-indulgence (think vodka-gulping Boris Yeltsin and the Russian economic collapse of the 1990s); cronyism and, well, priapism (think Italy's corrupt and randy Silvio Berlusconi); or simple ill temper (think the short-lived prime ministership of the UK's Malcolm Browne).

What's truly terrifying is when narcissism is accompanied by other, dangerously pathological traits such as remorselessness, sadism and bloodlust. That way lies the world's great despots—Hitler, Mao, Stalin, Pol Pot and most recently Syria's Bashar al-Assad. But however much history may rightly revile them, the fact is that none of those leaders would ever have gotten where they did if they hadn't had one other indispensable thing: followers. For that, a lot more people than just the narcissistic leaders themselves must shoulder some of the blame.

According to management professor Art Padilla of the University of North Carolina, who has studied human dynamics and politics, a monstrous leader needs three things to rise to power: a seductive but destructive personality, a conducive environment and willing followers. Without the convergence of these three forces—what Padilla calls the Toxic Triangle—there would be no dictators.

Hitler, as always, is the great, dark, case-proving example. The person who plunged the planet into World War II and authored the Holocaust would have been nothing but a small man with poisonous ideas—a species that has been spotted in almost all cultures—without the particular mix of his passionate (if often frothing) speaking skills, a public accustomed to supreme and centralized leadership, and a shattered economy, the consequence of World War I and the punitive sanctions imposed on Germany through the Versailles Treaty. Hitler was savvy enough about how to exploit the last two, as his writings in *Mein Kampf* make clear, but he evidently had doubts about how well he could project the dark charm he'd need to make his rise.

In 1925, after he was released from a nine-month prison sentence for his role in the proto-revolutionary Beer Hall Putsch, Hitler rehearsed his more operatic speaking poses before the camera of photographer Heinrich Hoffmann, while listening to recordings of himself delivering a speech. There was Hitler with the raised fist punctuating a point, Hitler with the body flung back as he hurled out his words, Hitler with the palms upturned in a gesture of professorial pleading. There was, too, a near-comical, silent-movie pose in which he looks skyward with his hands raised, as if he's seeing a glorious future for his country before him. Once he actually got a look at the portraits, the man who would soon use all that insane semaphoring to such destructive ends nonetheless had enough sense to order Hoffmann to burn the negatives. Hoffmann disobeyed—though he in turn had the sense not to release the pictures until after Hitler's death.

In the more contemporary era, Padilla sees Fidel Castro as the perfect example of a leader who benefited from the Toxic Triangle. "As a young man, Castro was seen as bright, charismatic, idealistic, courageous, bold, ruthless, skilled at self-promotion and able to attract a band of capable and equally ruthless and bloody minded supporters," Padilla and his coauthors wrote in a 2007 paper. "His charisma is apparent in newsreel clippings. His narcissism is evident from his exhibitionism—long speeches, starring him." Later in Castro's career, Padilla notes, he also exhibited the narcissist's characteristic grandiosity and overreach, sending troops into Africa and Central America when he was himself incapable of building a truly functioning twentieth-century state, even with every lever of government under his control.

The Cuban people were equally good at filling the role of susceptible followers, divided broadly into three groups: revolutionaries like Castro; the poor, for whom any promise of an improved life had appeal; and an apolitical middle class that was fed up with the corruption of the existing regime of dictator Fulgencio Batista and longed for change. Finally, Cuba's history of repeated coups and economic woes in a Western Hemisphere in which other large and small nations were thriving made the island a pile of political kindling ready to burn. The charismatic Castro was the spark—something the U.S. State Department recognized, but too late in the game.

"It would be a mistake to underestimate this man," a State Department analyst wrote in 1959, just after Castro seized power. "He [is] clearly a strong personality and a born leader."

The irony of that official warning is that by itself it's high praise.

There's a thin line separating the selling of a bad and murderous idea from selling a good and noble one. The messages may be entirely different, but the huckster's skills necessary to persuade millions of people to believe and follow are unsettlingly similar. It appalls and offends us to compare America's celebrated leaders with history's worst, but if a figure in our past were going to drive us over the edge the way Castro and Hitler drove their countries, would it have been the likes of Martin Luther King, Jr., Ronald Reagan, John Kennedy and Bill Clinton, or would it have been Al Gore, Jimmy Carter, Dwight Eisenhower and Bob Dole? The first group came equipped with powerful talents to persuade and seduce and used them in high-minded and civilized ways. The second group was just as wisely and principally inclined, but lacked the ability to make people feel anything terribly deeply, and mobilizing a nation to extreme behavior is all about the emotion.

"We say Hitler was horrific and part of that arose from his narcissism," says Barbara Oakley, author of multiple books on human behavior, including *Evil Genes, Cold-Blooded Kindness* and *Pathological Altruism*. "But we don't say that Churchill was equally narcissistic. People used to say that he and his wife had a great relationship because they were in love with the same man. But Churchill had empathy and caring for others that Hitler did not manifest." Both, however, were members in good standing of the self-adoration club.

It also helps leaders of the despotic stripe to have a boogeyman, an outside threat against which the people can be mobilized and energized. The United States is framed as an existential menace in both North Korea and Iran—something against which only the existing regime can keep the country safe. For Hitler the dangerous other was the Jews, for Cambodia's Pol Pot it was the intelligentsia and city dwellers, for Rwanda's Hutus it was the Tutsis, for the Bosnian Serbs it was Bosnian Muslims.

"Yugoslavia is the great modern example of manipulating tribal sentiments to create murder," says psychologist and morality re-searcher Jonathan Haidt of New York University's Stern School of Business. "In most cases of genocide you have a moral entrepreneur, a person who uses moral mechanisms to rally his tribe together to mur-der other tribes."

There have been too few women as heads of state to know how they would behave in a more gender-neutral world. Golda Meir was no-body's patsy in the five years she was prime minister of Israel, nor was Margaret Thatcher in the fifteen years she held the same office for Great Britain. Both women had the label "The Iron Lady" applied to them, and neither was reluctant to use her military. Thatcher, in particular, showed an equal—many said pitiless—toughness in dealing with Britain's trade unions. Indira Gandhi and Benazir Bhutto, one-time prime ministers of India and Pakistan, respectively, were similarly tough and both advanced their countries' nuclear weapons programs. Both, too, were assassinated, taking the kinds of chances and putting themselves in the kinds of danger that only people who fancied them-selves indestructible would incur.

All of those traits in all of those women certainly had more than just the air of narcissism about them, as did the mere fact that they sought such positions of power in the first place. But it will take a far more egalitarian world with a far larger sample group of female leaders before we learn if the few who attain real power are just conforming to geopolitical norms long since set by men, or if the narcissism that comes with leadership knows no sexual distinctions at all—which means that a female Pol Pot or Stalin or Castro could one day be among us.

The United States has never produced a leader who achieved that level of monstrosity. Some of that may simply be that we've been in the nation game for so short a time—less than 240 years, when other countries have been around for millennia. Some of it, too, is the struc-ture of our government, with its three competing branches always checking and constraining one another. But in both LBJ and Nixon there were the makings of madness, erratic temperaments that might have reached full lunatic bloom in a system that provided them something closer to absolute power. Instead, both were forced from office early—Johnson by a public that turned on the Vietnam War and him as its architect, Nixon by impeachment proceedings in Congress.

George W. Bush's Iraq adventure went badly awry, too, and Bill Clinton was formally impeached (unlike Nixon, who quit before the matter actually became official), yet both survived to serve two full terms. It wasn't just their personalities that were responsible for that. There were far fewer American deaths in Iraq than in Vietnam, which partly insulated the country from the calamity the war nonetheless was. And Clinton's impeachment was a partisan exercise, payback for Nixon's, for ostensible crimes that were so petty as to be inconsequential. Clinton's popularity actually climbed following the impeachment drama and the GOP's crashed. Indeed, before the 2013 government shutdown pushed the Republican's approval rating down to 28 percent in Gallup polling, the lowest the party had ever been was 31 percent on December 18 and 19, 1998—the days House GOP members debated and voted on impeachment articles.

All of those variables helped doom Johnson and Nixon and save Clinton and Bush. But it is undeniable that they both also projected a stability and emotional soundness—to say nothing of a pleasing personality—that their predecessors lacked.

Other countries have to find other ways out from underneath the autocrat's boot, and fortunately the leaders themselves often provide it. The narcissists' inability to learn from mistakes, to listen to the wiser words of others and to realize that there are hard limits even to the most expansive power often as not prove their undoing. Any fool could have seen that Hitler should not have invaded Russia when he already had a multifront war going that would soon include the United States. Any fool could have seen that Saddam Hussein needed to get right with the rest of the world unless he wanted to wind up at the end of a rope—which he did. Any fool could have seen that as Libya was crumbling Muammar Qaddafi should have gotten out while the getting was good. But the narcissist labors under a greater disability than the fool.

"I think of Napoleon blatantly ignoring his advisers and going deeper into Russia in the winter as a good example of this," says Nathanael Fast. "Power leads to positive illusions of the self—a sense of control. Power is *defined* as having control."

But illusory control is the same as having no control at all. The one thing narcissistic leaders need to manage first is themselves—their tortured egos, their broken self-esteem, their inability to see their own flaws. Those who do may indeed achieve historical greatness. Those who don't become history's morality tales.

CHAPTER EIGHT

The Chest-Thumping
of the Tribe

I never much cared for close-order drill instruction, and I had plenty of reasons to feel the way I did. There was the heat, the tedium, the buzzing of gnats and mosquitoes that must have found a closely spaced line of overheated and stationary human beings both a bounty and a puzzle. And then there was the utter pointlessness of the thing. Marching with perfect precision, in perfect obedience to a series of shouted commands, was not, near as I could tell, a skill that had any application beyond the immediate business of learning how to do it so I could get the day's session over with and move on to something that had a demonstrable purpose.

Drill instruction was not something I ever should have experienced at all. I did not attend a military prep school, and I reached draft age at precisely the point the United States was making the transition to an all-volunteer military. That should have been all I needed to spare me the chore of ever learning how to march, but I never reckoned on summer camp.

I hit the camp demographic in the early, roaring days of the space age, when science, technology, engineering and math—the critical disciplines that we hadn't yet labeled with the snazzy twenty-first-

century acronym STEM—all at once seemed at least as important as
the hiking, canoeing and ballplaying curriculum of the traditional
summer camp. That was fine with me, since I was an almost surreally
poor athlete and an unashamed geek. It was finer still when I was told
that the camp that had been chosen for me was the reassuringly soft-
sounding Camp Comet, with its advertised curriculum of "science,
nature, sports"—in that order.

The camp delivered just the program it advertised, but what had
somehow been left out of the brochures was any mention of a man the
campers called simply Colonel Plaine—and whom I suspected friends,
relatives and even grandchildren addressed with the same name, since
I could not imagine anyone calling him anything else. Colonel Plaine
was a retired lieutenant colonel and the headmaster of a military academy in the non-camp season. He was a solid, silver-haired man with
an expansive gut that was always straining against his regimental
Camp Comet T-shirt and a voice that was less an actual voice than
a cannon report. He taught, not surprisingly, riflery, and enforced a
fierce discipline on the shooting range that somehow made marksmen
out of even the least gifted, most myopic campers and resulted in exactly zero accidents in the nine summers I attended the camp. It was
Colonel Plaine who would play reveille in the morning and taps at
night and preside over the ceremonial flag-raising and flag-lowering at
the beginning and end of the day. And it was Colonel Plaine who was
the drillmaster, overseeing an hour's program of instruction every
Sunday and the daily march to the flagpole each evening.

As an adult—even as a college student after my camp years had
ended—I came to appreciate the genius of Colonel Plaine. He affected
a muttering brusqueness most of the time, but if you spotted him in an
unguarded moment, speaking only to other adults, he had a winning
smile and an easy way about him. He maintained order in a Lord of
the Flies group of 250 boys living in cabins far away from their parents, and even the drilling—the cursed drilling—taught us a thing or

two about teamwork, self-control, delayed gratification and the simple business of sucking it up and tolerating a little discomfort. And on two occasions—and only two occasions—I learned to love the otherwise pointless business.

First, of course, were those rare days on which the girls would come by. On the same mountain as our all-boys camp—though separated by a lake and a ravine—was an all-girls camp of roughly the same size. I didn't give much thought to the girls during my first few summers, when I was nine and ten and eleven. But around the time I turned twelve or thirteen, their very presence—close enough that we could wave to them from ridges framing the gulf between the camps— became a drug. We talked about them, we thought about them, we developed the pheromonal antennae of moths; if there was a molecule of girl anywhere on the wind, we could pick it up at half a mile. Most of the time that half mile was unbridgeable, but on Visitors Day, when the parents would come to call and the boys and girls who had brothers and sisters at both camps would shuttle back and forth, the border was thrown open. There were all manner of plays and other performances that had been prepared for the occasion—and one of them was a drill display. I dreaded it as I always did, until the demonstration actually began and I saw the girls watching. At that point, I was transformed.

For the first time, I wanted to stand as straight as I'd been instructed to; I wanted to keep my eyes locked forward and my fidgeting under control. I wanted to turn crisply and stop smartly and do every single thing Col. Plaine had been instructing me to do for so many summers because, well, the girls were there and while I could not have begun to explain the primal forces that simple fact put into play—the need to signal my strength, my genetic fitness, and yes, my reproductive worthiness—while I couldn't even have fully fathomed them if they'd been explained to me, I knew they felt novel and powerful and thrilling. And while each boy in that line with me was impelled to send that signal individually—indeed to send it more powerfully than all of the other boys on either side of us so that we would be the ones noticed and, in our unconscious imaginations, selected—we also sent it as a group. We could hardly go marching about all by ourselves in the hope of catching the eye of a girl. We'd look less fit than ridiculous. But as a tribe we conveyed a different, deeply rooted message: It's a dangerous, bloody, fang-and-claw world out there, a world filled with other tribes, savage tribes, tribes not to be trusted. We, as a band, are better than they are—worthier, handsomer and more desirable; and I, as a member of that band, might be the best of them all.

The feeling went away as soon as we finished drilling, stuffed back in its genetic trunk for the moment. But it was impossible to forget, and it left me—and I suspect all of us—feeling happy and a little tipsy. Something similar came roaring back, more powerfully still, a couple of weeks later, when the camp's annual color war competition began.

Nearly all camps have a color war, though at the girls' camp it went by the more peaceable name "Team Week." But the concept is the same everywhere. The entire population of campers, who until then were divided in a series of horizontal strata by age and bunk, would all at once be cleaved vertically instead; from the sixteen-year-olds down to the six-year-olds, a scythe would fall, dividing the boys into a blue team on one side and a white team on the other. The selections of who would fall on which side of the line would be made behind the scenes— by counselors working to create two rosters of boys equally matched in abilities. Initially, the warring sides would be known simply as Team A and Team B, and if those labels had remained, some of the passion would have gone out of the game. But colors were designated instead, and that changed everything.

Once the team assignments were announced, campers would be given a small white ribbon or a small blue ribbon that was to be pinned to their T-shirts at all times; being caught without yours was the same as being out of uniform, which meant demerits for your team. No sooner were the ribbons distributed than arguments and boasts would begin to break out in the cabins. Boys who hadn't gotten along for most of the summer but who happened to be wearing the same ribbon would suddenly make common cause against boys who, until moments before, had been their closest friends but now were on the wrong side of the color divide. In bunks with an even number of kids and an even division between the teams, the posturing stayed pretty much in balance. But woe betide the kids in the minority of an odd-numbered bunk, with, say, four white-teamers forced to endure a week of intimidation at the hands of five blue-teamers.

It was during drill—now mass drill—that this brother-against-brother animus truly crystallized. Where once we marched to the flagpole a bunk at a time, in lines of eight or nine boys each, we now formed two powerful battalions of 125. Each evening, we would fall into line on opposite sides of the parade grounds, almost out of each other's sight, arranging ourselves from the smallest boy to the tallest, dressing the ranks with the proper right arm to the next shoulder in line to maintain the proper distance, before reassuming the rigid attention stance. The team captain would stand at the front of the line with the team flag—a large white banner or a large blue banner—carried in front of him. Then the teams would march in.

The flags would almost always be snapping in the wind as we approached, whipped up as the cooler air of an August evening met the heat of the day the mountain was surrendering. The dirt of the parade grounds, where the grass had been worn away in long strips by a summer's worth of marching, would give up puffs of dust as 250 pairs of feet stomped on it. And the sound of those feet—the loud, steady, collective tromp—would produce as much a physical sensation as a sound.

We knew nothing about how that cadence played our brains—how the rhythm of the feet, like the rhythm of drums, poured into the auditory cortex, lighting up the brain's right hemisphere, where emotions like affiliation are processed, as well as the amygdala, which handles baser feelings like fear and rage and aggression. We knew nothing about how millennia of generals had learned to bang those same tribal drums to impel men to march into battles in which they might—in many cases surely would—die, but somehow that was all right because to the extent that they were thinking about death at all, they were dying with their fellows and for their country and that was just fine.

We were small children, of course, and there was nothing but play at stake in our marching. But we knew the sensations all the same—and we loved them. The narcissism of a tribe can be a wonderful, terrible, lovely, bloody, life-giving, life-taking thing—sometimes all at once. It's present in the harmless exhibitionism of the sign-waving, face-painted fans at the Super Bowl or the World Cup. It's present in the faintly darker, more jingoistic chants of "U.S.A! U.S.A.!" that may accompany an Olympic hockey win (a very good thing) or an ill-planned invasion of Iraq (a very bad thing). It's part of every company softball game ever played—techies versus sales, banking versus investment, edit versus ad—and every blue state versus red state argument ever had. It's the Whigs versus the Tories, the Mugwumps versus the Republicans, the Bolsheviks versus the Mensheviks, the Communists versus the Capitalists, the Union versus the Confederacy. It's soldiers who race into the field risking death and ducking cross fire to save a wounded comrade and then, that job done, turn their fire outward and take other lives with the same resolve and pride with which they just saved one.

Human beings are social creatures—a very important thing to be if soft, slow, fangless, clawless ground-dwellers like us were ever going to survive. But being social implies bands, and bands imply favoring your own above all the others. And since we're rational creatures, too—creatures who like to feel good about ourselves and don't like to think we seize land and resources and mates simply because we're greedy—we tell ourselves that we favor our own kind because we're smarter, prettier, better, more virtuous, more caring, a superior breed of people in a world filled with lesser ones.

"When a member of your group does something good, you attribute it to character," says Yale University psychologist John Dovidio, who specializes in intergroup relationships, prejudice and stereotyping. "When they do something bad, you dismiss it as a situational deviation. We do the opposite with non–group members. Once you start categorizing people, you automatically feel more positive toward people in your group and some distrust for outsiders."

That's true not just of us, but of many, many other species, too—apes that go to war with other bands, prides of lions that compete for territory. "You see this all the way down to tadpoles," says UCLA biologist Jay Phelan, coauthor of the book *Mean Genes*. "They preferentially associate with other tadpoles, depending on how closely related they are."

Those feelings may exist in us naturally, unavoidably, but they're also ones that can be dangerously easy to manipulate—with an anthem, a chant, a little scrap of ribbon. The narcissism of the individual is a personal thing—growing from within to take control of only one mind, one personality. The narcissism of the tribe is a gravitational thing—the kind that gathers more and more individuals to a central point, its tug increasing along with its size and mass. Dictators and despots may ignite wars and bring down nations, but they are still merely borrowing their power. They are merely the engineer in the cab of a hundred-ton locomotive. The people, the tribe are the machine itself, and they generate a collective power that can all too easily go off the rails.

THERE ARE COUNTLESS THINGS that distinguish in-groups from out-groups: dress, language, customs, music, hairstyles, height, the shape of the eyes, the length of the nose. But there is nothing that draws a brighter dividing line than skin color.

Race, to the degree that such a concept even exists biologically, is barely an afterthought in the human genome, a few bits of coding that reflect the climactic and geographical adaptations that a migrating species has to make if it is going to survive in a new land—darker pigmentation to afford protection from the sun in tropical latitudes, lighter skin to absorb what sunlight there is in cold, damp northern regions. "We didn't start off as a multiracial species," says psychologist Liz Phelps, director of New York University's Lab of Learning, Decisions and the Neuroscience of Affect. "We have races simply because we dispersed."

There are far more genes devoted to controlling, say, metabolism, disease risk, temperament and longevity than there are to coding for the color of the skin and the texture of hair, but we don't divide ourselves into tribes according to lactose intolerance, allergies to gluten or susceptibility to heart disease, at least partly because those variables are invisible. Race is a conspicuous, unmistakable badge of difference— even if it ought to be an inconsequential one.

The brain, says psychologist Joshua Correll of the University of Chicago, is "a meaning-making machine," something that from the moment we're born begins sorting things and people into categories: big and little, old and young, loud and quiet, familiar and unfamiliar. Once those silos are created, a value is assigned to them. Loud things are scary, quiet things are safe. Familiar things are comforting, new things are threatening. When it comes to color, those defining lines can be indelible.

In experiments conducted at the Max Planck Institute in Munich, developmental psychologists divided a large sample group in half and showed each a series of pictures of fruits and vegetables—some of the pictures in their proper colors, some only in black-and-white. When the groups returned the next day and were asked about the images, the subjects who had looked at the color pictures recalled them accurately, but those who had gotten the ones in black-and-white often didn't, believing they had seen the fruits and vegetables as they look in real life. To the brain, it seemed, a banana will always be yellow and an orange will always be orange—even when they're not.

For fruits and vegetables this kind of perceptual stubbornness is harmless, and may even have real survival value: You would rightly think twice about eating a green orange or a black banana, because one is underripe and one is spoiled and neither would be good for you. An uncompromising idea about the proper color of food just might keep you alive. The same was true—at least early on—about the proper color of people. Like it or not, the tribe you know—which shares your genes and wants you to live long enough to pass them on to the next generation—is much likelier to protect you and keep you well than the tribe you don't know, whose members see you as alien at best and a competitor for resources at worst. So no sooner are children old enough to toddle away from the campfire than they develop a sharp antenna for otherness—perceiving differences they may never have noticed before.

Initially, children don't assign value to the mere fact that a stranger looks different. They notice it, and if it gives them pause at all, it's a result less of disdain or dislike than uncertainty. "In-group love can come without hatred of the other group," says Dovidio. Indeed, he explains, it can sometimes come with a sort of sympathy—a sweet if misplaced feeling of concern. "If you see people who are different, you feel bad for them because they're not like you," he says.

I got a taste of that phenomenon when my older daughter was barely four years old and had not yet begun to comment on or ask about all of the different races and skin tones around her, but had begun to eyeball people in ways she hadn't before. One afternoon when we were in line at a very busy Bed Bath & Beyond, I noticed her staring at the cashier—a young African American woman. I watched her watching, guessed what was going on in her head and silently pleaded with her not to give voice to it. But no sooner did we reach the register than she did.

"Are you sad that you don't have light skin?" she asked. I winced and then hissed her name reproachfully but managed nothing more. The cashier could have responded in a thousand different ways—more bad than good, by my count—but she chose something that was equal parts insightful and gentle.

"No, honey," she said. "Are you sad that you don't have dark skin?" My daughter shook her head no. "Well, there you are, then," the woman said. "We're both happy with what we are."

That innocent, judgment-free phase of childhood does not last long—and it's disturbingly easy to hurry kids out of it. A few years ago, psychologist Yarrow Dunham, then with the University of California and now at Yale, separated a sample group of schoolchildren into two smaller groups, distinguished by two different colors of T-shirts. He then read them stories about kids who were part of both groups, including both good things and bad things all of the characters had done. When the children were interviewed later, they preferentially remembered more good things about the behavior of the kids wearing their color of T-shirt and more bad things about the other kids.

"There's a selective memory going on," says Dunham. "Kids will begin to show these preferences right away, in the lab, on the spot. It's not just a preference, it's also a learning bias—the children actually learn differentially about the in-group and the out-group. That creates a snowball effect—what starts out as a little bias can lead to a pretty rapid entrenchment of stronger biases."

In the brief history of the United States, color-based bigotry has been turbocharged by circumstances. America has always been a multicultural place, with all manner of races and ethnicities mixing. But it was originally just a two-way and then three-way division—and it got ugly, bloody and hierarchical fast. Europeans arrived on what was another people's continent, bearing guns, cannons and land hunger—a dangerous combination. The native populations could not compete technologically—nomadic and agrarian people simply don't need the same tools to survive—and they were eventually slaughtered. It was just as well, the Europeans told themselves. The Indians were poor stewards of the land anyway—their very primitivism was proof of that. And if there was any remaining doubt, the mere fact that they were a different, darker color sealed the deal.

Things got even worse when Europeans imported another, still-darker race to the new continent—in chains, no less—and set them up in a state of what was intended to be permanent servitude. Again, the master class had willfully misinterpreted lack of technology among African populations for lack of intelligence, and the bigger gulf between the white and black skin tone than between the white and red made it easier to believe that the racial superiority gulf was greater too.

"Black folks didn't show up en masse until 1619 as a result of the slave trade," says Juan Battle, a sociologist at the City University of New York. "You have almost immediately a stratification. There were whites who had been indentured servants and slaves, but that shifted over to dividing by skin color. We have these color differences that appear in the world, and that's normal. What isn't normal is stratification, the assignment of values."

That assignment moves in two directions. Every time you lower the other race a peg in your estimation, you elevate yourself a peg, giving racism the added dimension of grandiosity, egotism and self-adoration—narcissism by out-group diminution. It's not for nothing that Rudyard Kipling's 1899 poem "The White Man's Burden" is so reviled by history. Indeed, it's one of those bits of ostensible artistry that actually seem worse with the passage of time:

> *Take up the White Man's burden—*
> *Send forth the best ye breed—*
> *Go send your sons to exile*
> *To serve your captives' need;*

To wait in heavy harness
On fluttered folk and wild—
Your new-caught, sullen peoples,
Half devil and half child.

The thing goes on that way for a while, warning the white caretaker race about "The blame of those ye better, / The hate of those ye guard," but it could have stopped after a few lines. The message—race makes you great, and with that comes responsibility—was clear.

Once these kinds of biases get baked into our worldview—both over the course of generations and within a single lifetime—even good intentions aren't entirely sufficient to remove them. It was in 1998 that psychologist and social scientist Mahzarin Banaji of Harvard University co-created what she called the Implicit Association Test (IAT), an easy and unsettling on-screen experiment that has been part of almost any serious conversation about race and other kinds of bias ever since. Subjects taking the IAT are flashed pictures of white faces or black faces in no particular order and asked to press a key associating the whites with a number of words, including *joy, love, peace* and *happy*, and to associate the black faces with words like *agony, evil, hurt* and *failure*. It is a distressingly easy and speedy exercise: Click one key for the good words and another key for the bad words, depending on the face that shows up on the screen. But it gets hard when subjects are asked to reverse the associations—pairing up whites with sad or tragic qualities and blacks with happy ones. No matter what subjects think about their egalitarian nature, they slow down markedly.

The IAT, which Banaji has now made available online (at implicit .harvard.edu) in part as an educational tool and in part to broaden her dataset, measures all kinds of biases—age, religion, disability, weight—but it is with race that it has made its true impact. I first took the test several years ago and did poorly—shaking out as moderately racist despite my previously high opinion of myself. I took it again recently and found that this time the scoring has been made more specific, ranking how favorably people feel about black males, black females, white males and white females. In my test, I was shown to be most comfortable with white females, followed closely by white males, who, in turn, were followed by black females. Black males finished last—by a fair bit. I'm not happy about that, but if there is any consolation to this dark peek at my inner self, it's that I'm not remotely alone. Both blacks and whites react less favorably to pictures of the opposite race than to their own when they take the IAT.

"The IAT allows us to come face-to-face with the mental difficulties of making the association we want to make," says Banaji, who was born and raised in India. It matters that we indeed want to make those better associations, but that doesn't mean it's easy. Banaji cites the common Stroop test, in which people are flashed the name of a color written in letters of that same color—*red* printed in red, say—and are told to announce what the color is or hit a key indicating it. Easy. But when things are mixed up—*red* printed in blue, for example—and people are told to ignore what the word says and indicate only what the color of the letters is, they slow down just as predictably as they do on the IAT.

"I give the Stroop test to corporate audiences and say to them you feel silly that you're not doing this right but you're not embarrassed or guilty," Banaji says. "I want people to know that about race too."

That uneasiness is also something that applies equally to whites and blacks—even blacks who have devoted their lives to fighting racial bias. Jesse Jackson once famously said: "There is nothing more painful to me at this stage in my life than to walk down the street and hear footsteps and start thinking about robbery. Then look around and see someone white and feel relieved." African Americans, like whites, often do less well on the IAT than they want to—a legacy of cultural bias that, in a paradoxically evenhanded way, afflicts all races equally.

None of this means that anyone gets a pass for embracing the ugly, for celebrating the our-group-is-great-and-yours-is-vile ethos because that's the way your brain wants to work. The fact is, these biases, while terrible, are also malleable, or at least more malleable than they seem. Phelps, of NYU, has conducted studies in which she scans white and black subjects' brains with functional magnetic resonance imaging (fMRI), while she flashes them pictures of white and black faces. Both races have higher activation of the fear and rage centers in the amygdala when they see the opposite race than when they see their own. But when the opposite-race face is a friendly or familiar one—Will Smith for whites or Harrison Ford for blacks, for example—the amygdala is significantly quieter. More encouragingly, when Phelps flashes the nonfamous faces more slowly, giving the brain more time to work, there will be the same level of amygdala activation, but it will be followed by activation of the dorsolateral prefrontal cortex and anterior cingulate cortex, higher, more civilized regions that rein in the primitive emotions of the amygdala.

"The amygdala is critical for fear conditioning," Phelps says. "You attend to things that are scary because they're essential for survival. Then the other brain regions kick in that allow you to regulate your reactions—to control your thoughts and feelings."

Unless, of course, you choose not to—and that way lies trouble. Psychologist and Columbia University lecturer Michael Schulman, coauthor of *Bringing Up a Moral Child*, works with delinquent adolescents at a residential treatment center and was struck one day by the outrage that swept through the place when word got around that three of the boys had mugged an elderly woman. "I wouldn't mug an old lady. That could be my grandmother," one said. Schulman asked whom it would be OK to mug. "A Chinese delivery guy," the boy answered. Says Schulman: "The old lady is someone they could empathize with. The Chinese delivery guy is alien, literally and figuratively, to them."

THE SOMETIMES BRUTAL, even murderous differences that define the insider-outsider line are evident everywhere and do not require a racial difference. They're present in mobsters who kill promiscuously yet go on rhapsodically about "family"; in street gangs that fiercely protect their members and their turf and then spray rival gangs with automatic-weapons fire from speeding cars. But they have their most terrible expression in wars, in which the dehumanization of the outsider is essential for wholesale slaughter to occur.

One of the most unsettling pictures to come out of the Holocaust did not involve piles of bodies or cattle cars full of people, but a much smaller, more personal moment in one of the Jewish ghettos. A man dressed in a traditional black suit and a large-brimmed black hat, with the beard and side locks of the deeply religious, is standing, staring fixedly ahead, while a group of three or four Nazis surround him and one of them cuts his hair—as primal a violation as forcibly shaving the beard of a Muslim or a Sikh. The Nazi soldiers look neither angry nor vengeful. They look happy, amused, laughing at a jolly game, which seems to be bringing them genuine enjoyment.

Somewhere in their brains, the same pleasure regions that would be firing in response to a genuine bit of benign play—arm wrestling in a bar, needling a friend who got snubbed by a local girl when he offered to buy her a drink—were active here too. And no doubt the men went back to their barracks that night with the same sense of camaraderie they'd have had if they'd indeed been involved in such innocent horseplay, as opposed to humiliating and terrorizing another human being. The key is that at some point, they'd quit thinking of their victim as human at all. Compared with the Jews, the Germans were not only a superior race, they were a superior *species*. There's a reason that in Nazi propaganda films Jews were depicted as rats swarming up from sewer grates—and it's the same reason Rwanda's Hutus referred to the Tutsis as cockroaches during the 1994 slaughter and that American propaganda posters during World War II depicted the Japanese as fang-toothed, claw-handed, yellow-faced monkeys. These are beasts, the semiography says—and they're vile beasts at that.

That, admittedly, stretches the boundaries of simple narcissism, but not to the breaking point. It may not be possible to make your group any more human, but you can always make the outside group less so, and the wider that gap gets, the higher you climb by comparison. If you think this kind of dehumanizing doesn't happen in the United States, think of the ugly legacy of African Americans being depicted as apes or monkeys, something that crept back out of its hole in 2008 after Barack Obama was elected president and vile T-shirts, illustrations and Photoshopped pictures appeared on the more sinister provinces of the Internet. Still, it's when a nation goes to war that the animalizing impulse reaches full flower.

"In any war zone, the people on the other side aren't people," says psychologist Marc Hauser, author of *Moral Minds* and the wonderfully titled *Evilicious.* "Leaders start to turn the other into something disgusting. You recruit the same disgust reaction that impels you to get rid of parasites and vermin. Once you do that, you've got all you need."

That doesn't mean it's all that easy to get to that point. Dovidio believes a dominant group needs to go through three stages to reach a state of mind that allows its members to slaughter: Dehumanization of the other comes first, the disgust Hauser cites comes second, and finally comes extreme fear or extreme anger. The anger part is often stoked by framing the out-group as an existential threat—and it must be a knowing, calculated threat. An out-group that unwittingly carried a virus that was lethal to the in-group would surely be rejected and maybe even killed, but its members wouldn't be despised. An out-group that knows the harm it's doing and does it on purpose is an entirely different matter. *The Protocols of the Elders of Zion,* the fraudulent manifesto published in 1903 that purported to be the Jews' secret guidebook for world domination, trafficked in such an idea. So, too, did Adolf Hitler when, in a January 1939 speech, he explicitly declared: "Today I will once more be a prophet: If the international Jewish financiers in and outside Europe should succeed in plunging the nations once more into a world war, then the result will not be the bolshevization of the earth, and thus the victory of Jewry, but the annihilation of the Jewish race in Europe." The war to annihilate the Jews, in other words, would be a war initiated by the Jews.

In the United States, this kind of imputation of malevolent intent has rarely reached the level of formal government policy, but it's been an animating idea for some of those policies all the same. Witness the imaginary peril lascivious Native Americans and African Americans were said to pose to white womanhood. Protecting wives and daughters surely justified the occasional lynching or plains war, didn't it? The more generalized, if more existential, danger of deliberate crossbreeding to dilute and destroy the white gene pool is still cited by white supremacists as part of some larger miscegenetic plan. In North Dakota, residents of the town of Leith are even now, in the second decade of the twenty-first century, fighting to block an avowed supremacist from buying up enough property to wrest control of the local government and create the country's only official white supremacist community.

"We hate that which threatens what we love," said the leader of the group in an interview with CNN.com. "And we're being genocided in our own country. Wouldn't you be bitter about it?"

That kind of naked racial hatred cloaked as self-defense has long since been unwelcome in the more mainstream political community, but even there, the demonizing-the-other game goes on unabated. The radical right sees the left not simply as advocating for a different set of policies and ideas, but as scheming to establish a one-world government ruled by the UN or the socialists or who-knows-who. The radical left ripostes with its own particular lunacies, fancying a world of plutocrats dressed up like the millionaire on a Monopoly card, conniving with Wall Street and the international banks to hoard the world's wealth. In fairness to the left, the wing nuts have not gotten inside the Democratic Party the way their opposite number on the right has co-opted a significant portion of the GOP. But on both sides, the extremists are relying on the idea that it's hard to make monsters of the opposing group if the principles at stake are complicated and nuanced. So you turn the other guys into something willfully evil and you're off to the xenophobic races.

Psychologist Robert Sternberg sees a different three-step process at work to turn mere animus into homicidal loathing. It begins with what he calls a negation of intimacy, the familiar dehumanization of the target group, which disqualifies them from ordinary empathy and decency. Next comes passion, an intensity of emotion that adds a dimension of rage to the mix. "Passion is hot hate," Sternberg told me for a 2008 *Time* magazine story about racism, "the kind you see in road rage or upon returning home and finding your spouse in bed with someone else."

Last, and most disturbing, comes commitment, a coolly reasoned, intellectualized choice to commit a murderous act. It is commitment that gives rise to the decision to use chemical weapons against an ethnic minority, to burn down a village in Vietnam or gun down the people of Babi Yar during World War II. It is commitment that led to the infamous Wannsee Conference, held in a villa outside Berlin on January 20, 1942, during which leaders of the Nazi Party planned the "final solution" to the question of the Jews. "Commitment is more of a cold hate," says Sternberg. "It's what you are taught. The more of these three components you have, and the more intense they are, the more likely you are to get massacres and genocides."

It's hard to know what to say about a species in which an emotion like "cold hate" is even on the behavioral menu, except that it's a mercy it's a state of mind not easily achieved. And while it's impossible to lay all that ugliness at the feet of ordinary or even clinical narcissism, it's hard not to say that the arrogance, the self-regard, the diminution of others, the lack of empathy and remorse and the willingness to commit any act to achieve personal ends, all of which are essential parts of narcissism, are not in play here as well. Just as acts of individual good can come together to become acts of global or national good—the field workers who trudge into often dangerous tribal regions of Pakistan to vaccinate children against polio, the first responders who sweep into areas devastated by an earthquake or a tsunami—so, too, can individual evil become a national enterprise, with thousands and millions of people moved by self-regard and remorselessness, coming together to create the kind of mass horror no one of them ever could.

IF TRIBALISM can be wondrous or hideous, it can also be splendidly preposterous—more about ceremonies and bragging rights than anything else. Did it matter a whit when Alaska joined the union and bumped Texas down a spot to second-largest state? It did to Texans. Does anyone really care that Dubai is now home to the tallest building in the world, a distinction Malaysia once held, and the United States before it, and both have now lost? Yes, if you live in Dubai. These things matter to plenty of people in plenty of ways, as long as they don't stop and think too hard about why. There is nothing, however, that better captures the deep feelings, kabuki rituals and utter pointlessness of tribal competition than organized sports.

And there's nothing that captures collective narcissism better, either. States may boast about their square mileage; cities may boast about their tallest skyscraper. But only in sports are there actually chants and merchandise making that point. Consider the "We're number one" cheer rhythmically repeated by fifty thousand fans wearing giant foam rubber fingers. Consider the popular nicknames: America's Team (the Dallas Cowboys), Monsters of the Midway (the Chicago

Bears), Orange Crush (the Denver Broncos). Those are not names that cry out "We're number two!" Yes, the old Brooklyn Dodgers affectionately adopted the decidedly unflattering nickname "Dem Bums," but even here, it was all about building allegiance, identity and us-versus-them superiority—the scrappy, outer-borough toughs against the swells of Manhattan (the Giants) and the princes of the Bronx (the Yankees). All of this falls squarely within nearly any definition of narcissistic behavior—and a particularly self-celebratory brand of it at that, though it is a comparatively harmless brand too. Its roots, however, are sunk in something darker and deeper.

It is hardly a novel observation that if war is politics by other means, sporting events are war by other means. There are the flags, the costumes, the marching bands, the songs, the bloodshed (often), the passions (always) and the emotional affiliation with a home city, a team name and a set of iconic colors—the sports equivalent of the red, white and blue. When Cleveland lost its football Browns in 1996, there were marches and demonstrations not seen in the city since the civil rights era—even accompanied by the appropriated chant "No team, no peace!" which sounds a lot more meaningful in its original incarnation, "No justice, no peace!" While the National Football League quickly promised the fans that a new team would be granted the city within three years, local passions were not really cooled until the fans were also promised that the team name, uniform and signature orange helmets would be returned to them as well. It was Baltimore, which lost its Colts to Indianapolis in 1984, that stole the Browns, and while fans there were thrilled to be back in the league at last, they still grumbled that they, unlike Cleveland, had to pick a new name and new colors, since when the Colts cleared out they took everything with them, including the horseshoe logo. So Baltimore hates Indianapolis for their scheming and their larceny, and Cleveland hates Baltimore for the very same reasons. That loathing shows in the stands when the teams play each other—and that, in a sense, is understandable. But

Red Sox and Yankees fans hate each other, too, and the love is no greater when the Lakers play the Celtics and teams from Philadelphia play pretty much anyone at all, and none of them picked the other one's pocket of a well-loved team.

The bad blood between cities and teams can sometimes turn to real blood in the stands. English soccer fans are notorious for their brawling and even rioting. As long ago as the fourteenth century, King Edward II forbade early forms of soccer from being played in rural villages because of the fear of hooliganism and street fights. In 1885, after England's Preston North End franchise beat Aston Vista 5–0, the players had to duck a hail of stones thrown from the stands and were set upon bodily when they left the field. Exactly 100 years later, in 1985—after what you would think would have been a civilizing interval—English teams were banned for five years from competing in the European Cup owing to a brawl started by Liverpool fans during a game against Italy.

The Brits aren't alone, of course. Brawling has been a common feature in soccer stadiums across Europe, as well as in nearly all American stadiums and arenas. Major League Baseball now stops beer sales in the stands after the seventh inning—and it's not because they don't want the revenue. And the violence isn't confined to the stadium. In 2011, two Los Angeles Dodgers fans accosted a San Francisco Giants fan in the parking lot outside Dodgers Stadium and beat him badly enough to leave him in a coma. On at least two occasions in the long Dodgers–Giants rivalry—in 1938 and 2007—a fan of one team has been murdered by a fan of another after a game.

The passions of fans need not be so feral, and often they can be channeled into ceremonies that allow just enough we're-number-one steam to be blown off safely. The formal introductions of teams before a football game starts—complete with sprints down the tunnel from the locker room and onto the field between rows of pom-pom–shaking cheerleaders—serve that function, at least for fans of the home team, though opposing fans are free to boo. The zillion-dollar opening ceremony staged at the beginning of every Olympic Games is a similarly satisfying trooping of the colors, particularly for countries fielding small teams that won't have much opportunity to make it onto the medal stand. Other times, fans take it upon themselves to strike that safe balance between expressing their passions while containing them too.

A number of years ago I attended a baseball game in Osaka, Japan, between the home-team Hanshin Tigers and the visiting Chunichi Dragons. Hanshin had been leading the Central League for much of the season and would go on to win the Nippon Series in the fall. Chunichi had been stumbling along and would finish second to last that year, besting only the Yakult Swallows. Still, the rivalry between the teams was fierce, and while the results of one game would do nothing to change the Tigers' good fortunes or the Dragons' poor ones, the stadium was packed.

Before the game started, the upper deck was a pointillist mixture of thousands of fans dressed either in Tigers yellow or Dragons blue—I saw almost no one wearing any other color—mingling easily. But as soon as the players began to take the field, a tidy sorting-out began: All of the Dragons fans took their seats in the deck overlooking right field and all of the Tigers fans sat on the left, making a perfect division of yellow and blue. Then, throughout the game, they performed organized chants and songs—first one side, then the other. The performances weren't constant—there were plenty of times the fans simply watched the game and cheered as they chose. But it was clear they were watching it raptly—and it was entirely unclear what signal was given when it was time for a performance to begin. I have no recollection of which team won, but I do remember that it was the Tigers fans who beat the Dragons fans at least in terms of elaborateness of their performance. One perfectly staged song ended with the yellow-clad crowd inflating yellow balloons and then releasing them to corkscrew their way upward before they ran out of air and fell back down.

The question in all this isn't why we care—sports are fun, the pageantry is beautiful and watching gifted athletes perform can be as exciting as watching gifted dancers dance. The question is why we care so *much*. You're not the one who gets to hold up the trophy after a Super Bowl win, after all. Some guy you never met does that. And you're surely not the one who signs the seven-figure endorsement deal or the eight-figure contract extension. You had absolutely no role in the game at all, and thus you have no right to any feelings of exultation if your team wins or despair if it loses. And you rationally know that— but your emotional self is an entirely different thing.

It was in 1976 that psychologist Robert Cialdini, then and now a professor at Arizona State University, published his often cited study of the phenomenon he called BIRG—or basking in reflected glory— as it applies to sports fans. Over the course of most of a college football season, Cialdini observed students on the campuses of seven large universities, including ASU, looking particularly at what they wore on the Mondays after either a win or a loss by their team the weekend before and, more important, how they described the game.

On the whole, he found that students were more likely to wear an article of clothing emblazoned with their school's name, logo or colors following a win than following a loss. On some campuses the difference wasn't much—just a few percentage points. But on other campuses, it was dramatic. Louisiana State University students were 2.4 times likelier to wear the purple and gold after a team win; for Ohio State, it was a 2.3 bump. University of Pittsburgh students were almost three times likelier to wear a Pitt logo or Pitt colors following a victory. The students' connection to the victories, Cialdini wrote, was "causally meaningless"—in other words, they had not a thing to do with it. But that didn't stop them from wanting to publicize their "positive unit relationship" with a team that had brought pride to the larger university tribe. And those positive feelings of group belonging and group superiority extended beyond the team to the school itself. "It is possible," Cialdini wrote, "that a football victory caused students to like their school more, and this heightened attraction manifested itself in the tendency to wear school-related apparel."

Even if the students weren't aware of the reasons they wore what they did on Monday mornings, they were aware of the *fact* that they did; they're the ones who selected which articles of clothing they took out of the closet, after all. But there was a subtler, more powerful indicator of their reactions to a win or a loss, too, and this one was likelier to be unconscious. In the second part of Cialdini's study, he had confederates call students at the same seven universities, posing as representatives of a "Regional Survey Center," asking questions about their school and the surrounding community. Among the questions was one about how their football team had fared the weekend before. Following a win, Cialdini found, students were nearly twice as likely to describe the results in the first-person plural—*we won, we beat them, we scored the winning touchdown in overtime.* Following a loss, they were much likelier to disown the team and refer to it either in the third person ("They got beat") or simply to recite the results and credit the other team ("The score was 14–6, Missouri"). Other psychologists and sports commentators, spinning off Cialdini's BIRGing term, dubbed this distancing CORF—cutting off reflected failure, or cutting off responsibility for failure.

Significantly, Cialdini also found that he could manipulate the results of the study depending on how the callers from the imaginary survey center identified themselves. If they said they were calling from somewhere off campus and had no connection to the school, the tendency of the students to use *we* after a win and *they* after a loss was greater—the better either to elevate yourself in the eyes of outsiders by advertising your membership in the powerful tribe or to avoid diminishing yourself by disavowing any responsibility for the group's weaknesses. When the caller was supposedly part of the school, the subjects had less at stake since both people on the call rose and fell together. The use of first- and third-person language was thus less pronounced.

"[A game] is not some light diversion to be enjoyed for its inherent grace and harmony," Cialdini said years later in an interview with *The New York Times*. "The self is centrally involved in the outcome of the event. Whoever you root for represents you."

For some truly, deeply loyal fans, it's easy to BIRG, but not so easy to CORF. The Green Bay fan has not been born who will refer to the Packers in anything other than the first-person plural. But there's another way to cut off reflected failure. Cialdini calls it "blasting," demeaning the opposing team to minimize the value of their victory. So the Red Sox came to New York and beat the Yankees? Fine. Hope they enjoy their bus ride home to that hamlet in Massachusetts they call a city. So the Indianapolis Colts beat the Chicago Bears in the Super Bowl? At least the Bears are loyal to their first and only city. If you can't demean the other team, blame the officiating. If you can't blame the officiating, blame the weather—the game should have been called in the fourth when the rain started.

Blasting serves the same function for a group's collective narcissism as it does for that of an individual: elevate yourself by diminishing the other. It resembles, too, the way narcissists behave in the workplace— blaming others when a project tanks or a deadline is missed, but claiming credit when things go well. It even has echoes of infantile narcissism, in the *enfant terrible* who can never, ever accept that limits or disappointments are justified, since what the baby wants the baby is entitled to get. When it's not forthcoming, the inevitable cry is "unfair!" Sound familiar, sports fans still stewing over a years-ago Super Bowl, which really, truly would have come out differently if the inept ref had only made the pass-interference call?

While both sexes exhibit sports tribalism, it's still men who experience it more powerfully. That makes sense because in real tribes, it's males who typically do the fighting that keeps the larger group safe or fed, and in both that sense and the sporting sense, testosterone plays a big role. In times of real combat and real aggression, testosterone levels rise, and for couch-warrior sports fans, they do too. In a 1998 study out of the University of Utah, researchers took saliva samples of males both before and after they watched their team play in the World Cup or in a college basketball game. In both cases, testosterone levels were higher after a win than they had been before the game, and lower after a loss.

For all male animals, both of these hormonal states serve a powerful purpose. Combat—even pantomime combat like putting on your team colors and watching a game—is about establishing dominance. After the fight is over, it's best for the victor's testosterone levels to remain elevated for a while, so he can consolidate his position and, in the case of a tribe, make sure his allies stay loyal. It's similarly best for a loser's hormone levels to fall, the better to make a strategic retreat and not be goaded by pride or rage into taking an even worse beating. That doesn't mean it feels good, and that doesn't mean the losers don't stew. Every war ever launched to reclaim land another country seized a century ago proves that tribal humiliations die hard, and a World Series victory is always sweeter when you beat the same team that beat you last time around. But settling scores does not mean being stupid, and feeling low or defeated can sometimes ensure that you take your time before you fight again.

COLLECTIVE NARCISSISM has its most circuslike expression in sports and its most deadly expression in war, but it has its most profitable expression in the marketplace—particularly in the case of advertising. We have created an entire industry devoted to the singular, self-adoring art of proclaiming that the thing you create, build and sell is better than anyone else's, and companies are willing to spend tens or hundreds of thousands of dollars to announce that fact in a newspaper or during a TV show. During the 2013 Super Bowl, a single thirty-second spot went for a stunning $3.5 million. That's a lot to spend just to say you're great.

Advertising, of course, is about more than just vanity. In most cases, it's the sine qua non of staying in business—just as "Look at me" exhibitionism is central to being a model or a performer. Still, there's promotion of the product—this is a great camera or car or smartphone—and the promotion of the manufacturer: We are the best there is, and the things we make are therefore the best by conse-quence. That, too, can be central to success. In a crowded market-place, there is no better way to ensure sales than to have consumers stop asking questions the moment they see your name. There are way too many yogurt choices out there, but I recognize Dannon and that's good enough for me. There are too many TV brands, but this one's a Sharp—or a Toshiba or a Sony—so never mind the specs, I'll buy the name. "Ya know, it's the Radisson, so it's pretty good," says one of the prairie characters in the movie *Fargo*—a bumpkin's line that makes most audience members laugh, never mind the fact that those same people make the exact same kinds of purchasing decisions every day. Still, there's a subtler, more pervasive kind of institutional narcissism that creeps into the members of the company itself, and that can, over time, lead not just to arrogance but to the collapse or at least corrosion of the very qualities the group celebrates in itself.

Steve Jobs was famous for his lack of concern for what consumers were thinking at the same time he was making them products they couldn't resist. "A lot of times, people don't know what they want until you show it to them," the late Apple chief said. Some of that was true: A decade ago you probably couldn't have envisioned the iPad, but once you saw one you'd practically kill to own it. But that same institutional arrogance led Jobs and Apple to make we-know-better choices that hurt them in the long run: sealing the iPhone and iPod case so that batteries couldn't be replaced, requiring customers to use AT&T exclusively in the first few years of the iPhone's release, force-feeding users the much-reviled first version of the Apple Maps app and deleting Google's far better one when they upgraded. A federal court's 2013 ruling that Apple was guilty of fixing prices on e-books only weakened Apple's hand and strengthened Amazon's in a ferociously competitive market—a blunder that a humbler company might not have committed.

Said Lawrence Buterman, a Department of Justice lawyer, after the ruling, "Apple told publishers that Apple—and only Apple—could get prices up in their industry." Later Apple—and pretty much only Apple, among the makers of e-readers—paid the penalty for that.

The same listen-to-no-one folly led to the 1985 disaster that was New Coke—a universally rejected replacement for old Coke that precisely no consumers had been asking for—and the serial messes that are Microsoft Word, the all-but-universal word processing program that becomes more confusing, less intuitive and more stuffed with dubious functions with each unnecessary upgrade. Like the QWERTY keyboard, it is a bad system that unfortunately became the dominant system, but at least QWERTY has remained the same since its introduction in 1873. Microsoft Word doubles down on bad every few years.

There are "I Hate Microsoft Word" forums and "I Hate Microsoft Word" rant threads. There is an "I Hate Microsoft Word" Facebook page. On one tech website, the author of a story called "The 10 Most Hated Programs of All Time" wrote: "Some people say 'I hate Microsoft Word because it's far too complicated!' Some say 'I hate Microsoft Word because it introduced Clippy the bloody Office Assistant!' Still others say 'I hate Microsoft Word because I keep sending .docx files that only three people on Earth can actually read!' We say, people! Come together! Let's hate Microsoft Word for all of those reasons!"

There may be no company that does vanity better than *The New York Times*—and it's worth conceding that, as with Apple, its employees have a right to strut. The *Times* was long ago nicknamed "The Gray Lady" because of its appearance from a distance, with its very high ratio of copy to photos or other art—an all-business appearance that reflected a very serious approach to the news. It has embraced that nickname, as it has the even more ennobling label "the newspaper of record," said to have been coined by librarians, who used the *Times* as a final authority on disputed points of fact. Over the decades, the paper has pretty much lived up to both names, now more than ever as a shrinking print universe leaves readers with an ever-dwindling number of reliable news sources and an ever-growing number of sloppy bloggers and cable news screamers.

But it's true, too, that the *Times* can present itself with a self-important solemnity that can become self-parodying—a style of writing that suggests it's writing more for the ages than for the person who's opening up the paper in the morning just to get the news. Thus, the business writers refer to Consolidated Edison or International Business Machines on first reference in a story—a head-scratcher for the 99 percent of the world that says Con Ed or IBM. Thus, Bill Gates becomes William H. Gates on first reference and Mr. Gates thereafter. Thus, too, in the *Times* entertainment section, P. Diddy became "the rap impresario Sean Combs," which was so formal a way to identify him as to leave him wholly unidentified to people only casually familiar with rap.

"These things are all in the *Times* stylebook," says Daniel Okrent, until recently editorial consultant for Time Inc. and its twenty-three publications, and formerly public editor at the *Times*, an ombudsman position created in the wake of Jayson Blair, the *Times* reporter who left great gray egg on the great gray lady's face before being sacked in 2003 for inventing names and facts in his stories. "These are conventions that are baked into the paper's DNA—things like never calling

Greenwich Village 'the Village,' or giving all people honorifics like Mr. or Ms. except for convicted criminals and the dead. Devices like this do fade from the stylebook over time. I remember in my adult life when the word 'gas'—as a shorter version of 'gasoline'—had to be in quotes in a *Times* headline. I think we may see the same thing happen to 'William H. Gates.'"

The unique position the *Times* holds in global journalism may make it harder for it to shed such affectations than for other papers—much the way Ivy League schools and venerable corporations cling to old conventions longer than less tradition-bound institutions because more is expected of them. And the fact is, the stylebook quirks are entirely harmless. In the case of the Blair scandal, however, the *Times* revealed a far deeper well of institutional self-importance.

When the paper's editors discovered what Blair had been doing, it responded the way any good publication should—which was to fire him on the spot and retract or correct all of the errors he had introduced into the paper's pages. But for the *Times*, there was more. In its Sunday, May 11, 2003, edition, the paper published a 7,249-word story telling the tale of Blair—the kind of length not even the most globally important stories get. In the paper's July 21, 1969, edition, the front-page story reporting the Apollo 11 moon landing ran just 3,151 words, less than half the column inches the editors determined that the decidedly less epochal tale of Blair warranted. And that didn't even include the actual retractions—the whole point of the exercise—which went on for thousands of additional words in the same edition.

It was the end of the main story, however, that most captured the profound cultural significance the *Times* saw in an incident that was, in the end, little more than a case of a good newspaper getting punked by a bad employee, something that few news organizations are spared if they stick around long enough. "For now, the atmosphere pervading the newsroom is that of an estranged relative's protracted wake," the last paragraph of the article read. "Employees accept the condolences of callers. They discuss what they might have done differently. They find comfort in gallows humor." It's a description that might better have captured the scene at NASA after the loss of the shuttle *Challenger* or at an airline company when one of its planes goes down.

Here, too, Okrent gives the paper some latitude. "There may have been a defensiveness, a need to show that you're better than your critics," he says. "But I think there's a distinction between narcissism and self-consciousness. The paper is always looking at its shadow. There's this feeling that the *Times* is the best and it's the only one that matters, and that can manifest itself as narcissism, it can manifest itself as strutting. But there's also this enormous burden. Look at the number of other newspapers that follow the *Times* obsessively, from the right, from the left. No other journal has anything like that."

That's surely true, but it's also true that time can bring perspective and the view from the middle of a Blair-style storm is naturally less clear than the view you get later. Yet even after a decade's reflection, the paper seems not to have been able to step back from the long-ago incident. "The scandal that exploded 10 years ago last week was epic," wrote Margaret Sullivan, the current public editor, in her May 4, 2013, column, "as world-class as the newspaper where it happened."

Sullivan is right that the *Times* is world-class—and people who care about solid, well-reported news would be much poorer without it. She's wrong that the scandal was epic—it wasn't—or that it exploded anywhere but within the *Times* newsroom itself. Everywhere else, it did rattle the windows, but nothing more.

TRIBAL NARCISSISM has been central not only to the survival of our species, but also to its ability to become the planet's overwhelmingly dominant one. The dinosaurs once thundered, but the dinosaurs were an entire clade—just like the clade of mammals—and now they're all gone. *Homo sapiens* is a single species within that clade, and one that has been around for only 200,000 years. How powerful has that single line of beast become? Consider that some scientists increasingly refer to the modern era as the Anthropocene, joining the Pleistocene and the Holocene in the planet's great geological epochs. Never mind the glaciers or tectonic plates—we are the most powerful force shaping the earth today.

The numbers are as clear as they are scary. It took us 109 years to go from one to two billion people (from 1818 to 1927). The jump from two to three billion took 33 years (1927 to 1960). In 1999, we hit six billion, and by 2011 we were already at seven billion. It's hard to know how many other species there are on the planet—a single dipper full of ocean water may contain uncounted microbial species wholly unknown before—and the figure has variously been placed anywhere from three million to 100 million. One of the best new studies, published in 2011 and conducted by a team led by marine biologist Camilo Mora of the University of Hawai'i, puts the figure at 8.7 million. Mora bases his conclusions on a new algorithm that calculates down from the number of taxa existing in both the plant and animal kingdoms, and while the formula is complicated and the estimate it yields is on the low end of a very wide spectrum, 8.7 million is still a very big number—yet humans are chipping away at it fast.

The natural law known as the species-area relationship posits the very straightforward premise that the wider the area you sample, the more species you're going to find in it. The broad law has a local coefficient—the number of species you find in a fixed area in one part of the world will be different from what you find in other areas, which makes an awful lot of sense if you compare, say, the parched Australian interior with the dense biosprawl that is the Amazon rain forest. Still, factoring all the numbers together, you do get some sense of population distribution—and population die-off, thanks to human activity. In a typical year, humanity wipes out about 25,000 acres of forest, which, according to the new algorithm, comes out to the loss of 27,000 species at the same time. Clicking along at that rate, it's pretty easy to burn through the entire 8.7 million total in just under 325 years. And that destruction is through habitat loss alone—never mind climate change, which wipes out even more ecosystems, or the invasive species we introduce into previously environmentally balanced areas, which crowd out existing forms of life that once lived peaceably together.

"We're losing species at a rate we've never seen before, except during times of mass extinctions," says Mora. "In the history of the planet we're ranking in the top six extinctions right now. Humans are responsible and we are too self-absorbed to do anything about it." Mora does not hesitate to call that self-absorption narcissism—not of the individual or even of the tribe, but of the entire human species, and he admits that it's characteristic of nearly all life-forms. "If there was any species with the capability we have, it would very likely be taking all the resources too," says Mora. "But typically in nature there are automatic control mechanisms that stop the overexploitation. Unfortunately, we became too smart and now we're overcoming everything."

It is only in this one expression of narcissism—the species-wide expression—that our me-first, self-adoring impulses might win. Narcissists in the workplace, in relationships, in the dictator's palace, eventually burn out and go away. Humanity as a whole, however, has little to check its ego. We may indeed achieve the utter dominance at the expense of all else that every narcissist craves. Whether we'll like what's left of the planet we've won will be another matter entirely.

CHAPTER NINE

Death Row and Hollywood: Where the Narcissists Won

H e really was a very good boy—at least the therapist who was assigned to him thought so, and she was in a position to know. She worked with the boy for months—from shortly after his arrest until the time she passed him on to a different counselor so she could focus on other kids who really needed the help.

"Muy facile hombre" is what she wrote on the boy's chart. And that description—"very easy man"—seemed to say it. He was impossibly charming—witty, intelligent, and very talkative, but in a way that went beyond the self-absorbed prattle of the high school senior he was. He actually had things to say, insights to share. More important to the therapist's way of thinking was how remorseful he was about the petty crime that had landed him in her care in the first place—breaking into a van and stealing $400 worth of stereo equipment.

"I realized very soon afterwards what I had done and how utterly stupid it was," he admitted in the letter of apology he was required to write to the owner of the van. "I let the stupid side of me take over."

That, of course, is the kind of thing any boy would say if a state-appointed counselor was standing over his shoulder, and anyone who'd handled more than a few of these bad-news kids would know that such an anodyne apology counted for very little. But this boy said more. "If it was my car that was broken into, I would have felt extreme anger, frustration, and a sense of invasion," he wrote. "I would have felt uneasy driving in my car again knowing that someone else was in it without my permission. I am truly sorry for that."

Those few sentences changed everything. They sounded an awful lot like genuine empathy, and as the therapist knew, once these kids crossed that threshold, you practically had the battle won.

The apology note, however, was not the only writing the boy did about the crime he'd committed. He also put down his thoughts in a journal he kept at home—and in those pages, he expressed a decidedly different view of things.

"Isnt america supposed to be the land of the free?" he wrote. "how come, If im free I cant deprive a stupid fucking dumbshit from his possessions If he leaves them sitting in the front seat of his fucking van out in plain sight and in the middle of fucking nowhere on a Frifuckingday night. NATURAL SELECTION. fucker should be shot."

As it happened, the van owner wasn't shot, but a lot of other people were. It happened more than a year later, and the boy himself—Eric Harris—along with his friend, Dylan Klebold, pulled the triggers, killing fifteen people, including themselves, and wounding twenty-one others at Columbine High School in Littleton, Colorado, on April 20, 1999. It was a shooting spree that until the slaughter of first-graders in Newtown, Connecticut, in 2012 was the most savage mass killing Americans had ever experienced. And too few saw it coming.

Harris's first therapist was not the only one gulled by his easy charm and humble mien. The supervisor of the state-sanctioned youth program, who also evaluated him, swallowed the act, too, and predicted good things for him. "Eric is a very bright young man who is likely to succeed in life," he wrote. Klebold was a little more worrisome— quieter, secretive, certainly less charming—but that's true of a lot of moody teens, and he had more going for him than most. Indeed, as the counseling program's head therapist concluded, Klebold was "intelligent enough to make any dream a reality, but he needs to understand work is a part of it."

The intelligent boy and the bright young man actually did work hard, but in ways no one imagined. They studied and they plotted and they slowly amassed an arsenal—buying weapons, learning how to build pipe bombs and explosive propane tanks, then assembling them and testing them with the care of engineers. And all the while, they spilled their rage, first Harris alone in his journal, then on his AOL page, then later, the two boys together, into the lens of a video camera, creating a historical document they intended to be viewed only after their deaths.

"I'm coming for EVERYONE soon and I WILL be armed to the fucking teeth and I WILL shoot to kill," Harris wrote. "I can't wait til I can kill you people. Feel no remorse, no sense of shame. All I want to do is kill and injure as many of you as I can."

They had enemies, surely, lots of enemies: "Ni**ers, spics, Jews, gays, fucking whites" was how they enumerated them. There were the jocks, too—the beautiful people in their beautiful high school—and they deeply, deeply hated them. "I hope we kill 250 of you," Klebold said.

They assumed there would be a movie made about what they'd done—there had to be a movie—and they fantasized about which famous Hollywood name would direct it. Whoever it was, the mayhem they planned would certainly provide plenty of high cinematic drama. "It's gonna be like fucking Doom," Harris said, in a nod to his favorite video game. "Tick, tick, tick, tick. Ha!"

That Harris and Klebold were inept—that their propane tanks fizzled and their pipe bombs were puny and they wound up doing their murderous work armed with little more than their guns and their hate—changes nothing about their monstrousness. "Peekaboo," said Harris at one point during the rampage, as he slammed his hand on a table in the Columbine library under which students Emily Wyant and Cassie Bernall were hiding. Then he bent down, thrust the gun under the table and shot Cassie in the head.

"Who's next? Who's ready to die?" one of the boys asked as they prowled the library; the survivors can't say which killer said what, because they were hiding as best they could and dared not look up. "All the jocks stand up! We're going to kill every one of you!" one of them demanded. They shot a pair of students having lunch on the school lawn; they shot three boys who had gone outside for a smoke. "This is awesome!" Harris shouted as he stood at the top of a stairwell firing down at a crowd of students.

But it was the library that would forever be remembered as the center of the carnage—where they shot or killed twenty-two of their victims. It was in the library, too, that, their rage finally spent, Harris and Klebold took their own lives, leaving a mountain of evidence—and a mountain of mystery—behind.

"The slaughter at Columbine High School opened a sad national conversation about what turned two boys' souls into poison," wrote *Time*'s Nancy Gibbs in the week that followed. "It promises to be a long, hard talk, in public and in private, about why smart, privileged kids rot inside."

That was true then, and it's true a decade and a half later. It begs the point to say that Dylan Klebold and Eric Harris were psychopaths; there are many such grievously ill people in the world and they don't commit the kind of crime these boys did. It begs the point to say they were embittered by the social caste system of high school, whipped wild by violent video games, and living in a country in which it's far too easy for the criminally crazy to get their hands on guns. That, too, is true of many people. And it surely begs the point to say that the boys were narcissists—though they manifestly were, with their pitilessness, their conceit, their blamelessness and lack of accountability. "You made me what I am," Klebold said in a charge directed at his family. "You added to the rage."

There was, too, the seductive pose of the narcissist—not only the power to charm psychologists, teachers and parents, but a gloating awareness of that power. "I could convince them that I'm going to climb Mount Everest, or that I have a twin brother growing out of my back," Harris said. "I can make you believe anything."

Harris and Klebold would surely have been wretched and raging even without their narcissism, but in a wholly different way. They may still have murdered, or they may simply have collapsed in on themselves, their psychic bile leaving them angry and powerless and ultimately alone. Their narcissism—with its sense of grievance and grandiosity and overweening entitlement—was what helped bring all of the other ingredients in their psychic chemistry together. It activated them, it armed them, and ultimately, it set them to blow.

HUMANITY'S EMERGENCE from the blood-soaked wild is due to a lot of things—our opposable thumbs, our social nature, our unique capacity to plan and create and build. Then, too, there's our insula. Of all of our brain's remarkable structures, the insula often gets overlooked: It doesn't have the glamour of the higher regions or the emotive power of the lower ones. It doesn't even have a crisp function like the occipital lobe, where visual input is processed, or the olfactory bulb, where smell lives. But it does important work—particularly when it comes to empathy. That, in turn, is due in large part to what are known as mirror neurons.

Until thirty or so years ago, no one even knew mirror neurons existed—but everyone knew what they did. You see someone yawn, you yawn; you see someone in acute pain, you squirm. Someone cries—even just an actor playing a role, whose sorrow, you know, is entirely, artfully counterfeit—and you tear up too. Someone goes off on a laughing jag—particularly someone on live TV, who is trying to hold it together and simply can't—and you dissolve into a laughter puddle too.

It was in the 1980s and 1990s that neurophysiologists at the University of Parma in Italy first began looking for the source of this behavior in macaques, struck by the monkeys' imitative nature. Macaques readily mimic the behavior of both one another and humans, sometimes productively (as when they learn to manipulate an object by observing and repeating what they see) and sometimes pointlessly (opening their mouths or sticking out their tongues when another individual does). The Italian investigators first implanted electrodes in the brains of some of the monkeys and determined which neural circuits controlled their ability to reach for and grasp food. Then, with the electrodes still attached, the monkeys watched humans eating, using the same reaching and grasping gesture the monkeys had used. In the brains of the macaques, the appropriate circuits lit right back up—even though the animals were only observing the gestures, not producing them. The neurons responsible for that imitative firing were located in the premotor cortex—which, as its name suggests, regulates the planning and execution of movement.

Mirror neurons could explain a lot of things not just about monkey behavior but human, too—why people in business meetings tend to assume subtly similar postures, say, with a shift in position by one person triggering an unconscious cascade of similar shifting, particularly if it's the highest-ranking person in the room who moves first. It also explains why newborns mimic the same open-mouth or tongue-out expressions monkeys do, even before the babies have ever seen themselves in a mirror, which means that they don't yet know in any conscious way that their face has the same components as the face that's in front of them—or even, for that matter, that they have a face at all.

"Mirror neurons have incredible visual properties," says Marco Iacoboni, professor of psychiatry and biobehavioral sciences at UCLA, who has been studying them since 1999. "They get activated merely by watching, causing us to imitate gestures and postures—not explicitly, but subtly. Social scientists call this the chameleon effect. Some people tend to be more chameleonlike than others. Some less." And all of that is the work of just the mirror neurons in the premotor region. Subsequent studies have found that about 10 percent of all neurons scattered throughout the brain have some mirroring properties, including the neurons in regions that regulate emotion—and that can be both good and bad.

In 1999, Iacoboni and his colleagues began using functional magnetic resonance imaging (fMRI) to study how the brain reacts to a smile, and how that, in turn, affects feelings. From babyhood, we learn to return a smile for a smile, and as we get older, we often do it reflexively, unthinkingly—a social grace like nodding to someone you pass in the office. But a nod is mostly a physical exchange—one that conveys meaning, yes, but little feeling. Smiles are very different, sending powerful and infectious emotional signals. A stubborn disagreement often softens considerably if someone accompanies a point with a conciliatory smile of even the faintest wattage. You see one of those and, despite yourself, you put down your defenses at least a little.

When Iacoboni observed the brains of subjects as they watched another person smile, he saw the premotor cortex mirror neurons that control facial muscles react, lighting up the circuits that would create a return smile, even if the subject's face was not yet exhibiting the expression. More important, he noticed that the signals traveled to the insula as well, a small area tucked into the cerebral cortex in both sides of the brain. The insula is the seat of multiple emotions, including happiness, sadness and fear. It in turn communicates with the amygdala, where other emotions—particularly anxiety and anger—live.

Those flashing signals regulate a lot of reciprocal socializing—and a lot of reward, too. I want to make you smile not just because it's pleas-ant or it might help end a fight, but because if you do, my own mirror neurons light up and I get a little shot of ricocheted happiness too. The same is true of the amused delight we feel when we make someone laugh—as if we're the one who heard the joke, not the one who told it—or the warmth we experience when we give someone a gift or pay someone a compliment and share in the feeling of sweet appreciation. It's a brilliant adaptive strategy: being kind or attentive or generous costs me time, energy and in some cases even money. So I get a small neurochemical treat in exchange and the wheels of human society are greased a little more.

Positive reinforcement like this—the kind that encourages good behavior—is not the only mirror emotion at work. So is negative reinforcement—the shot of sorrow or unease we experience when we observe someone else suffering. That, at its most basic, is empathy, and behavioral scientists have devoted much time to studying its powerful social value. We're much likelier to help another person—to come to the aid of a lost, crying toddler or comfort a colleague who's experi-encing a life crisis—if it relieves the reflected pain we feel simply by observing them. And we're much, much likelier to avoid being the source of the other person's suffering, taking care not to inflict physi-cal or emotional pain because, selfishly, we'll feel it, too, usually at the same time the other person does.

"There's evidence of empathy even in newborns," says psychologist Jean Twenge of San Diego State University. "Newborns will cry when others cry. They show this from the very beginning."

But what happens if they don't—and if they don't in adulthood ei-ther? What if pain is only first-person pain, if what hurts me hurts me, and what hurts you—sorry—hurts only you? A person like that is a person with no internal brake, no onboard punishment system that inflicts a high price for bad behavior, a price that has to be paid again and again until good behavior takes its place. A person like that is also often called a psychopath—someone able to engage in any kind of atrocity at all because the anesthetic effect of lacking empathy means that an emotional bill is never presented. If those people exist—and they surely do—and if the operation of empathy in the healthy mind can be observed in an fMRI, it stands to reason that its absence might be too.

To establish if that was so, a team led by neuroscientist Christian Keysers, director of the Center of Neuroimaging at the University of Groningen in the Netherlands, scanned the brains of prisoners who had been officially diagnosed as psychopathic—and not just any flavor of psychopathic. In order to qualify for the study, the prisoners had to score at least 30 out of 40 on what's known as the *Hare Psychopathy Checklist-Revised (PCL-R)*, which is to the study of psychopaths what the NPI is to the study of narcissists. In both cases, a 30 out of 40 is hall of fame territory.

Prisoners who cleared that dubious hurdle and who agreed to participate in the study—something they tended to do readily in exchange for the rare chance to get out of maximum-security lockdown—were transported from confinement under heavy guard wearing nonmetallic handcuffs, since metal of any kind can be dangerous and even deadly in the high-magnetism environment of an fMRI. As an added precaution, a nonmetallic hobbling rod was inserted into one pants leg and shackled to one leg, making running impossible. Prisoners with tattoos were also screened for exactly when the inking was done. Older tattoo pigments had metal ingredients, which would also be unsafe in a scanner.

When the subject psychopaths were cleared for metal and were finally slid into the fMRI, they were shown simple videos of one person hurting another—but the images were chosen carefully. From the start, Keysers knew he didn't want the subjects to see any faces. For all people, psychopaths or not, a disproportionate share of neural real estate is given over to facial interpretation, so much so that those circuits might swamp the subtler firing of brain regions specifically involved in processing empathy. Instead, Keysers showed his prisoners people interacting with their hands only. In the first clip, one person's hand is seen stroking someone else's. In the second, one hand is twisting the finger on another. In a third, one hand is slapping another with a stick. A fourth video shows a neutral view of a handshake, which could be used as a baseline.

Existing brain research, along with Keysers's own, had already pinpointed the spots in the brain where both the pleasant and unpleasant sensations are processed when people experience the stroke or the slap of the finger twist themselves. In observers—at least observers capable of experiencing empathy—mirror neurons in the same regions should light up. In people without empathy there should be little or nothing.

Keysers scanned his subjects in 2007, but only in the summer of 2013 were the results at last published, in the journal *Brain*. As expected, he reported, the mirror neurons of the criminal subjects indeed barely stirred when they saw someone else experience either pleasure or pain. But there was another piece to his findings—and that piece offered a little more hope. The lack of neuronal empathy was present only when the prisoners were shown the videos with no particular instructions except to watch what was in front of them. In subsequent showings, they were specifically told to try to imagine what the people in the clips were feeling. After they received that guidance, their brains reacted precisely the way those of nonpsychopathic control subjects do. The differences between the healthy and unhealthy brains, said Valeria Gazzola, the second author of the paper, in a statement that accompanied the publication, "almost completely disappeared."

That's very big, something that may subtly but significantly change our entire understanding of how a psychopath's mind operates. "Psychopathy may not be so much the incapacity to empathize," Gazzola said, "but a *reduced propensity* to empathize, paired with a preserved capacity to empathize when required to do so."

Just a few months before the *Brain* study was released, psychologist Kent Kiehl, of the University of New Mexico, published related work in the online edition of *JAMA Psychiatry*. Kiehl, unlike Keysers, uses a portable fMRI for his work, which means he can visit subjects in their maximum-security settings, rather than taking the risk of transporting them around. He, too, showed his prisoners videos, as well as still pictures, though they were not limited to just images of hands. In one, for example, they saw a person hitting another person with a baseball bat. In other pictures, the people were engaging in harmless behavior. The psychopaths were asked to perform the decidedly low-order task of identifying the pictures in which someone was likely to be feeling pain—something they could determine as well as anyone else. But in other ways, their brains reacted differently from how those of control subjects reacted, with lower activation of the orbital frontal circuit, which helps govern sensory integration, decision making and the connection between reward and punishment.

A 2013 study used a different—and imaginative—way to explore how empathically flexible the brain is. A multinational team of investigators from Italy, Switzerland and Germany had some volunteers look at pictures of unappealing things like maggots and raw liver, while feeling either toy worms or toy slime to simulate the tactile experience of what they were seeing. At the same time, other volunteers looked at pictures of pleasant things like bunnies or swans and felt fur or feathers. All of the subjects were tested in pairs: In some cases, both subjects got pleasant stimuli; in others, both got unpleasant; in others still, one got the nice while the other got the nasty. No matter what, all of the subjects were allowed to see on a screen not just the image being shown to them but the one their partner was seeing too.

After the exposure to the stimuli, they all rated how they were feeling, from a low of -10, for utterly creeped out, to a neutral zero, to a high of +10, for utterly cuddly. Finally, they were asked what they thought their partner's score was. Consistently, when both people had

had the same good or bad experience, they made a pretty accurate guess of what the other person was feeling. But a person who had seen something nice tended to underestimate how nasty a person who had seen something unpleasant was feeling. And a person who'd seen something bad similarly lowballed the happy feelings of the person who'd seen something good.

That may not be a surprise, but what did make the study game-changing was that when all of the subjects were scanned by functional magnetic resonance imaging, the experimenters could spot where in the brain either lower or higher activation was causing this empathic mistake to be made. And when they stimulated that region with harmless transcranial magnetism—a painless, noninvasive pulse of magnetism that causes a brief flutter of extra activity—the empathy scores improved.

"The results of our study," said one of the investigators in a release that accompanied the paper, "show for the first time the physiological markers of highly adaptive social mechanisms, such as the ability to suppress our own emotional states in order to correctly evaluate those of others."

None of this means that there's a practical or desirable way to boost empathy artificially, but it does suggest that our ability to feel other people's pain is more adaptable than we think. Indeed, even hardened killers illustrate that, with their indifference to the people they murder juxtaposed against their genuine grief when a loved one dies. And the fact that many violent felons seem to age out of criminality, developing greater patience and self-restraint and at least a small sense of conscience, suggests that at least in some cases lack of empathy is not destiny.

Just how narcissism fits into this—particularly into the larger condition that is psychopathy—is not fully settled. Even people with full, florid narcissistic personality disorder are nowhere near the monsters people who can't be transported without manacles and hobbling rods are. But it's undeniable that in both conditions the ability to feel what other people are experiencing has been dulled or even numbed away entirely, and with that comes a liberty to act—and to hurt. For some psychologists, the best way to understand how the psychopathic and narcissistic mind might overlap is through a relatively new diagnostic category known as malignant narcissism.

Not all psychologists agree that malignant narcissism actually exists—certainly not in a way that would allow it to become a formal medical condition. But those who do think there's something to it define it as a type of narcissism that is associated not just with a willingness to hurt others but with a delight in doing so. As such, it's less mere self-regard to the exclusion of all others than it is something closer to the definition of evil.

"Malignant narcissism is the bad boy end of the spectrum," says psychologist Mark Lenzenweger of the State University of New York at Binghamton. "It's heavily infused with paranoia, aggression and a callous disregard for harming others. People who have that orientation are not just grandiose and self-enamored, they're actually willing to do harm to others just to keep themselves feeling good." Klebold and Harris, as one terrible case in point, spoke and wrote extensively about how much fun they expected to have during their killing spree.

Lenzenweger does not think all malignant narcissists belong under lock and key, and indeed, he believes that some are at large in the world—the very worst of the sadistic, crash-and-burn bosses, say. But most other researchers do put malignant narcissists in the hit-man, serial killer, Hitler box. It's malignant narcissism, they believe, that may help explain why Nazi doctor Josef Mengele was able to amputate limbs or remove organs from fully conscious concentration-camp prisoners and pursue such human vivisection as if it were any other satisfying line of work. It's malignant narcissism that helps explain the bloodlust of Caligula as he tossed victims, even spectators, to the lions in the Roman Coliseum. It's malignant narcissism that may also account for the grotesque incongruities of Saddam Hussein's regime, defined by its palaces and its torture cellars, its official parades and its government-sanctioned rapes.

The possibility that malignant narcissism might exist was first floated as long ago as 1978, by Weill-Cornell Medical College professor of psychiatry Otto Kernberg, still regarded as one of the world's leading authorities on personality disorders, particularly narcissism and borderline personality disorder. He defined malignant narcissism as a strain of narcissism with a poisonous dimension of "joyful cruelty and sadism" folded into it. The NPI, which was not created in its current forty-question form until the late 1980s, has recently helped apply some hard numbers to Kernberg's initial definition.

Psychologist Brad Bushman administered the NPI to a sample group of violent offenders—specifically, prisoners in Massachusetts and California convicted of murder, aggravated assault, robbery or rape, sometimes in combination. As a control, he also gave the test to groups of bodybuilders, dentists and students at the University of Michigan, an exceedingly competitive school with an excellent academic and athletic reputation. None of these law-abiding folks exhibited any of the antisocial or violent tendencies of the criminal sample group. But they were all members of populations that tend to score high on self-adoration and ego, and that made them a valuable comparison population.

On average, the California prisoners scored 21.4 on the NPI and the ones from Massachusetts scored a 23. Out of a possible score of 40, that doesn't seem like much, but compared with the general population it is. One of the biggest studies of narcissism levels in the general population was conducted in 2003 and involved a whopping 3,445 subjects on six continents. That's a huge sample group with an impressively large geographic sweep, yet it was limited on one metric: age. The subjects were all young—with an average age of 24.5 years. That shortcoming was actually an advantage, since narcissism may change over time, as life teaches us lessons about the primacy of the self (we're not as important as we think we are) and the enormity of our talents (we're not as special, either). What's more, the 24.5 average age jibed nicely with the average age of two of the three sample groups in the Bushman study—the students and the bodybuilders. For better or worse, then, the global study sought to capture people at the peak of their self-esteem, and yet even for these folks, the average NPI score was just 15.2. For the United States in particular, it was a marginally higher 15.3. That means the California and Massachusetts inmates scored a full 41 percent and 51 percent higher than the global average, respectively. The dentists, bodybuilders and University of Michigan students in Bushman's study scored higher than the general population, with the students leading the group at 19.2, but even they finished below the California and Massachusetts cons by 11 percent and 20 percent, respectively.

The meaning of these findings is admittedly not certain. For one thing, it's impossible to say if the inmates' narcissism drove them to prison or if breaking the law and winding up behind bars turbocharged their sense of rage, grievance and compensatory grandiosity, or if some combination of the two were at work. "For violent offenders," Bushman admits, "we don't know if their high scores are the cause or effect of their situations." Teasing out those answers would require long-term studies of people both before and after they run afoul of the law—a sample group that's not easy to assemble since you hardly know who the violent offenders will be until they actually offend. Still, Bushman does think that the robustly established link between narcissism and aggression suggests that it's grandiosity and self-adoration that comes first and the criminal career follows.

Other elements of narcissism also help drive the criminal mind, sometimes providing the critical push that causes it to cross the line from merely sick to truly psychopathic. The *PCL-R* measures psychopathy on two main dimensions, one labeled Lifestyle/Antisocial, which is more particular to criminal or otherwise dangerous behavior and includes traits such as lack of empathy. The other is called Interpersonal/Affective, which much more closely tracks the less dangerous but still bad traits that turn up on the NPI, such as glibness and superficial charm. Still, it's that charisma that can wind up playing a particularly big part in what makes psychopaths so deadly.

Saddam Hussein was a good illustration of this as he posed with Western hostages in the run-up to the first Gulf War in 1990, using them as bargaining chips and human shields but trying to project a protector's loving care. "We hope your presence as guests here will not be for too long," he said. "Your presence here and in other places is meant to prevent the scourge of war." He then singled out a clearly terrified five-year-old boy, the son of a British oil industry engineer, tousled his hair and asked if he was getting his milk. Later, the gentle protector laid waste to much of Kuwait.

A far more horrible example of psychopathic charm is Joseph Stalin, murderer of millions, whose "Uncle Joe" persona was also part of his power. In his 2005 book *Stalin: Court of the Red Tsar*, Simon Sebag Montefiore painted a picture of a man of almost surreal contradictions. Stalin's charisma was effective against people who ought to have known better—Franklin Roosevelt and Winston Churchill among them—and against those who could not have seen through him. Montefiore cites the case of a provincial official named Beria who visited Moscow and was invited to a formal dinner with the dictator and other officials. Stalin befriended Beria's little boy, sat him on his knee throughout the dinner, wrapped him in his fur coat when he was cold, then watched cartoons with him and tucked him into bed. No harm came to the little boy, but Stalin would sometimes disarm other politicians and even members of his inner circle with the same kind of attention—writing them gracious letters, answering his phone himself when they called, visiting their homes to make sure they were living in the kind of dignity and comfort they deserved. Then he would order them killed. "When he set his mind to charming a man, he was irresistible," Montefiore said in an interview when his book was released.

Then, too, there was the savagely evil serial killer Ted Bundy, handsome, articulate, a onetime lawyer, who used his charisma to attract many of the thirty or more women he raped and killed. Edward Cowart, the presiding judge in Bundy's 1979 trial, memorably captured the odd discordance between the charm and the crimes of the psychopathic narcissist in his closing statement after sentencing Bundy to death.

"Take care of yourself, young man," Cowart said. "I say that to you sincerely; take care of yourself, please. It is an utter tragedy for this court to see such a total waste of humanity as I've experienced in this courtroom. You're a bright young man. You would have made a good lawyer and I would have loved to have you practice in front of me, but you went another way, partner." Cowart went on to say that he felt no animosity toward Bundy—a strange admission considering the crimes for which this particular defendant was being sentenced to die. Yet it was an admission entirely consistent with the criminal narcissist's power to charm you—sometimes literally to death.

IF SOCIETY LOATHES its criminals—as well it should—it deeply loves its celebrities. And it's a good thing for the celebrities that we do; otherwise, we might be inclined to beat them insensible. Entertainers of all types can be variously arrogant, entitled, spoiled, demanding, wildly exhibitionist and unapologetically self-adoring. They earn millions, and hold out for millions more. They make a commitment to appear in a movie and then walk out on it if the makeup or the costar or the script changes are not to their liking. They move about in posses; wreck hotel rooms; get busted for speeding, shoplifting, driving drunk or picking up prostitutes. And before long, they're back on the red carpet doing it all over again.

They are Justin Bieber, onetime boy wonder, current punk teenager, ongoing train wreck. Jaws dropped around the world when, in 2013, Bieber visited the Anne Frank house in Amsterdam and signed the guest book this way: "Truly inspiring to be able to come here. Anne was a great girl. Hopefully she would have been a belieber." Because yes, the most important thing to consider when reflecting on one of the Holocaust's most tragic and iconic figures is whether she would have liked young Justin's music. But it was so much a part of the sulking, tantrum-throwing *enfant terrible* Bieber had already shown himself to be that the public disgust with what he said was mixed with both resignation and a can't-look-away fascination with what would come next.

Celebrity narcissists are Sean Penn and Russell Crowe—throwing punches at photographers or telephones at hotel clerks. They are Alec Baldwin, a man of great comic skills on camera and a near-pubescent temperament off it—calling his own eleven-year-old daughter a "rude, thoughtless little pig" on a widely circulated voice mail, getting himself tossed off an American Airlines flight after refusing to turn off his cell phone, publicly huffing over slow service at an Upper West Side Starbucks by tweeting out the bulletin that the "Uptight Queen barrista [*sic*] named JAY has an attitude problem." Presumably, the capital *Q* was a finger slip and the word was intended not as a reference to the legendary band but to the sexual orientation of the server. Narcissist, too, is the apocryphal rock star who would not perform unless a bowl of M&M's in a single, randomly chosen color was provided in his dressing room.

That story, oft told, is not true, but it has real roots: Van Halen's contracts did call for M&M's backstage with all of the brown ones removed. However, this was not an act of infantile entitlement, but a clever way of making sure the band's contracts were being read and complied with. The performances were so production-heavy, with so much electrical equipment trucked from show to show, that if the arena technicians didn't read the contract carefully and install everything exactly as specified, there could be short circuits or collapsed scaffoldings. So as lead singer David Lee Roth explained in his autobiography, clause 126 in all of the contracts would read, "There will be no brown M&M's in the backstage area, upon pain of forfeiture of the show, with full compensation." Thus, Roth wrote, "When I would walk backstage, if I saw a brown M&M in that bowl . . . well, linecheck the entire production. They didn't read the contract. Guaranteed you'd run into a problem." All the same, it speaks to the low and well-earned reputation of most celebrities that the story sounded so plausible on its face.

Surely, not all celebrities are narcissistic twits. There are lifetime gentlemen like Paul McCartney, who may crave the spotlight but has spent more than fifty years as royalty in the bad-boys' world of rock and, except for an embarrassing bust in Japan for marijuana possession, has maintained a spotless record. There are grand ladies like Helen Mirren, Maggie Smith and the younger, more irreverent but still exceedingly gracious Kate Winslet. And there is, too, Tom Hanks.

I got to know Hanks well when we were working together on the movie *Apollo 13*, and I've kept in occasional touch with him over the years. If there were stories to tell that contradicted Hanks's good-guy rep—his long-standing image as a Jimmy Stewart / Gary Cooper / Henry Fonda combo plate—I'd tell them. But they just don't exist. The very first time I had any contact with Hanks was when he left a message on my office voice mail to set up a time for us to meet and discuss some of the details of the Apollo 13 story. His message began with "Hello, Jeff Kluger, this is Tom Hanks. I'm an actor . . ." and then he went on to say why he was calling.

I've often joked afterward that I was thinking, "No, you're Tom Hanks the podiatrist." But his remark said a lot about him in a very offhanded way. The fact is, he couldn't be absolutely sure I did know who he was. The gaps in my pop culture knowledge sometimes amaze even me, and something similar is surely true of a lot of other people. It wasn't until the 2013 Academy Awards that I saw Channing Tatum on TV for the first time and discovered that he was a man. I'd seen none of his movies but had heard his name in passing and pictured him as a sort of female mash-up of Carol Channing and Tatum O'Neal. For all Hanks knew, he occupied one of those gaps—an idea that a narcissistic celebrity could neither abide nor consider, but that he preemptively guessed could be the case. He added that he was reading the as-yet-unpublished manuscript of the book I'd written about the Apollo 13 mission, which his agent had given him, and which, he added, "I realize I'm reading without your permission." So I was charmed from the start and was delighted to discover later that the easy, modest approachability Hanks projected was the real deal, not the illusory kind of so many celebs.

But Hanks and his gracious ilk are in a decided minority, and Drew Pinsky, the internist and psychologist who hosts both a TV and radio show under the media-friendly name Dr. Drew, was able to apply some hard numbers to that commonsense observation. Over the course of twenty months, he asked the celebrities who appeared on his radio show if they would be willing to fill out the NPI—anonymously, of course—so that he might use the results in a survey he was conducting. A remarkable 200 of them—142 men and 58 women—agreed. As a control group, he and his collaborator S. Mark Young, a professor of accounting, management and communication at the University of Southern California, also administered the test to 200 MBA candidates, members of a group that other studies have shown tend to score high on narcissism scales as well.

The MBA candidates, true to their reputation, did finish on the high end of the NPI, with an average score of 16.18, close to a full point above the global average. The celebrities, however, had them beat—and the kind of entertaining they did made a big difference. At the top of the NPI heap were the reality stars, who averaged out at a 19.45 NPI score—or, for what it's worth, just 1.95 points below the violent offenders in California prisons. The comedians were next, at 18.89, followed by the actors, at 18.45. Last were the musicians at 16.67—or less than half a point above the MBAs. Overall, female celebrities beat males by nearly two points—19.26 to 17.27, which is a reversal of the pattern in the general population, in which men tend to score higher. (Among the MBAs, the males did score higher than the females.)

Significantly, Young and Pinsky added one more variable to their equations—the number of years all of their celebrities had been in the business. What they were looking for with that additional data point was whether the amount of time people have spent being celebrated drove their scores either higher (as they became drunk on their fame) or lower (as they became inured to it). But as it turned out, the number of years moved the scores in neither direction. The conclusion: The celebrities began their careers as preexisting narcissists, and that might be one of the reasons they chose that line of work in the first place, "self-selecting into the industry," as Young and Pinsky wrote when they published their study. "Narcissists," they added, "may gravitate to environmental contexts in which the opportunities for high performance will lead to self-glorification."

The degree of the celebrities' prebaked narcissism may also have explained which kind of entertaining they chose to pursue. For reality show stars, the whole point of the exercise is the exhibitionism of the performers and the voyeurism of the fans, which goes a long way to explaining the stratospheric NPI scores that turned up in the study. What's more, while the stars of *Project Runway, Top Chef, Dancing with the Stars* and some other reality shows have real skills and demonstrated talents, others, like the Kardashians or the cast of *Jersey Shore*, are famous simply because of their willingness to act outrageous on camera. Still, without the "Look at me" component of narcissism, none of the reality stars would have gotten past episode one.

Comedians come by their high scores rightly too. As they themselves readily acknowledge, part of the appeal of their craft is the sense of dominance it gives them—the ability to elicit an often-involuntary physical response from a roomful of strangers with their words alone, sometimes reducing audience members to a sort of happy helplessness. The oft-cited language of the comedian—"I killed tonight," "I slayed that crowd"—is hardly the phrasing of a person indifferent to acquiring power.

Actors are more of a mixed bag. Pretty-boy couch jumpers like Tom Cruise, showboats like Jim Carrey, preeners like Nicole Kidman probably score high on the NPI. Hanks probably doesn't. George Clooney, eye candy for the camera but unpretentious in his public behavior, probably doesn't either. Keith Campbell of the University of Georgia cites Meryl Streep as another example of a celeb who artfully manages to balance great fame and low narcissism. "She seems like a craftsperson and a storyteller," he says. "If you're focused on the craft, the ego gets out of it a little more."

The fact that musicians score comparatively low on the NPI is actually not surprising, since what they do is essentially a collaborative exercise. "If you're a musician," says Campbell simply, "you've got to play in a band." That necessary immersion of the self—or at least its integration into a larger, collective self—is essential to performing well and, indeed, to performing at all. And while some bands may be known by their members' names, even when the list can be a mouthful (Crosby, Stills, Nash and Young; Emerson, Lake and Palmer), that convention is more commonly used by twosomes (Simon and Garfunkel; Hall and Oates). Most of the time, the performers play under the brand name of the band, with only the lead performers (Jagger and Richards, say) universally known. (John, Paul, George and Ringo, you're excused from this rule.)

That's not to say rockers don't crave their crowds, or that they don't make a point of giving them something to look at. Even now, decades on, the windmilling Pete Townshend and the leaping, microphone-twirling Roger Daltrey, who, at age seventy, still performs with his shirt ripped open and—give the man his props—can more or less pull it off (though it's best to grade him on a generous septuagenarian's curve), are proof of that. But The Who is still larger than the them, just as the Stones are still larger than the Mick, and just as the Grateful Dead were always larger than front man Jerry Garcia, which is the only way such bands could last so long. The groups that are home to too many conflicting egos are typically the ones that die young—the centrifugal forces of their self-adoring personalities causing them to spin apart.

None of this ego sublimation is necessary for solo performers, which is why they, as a rule, are the most flagrant narcissists: Bieber again; Madonna always; Lady Gaga sometimes; and, of course, Kanye West—the Kanye who famously interrupted Taylor Swift's acceptance speech at the 2009 MTV Awards to announce that Beyoncé should have received the award that Swift won; the Kanye who responded on his blog to the B+ score *Entertainment Weekly* had given one of his concerts with this blast: "What's a B+ mean? I'm an extremist, its either pass or fail! A+ or F–! You know what, f**k you and the whole f*****g staff!" And, of course, the Kanye West who had this to say (in the third person, of course) about, well, Kanye West: "I think what Kanye West is going to mean is something similar to what Steve Jobs means. I am undoubtedly, you know, Steve of Internet, downtown, fashion, culture. Period. By a long jump."

It's true enough that like Jobs and other famous narcissists—athletes who give themselves to the game, yet always seem to know where the camera is; philanthropists who attach their names to every museum or hospital wing they build; even human rights leaders who clearly thrill to the throngs they attract—narcissistic celebrities often leave the world better than they found it. They touch and move and transport their audiences, despite—or perhaps because of—the self-adoring demons that rage within. Demonic is all there is to malignant narcissists like Bundy and Hussein and the pitiless killers locked down in supermaxes around the world. Neither group asked for their pathologies, and both may suffer their own torments as a result of them. But the worst of the celebrities do great things before they self-destruct. The worst of the monsters only destroy—and the self is the least of their victims.

CHAPTER TEN

Tomorrow Belongs to Me

I t's probably best for all of us to get used to narcissism and practice the art of dealing with it—recognizing the narcissistic lover before we become too entangled, the narcissistic boss before we take the job, the narcissistic politicians before we elect them to high office. And if we're too late—if we realize that we've got a megalomaniacal monster on our hands only when the problems start occurring—we must similarly become adept at extricating ourselves. That may mean leaving the job with the narcissistic boss, shutting out the narcissistic coworker, firing the narcissistic lover, voting out the narcissistic pol.

No matter what, however, narcissism sure isn't going anywhere. The disorder will remain part of the whole bestiary of humanity's psychic maladies—depression, obsessions, phobias, paranoia, rage, addiction, delusions, dementia—that have always afflicted us and always will. Some have their value. In periods of depression can come reflection and insight. In obsessions can be focus; in paranoia, caution; in rage, self-assertion. A little bit of anything can shape and strengthen and anneal the personality. Too much can wreck it.

So, too, is it with narcissism. It's not necessarily bad when self-confidence comes with blinders, shutting out worry and self-doubt, since that can be essential to succeeding in spite of pitfalls and long odds. But the blinders have to be removable. Charm, similarly, wins friends and followers; but it repels them if there's nothing underneath it. Abiding love of the self is not only all right but essential, as the sad lives of the self-loathing show; but love of self to the exclusion of others produces its own kind of sorrow.

So narcissism deserves to be a permanent fixture on our psychic landscape. And yet, oddly, in 2013 it almost disappeared, wiped from the list of human illnesses as surely as smallpox has been. Smallpox, of course, was vaccinated away. Narcissism, by contrast, was nearly defined away. That eradication by fiat was one possible result of the long, fourteen-year debate that went into rewriting the fourth edition of the *Diagnostic and Statistical Manual*, or *DSM-IV*, in preparation for the publication of the *DSM-5*.

The *DSM* was first published more than half a century ago, in 1952, and has always been a work in progress. That's the case with all medicine, but sicknesses of the mind have historically been far harder to understand and frame than sicknesses of the body. Once you've found the bacterium or the virus or the structural anomaly responsible for an illness, you've taken a huge step toward curing it. But psychological ills? Not so much. There's no germ for paranoia or depression; no surgically reparable breakdown that causes a phobia.

Yes, psychologists and brain researchers have gotten better and better at disassembling the brain into its constituent lobes and regions. And yes, PET scans, CT scans and fMRIs have revealed what lights up and what doesn't when the brain is functioning healthily and unhealthily. Biologists have even peeled things back far enough that they have identified the very molecules that make up neurochemicals like dopamine, serotonin and norepinephrine, leading to a whole new class of drugs that disrupt or potentiate how they behave, and changing the very function of the brain in the process.

Yet a lot of that precision is really illusion. Even when you've taken the drugs, gone through the talk therapy, how do you know you're cured? The effectiveness of an antiretroviral drug is measured by counting the virus particles in a blood sample. The effectiveness of an antihypertension drug is determined by taking your blood pressure. But the effectiveness of talk therapy and psychotropic drugs is subject to a somewhat less rigid test:

YOUR DOCTOR: How are you feeling?
YOU: OK, I guess.
YOUR DOCTOR: Better than last week?
YOU: Hard to tell.

So there's a certain lack of precision to it.

The very definition of the conditions people come down with has a feeling of ancient sorcery about it. Narcissism is one of just ten personality disorders, which are in turn organized into three groups with decidedly unscientific names: the odd disorders (paranoid, schizoid and schizotypal); the dramatic disorders (antisocial, borderline, histrionic and narcissistic); and the fearful disorders (avoidant, dependent, obsessive-compulsive). It's a case of twenty-first-century medicine with names that seem better suited to the era in which there were just four elements (fire, earth, air, water) and four bodily humors (sanguine, phlegmatic, choleric and melancholic).

Psychology and psychiatry are not alone in this. Particle physicists sound awfully smart when they talk about quantum states and electron volts, but get them talking about quarks and you'll get a lot of magical-sounding prattle about how they come in six flavors (yes, flavors) called up, down, strange, charm, bottom and top. But you can still test it all with a multibillion-dollar particle accelerator and see if your theories check out. There is, as yet, no supercollider for the brain.

The *DSM* tried to bring order to all of this. In its first edition, it defined 106 different mental conditions and disturbances, which seemed like a pretty fair count of the number of ways people can go crazy. But it apparently wasn't. The second edition, in 1968, increased that number to 182. We got sicker still with the *DSM-III*, in 1980, when the number jumped to 265; with the *DSM-IV* in 1994, the list reached 297. There is both caprice and the potential for profound error in how these disorders are designated. In the sexually unenlightened 1950s, the *DSM-I* listed homosexuality as a "sociopathic personality disturbance." In 1974, a revised version of the *DSM-II* righted that wrong, eliminating that listing and, as gay people at the time drily observed, instantly curing up to 21 million Americans. Yes, the 1974 edition got things right; but for twenty-two years, the earlier editions had gotten them grievously wrong.

The *DSM-IV*, perhaps in an effort to simplify and clarify its huge catalogue of illnesses, subdivided things into five different axes (the personality disorders, for example, are Axis Two conditions; anxiety disorders like phobias are Axis One). And all of the conditions have a number code—a nifty shorthand that makes insurance billing easier. OCD is 300.3; stuttering is 307.0; Asperger's disorder is 299.80; selective mutism is 313.23; and cannabis-related psychotic disorder (with delusions) is 292.11.

Assigning any one of these diagnoses to a particular patient can be very much an interpretive exercise. The *DSM* lists a handful of symptoms of any one condition and specifies that a person who exhibits a particular number of them—say, five out of seven or six out of nine—can be officially said to have the condition. The ability to make that call well is no small thing, requiring a doctor to be familiar with the nature of the patient and the nature of the disorder and to be painstaking in considering both. Not every doctor is quite so careful, but even if all of them were, that still leaves room for error. Identifying a physical ailment like anemia is similar to determining who has the fastest time in a 400-meter Olympics race; in both cases the answer is empirically provable, since blood tests and stopwatches don't lie. Diagnosing a mental condition is like judging the ice dancing competition; there are plenty of talented people who can do it quite well, but subjectivity, judgment calls and flat-out error are inevitable. Still, that's the best that is practical and possible for most doctors and patients.

"I can't do neuroimaging in my office," lamented psychiatrist David Kupfer of the University of Pittsburgh in a conversation with Time .com for a story on the *DSM*. "We are lacking the validation of these methods, which are promising but not decisive."

It was Kupfer who got the unenviable task of trying to improve the state of the diagnostic art, when he was tapped to be chairman of the task force that oversaw the drafting of the latest edition of the *DSM*, the *DSM-5*, in preparation for its May 2013 release. One of the most innovative ideas he and his committee came up with was to do away entirely with the formal divisions among the various personality disorders and instead put them all on a sort of continuum, with the completely healthy at one end and the floridly symptomatic at the other.

That made a certain kind of sense since there is an enormous amount of overlap in symptomatology among the ten disorders. Arrogance and volatility, for example, can be features of narcissism, borderline personality disorder, histrionic personality disorder and obsessive-compulsive personality disorder (or OCPD, a misleadingly named condition that has little to do with common OCD and instead involves a sense of rigidity and rule-boundedness). Delusional behavior and fanciful thinking can be features of schizoid and schizotypal behavior as well as of paranoia. And all of the conditions across the personality disorder spectrum—particularly narcissism—involve a refusal to recognize that there is any problem at all. Under the new plan, the ten categories of personality disorder would be erased as surely as homosexuality was, and replaced with a kind of fever chart of ill health, with the severity of the symptoms determining the recommended treatment.

No sooner did the *DSM* committee announce their idea, however, than they were hit by a fusillade of criticism—and a lot of it surrounded narcissism. There has not been much of an increase in cases of, say, borderline personality disorder or OCPD in recent years, but with an apparent epidemic of narcissism breaking out culture-wide, it seemed like an awfully funny time to abolish the diagnosis altogether.

Psychologist Thomas Widiger of the University of Kentucky, who was part of the *DSM-5* revision committee, conceded that the plan could relegate narcissism "to a sidebar that will unlikely draw much research or diagnostic interest."

Mark Zimmerman, director of outpatient psychiatry at Rhode Island Hospital, told me: "The difficulty of dealing with personality disorders created an argument for just blowing up the tracks and starting over with *DSM*. But just because there's a problem there's no case for changing the nomenclature. You must show it's better before you make that change."

Ultimately, the *DSM* committee could not show that and backed down, retaining all ten original personality disorders and tucking its recommendations for eliminating the categories into an appendix in the book, where topics marked for further study live. That leaves, for better or worse, the old diagnoses in place. And that—also for better or worse—leaves the therapy protocols for narcissistic personality disorder essentially unchanged.

The generally low recovery rate for people with NPD is due first to their characteristic refusal to admit that they have a problem at all. That means that talk therapy is typically something they tolerate— if at all—only until they decide that the doctor is a blithering fool and they had no reason to come in for treatment in the first place. They then walk out and resume their lives, no healthier or more self-aware than they were before.

"We've looked at clinical samples showing that following failure at love and work narcissists may experience depression over time, so that does show some learning," says Campbell. "Some of them do get into therapy, but they leave early. I've seen hundreds of people who have been hurt by narcissists at home or at work. And in all that, I've seen maybe three narcissists who really want to change—someone who says, 'I see my friend and he has this great relationship with his family, and I don't have that. I'm missing something.' So it's possible, but it's not the natural course of events."

More commonly, depressed narcissists who come into therapy are looking simply to get their persistent low feelings treated, reckoning that once the symptoms lift, they can go on with their lives just as they've done all along. "The patient will go through a lot of drug treatments, often without a lot of success," says Zimmerman.

And yet the outlook for narcissists—as well as all people with personality disorders—may be brighter than once thought. The old thinking was that the refusal of personality-disordered people to own up to their problems would forever foreclose the possibility of recovery. "By the age of thirty," wrote William James in the authoritative 1890 textbook *Principles of Psychology*, "the character has set like plaster, and will never soften again." And as work by people like Campbell still shows, there's a lot of truth in that.

Yet in 1990, Lenzenweger launched a sixteen-year longitudinal study, funded by the National Institute of Mental Health, and found that even without a lick of therapy, the severity of most personality disorders—including narcissism—diminishes over time. The mechanism is unclear, and the problems by no means vanish. But as with so many other things, age appears simply to have a seasoning and mellowing effect.

"Contrary to about a hundred years of teaching and psychiatric theory," says Lenzenweger, "personality disorders were looking fairly malleable. Some people in our sample group were in treatment, but we were able to get a handle on that and look at just the improvement that seemed to be happening without it. And we did see something that was not so much spontaneous remission as it was maturation. The disorders may just clear some for some people."

The findings were limited in a lot of ways, principally in terms of age. The study tracked improvement only until about age thirty-five, which is about five years after the frontal lobes of the brain complete their three-decades-long myelination process—laying down fatty insulation in neural connections that improve the operation of the overall system. Until that time, executive functions aren't truly up and running. So while the study was constrained by the age of the subjects, it was at least dealing with fully mature brains as opposed to ones in flux, and that gave it real credibility.

"Borderline and psychopathic people are not nearly as flamboyant in their forties and beyond as they are when they're younger," Lenzenweger says. "They remain live wires into their thirties and then they begin to settle down. Is that just feedback from the environment, or is it developmental and physical changes? It's probably both." Even if this kind of slow remission isn't enough to fix what ails most narcissists, it may at least help them lower their resistance sufficiently to get real work done in talk therapy, exploring the roots of their disorder and practicing cognitive behavioral strategies that may help them acquire greater humility, tolerance and impulse control. In some cases, psychotropic drugs can help too. Antidepressants and mood enhancers like Prozac, Zoloft and Celexa may not be enough to treat the disorder, but they, too, can dial back florid behavior just enough for a therapist to do some good.

For some narcissists, however, the condition is for life, and the indignities and infirmities of old age may simply exacerbate it. After a lifetime of grandiose and arrogant behavior, many superannuated narcissists may find that whatever friends they once had have long since drifted away and whatever family members are still around will tolerate them at funerals and Thanksgiving, when they absolutely must, but little more. The passing of the years and the few that remain ahead mean that the rich fantasy life that sustains many narcissists—one filled with dreams of fame and wealth and plans for settling scores once greatness is achieved—may no longer be available, either. Instead, the narcissist can dwell only on triumphs—and, surely, grievances—of the past and goals never achieved. Loss of physical strength may mean a humbling dependency, while loss of physical beauty may be utterly devastating to the narcissistically vain.

And still the self-absorption may endure. In one study, an eighty-five-year-old woman who scored a lofty 23 on the NPI was reflecting on her past, including her unhappy first marriage, which ended when her husband enlisted in the Army during World War II. She wondered aloud whether the purpose of the war was to "put Hitler in his place or to set me free." It takes a particular kind of mind to frame a global conflict that claimed the lives of 56 million people as a personal gift—yet those minds are out there.

For average people, the bill for a life of self-adoration and grandiosity is paid more or less privately, with only family and former friends knowing what became of the faded narcissist. For the famous, the fall is more poignant. Richard Nixon spent his final years widowed, alone and at the fringes of the power centers he craved, sending unsolicited advice to a young President Clinton, waiting hopefully for his phone to ring in return and grumbling to his sole remaining aide when it didn't. John Edwards, a political comet who consumed himself in his own strange flame, aspired to be president and instead became a punch line, an aging southern lawyer whose boyish beauty is vanishing and whose superficial charm was long ago exposed as a ruse. O. J. Simpson, who once lit up scoreboards, appears in the paper now only as he shuffles into or out of police vans for this or that hearing—handcuffed, jumpsuited and increasingly bloated. "Just a Fat Old Man in Court," read a *New York Post* headline when Simpson appeared for a 2013 parole hearing—an insult, surely, to other fat old men who also happen to have lived lives of grace and purpose and generosity, but a sly reminder all the same of what Simpson had become compared with what he had been.

The indicted lawyers, the jailed brokers, the busted celebrities, looking surly and haggard as they glare for one more mug shot after one more DWI arrest, may all find their ways to the same disgraced place. So, too, may too many others. Confidence, ambition, charm, self-love are all vital chords in the complex symphony that makes us who we are. Played well, they are rich and pretty and vital to the whole. Played badly, they are nothing more than the drumbeat of the self.

AFTERWORD

I did not intend to wind up feeling much sympathy for narcissists when I set about researching their affliction—and I certainly didn't expect to feel any fondness for them. Narcissists are, in a sense, emotional muggers, people who assault their victims with a combination of stealth and misdirection—leaping out at them in situations and at times when they have a right to feel safe and taking what they want. Perhaps, in the aftermath of a real mugging, the victim may find the generosity to contemplate the life of deprivation and desperation that drives a person to a life of petty street crime—surely not a life anyone would choose. But when you've been attacked, robbed and perhaps physically injured—when the basic rules of the social contract have been violated by someone who gives not a hoot for such civilized niceties—it's hard to summon up much emotional charity.

So it can be with narcissists and the harm they leave in their wake. The very day, late in 2013, when I was making the final revisions to this book, the Commonwealth of Massachusetts sentenced Annie Dookhan, a forensic chemist, to three to five years in prison for tampering with and fraudulently processing evidence in an astonishing 40,323 drug prosecutions. In all of the cases, she reported that samples had tested positive, some of which surely would have if she had done her work properly, but an uncounted number of which were either deliberately mishandled or not tested at all. More than three hundred defendants had been released from Massachusetts prisons at the time of her sentencing, and $30 million in state funds had been set aside to investigate the tens of thousands of other cases that were compromised by her crimes. Dookhan's motive, prosecutors concluded, was nothing more or less than ambition—to process more samples in less time and win more convictions than anyone else in her lab, and thereby advance her career and boost her prestige.

If any crime argues for a much stiffer, certainly double-digit sentence, one of the scope of Dookhan's certainly does. And yet, in accepting the plea bargain that led to the comparatively lenient punishment, the judge of the county superior court showed surprising compassion. Dookhan, she wrote, "presents as a tragic and broken person who has been undone by her own ambition." It was a remarkable conclusion to reach—made, perhaps unintentionally, all the more remarkable by the judge's use of the words "presents as." It's precisely the phrasing physicians use when writing up a diagnosis—*patient presents as a 35-year-old woman with early-onset hypertension and pre-diabetes.* Blood pressure problems and narcissistic ambition, the judge seemed to suggest, are equally clinical conditions and may equally pluck a few strings of sympathy in the well observing the unwell.

It's hard to say whether anyone else will be as forgiving toward Dookhan, certainly not a defendant who spent so much as an hour wrongly confined as a result of her crimes. But forgiveness, or at least understanding, does come to some narcissists. We all have a fascination with—and a degree of compassion for—the ambitious and accomplished after they become the low and tragic. If you didn't feel at least a flicker of sadness for Richard Nixon as he wept before his White House staff on the day he surrendered the presidency and, before long, had to fight for his life in a California hospital as a result of a blood clot that nearly killed him, then you're either a hard person to move or you'd closed your heart against him with a completeness that doesn't come naturally to most people. If you don't pity the ludicrous Anthony Weiner—congressman turned laughingstock—then you're just not thinking hard enough about what it would feel like to be inside his life.

Nixon, in many ways, pushed back against the redemption he so craved in the final decades of his life. A single, sincere expression of true contrition—an acknowledgment that he had committed crimes and that he was ultimately responsible for the ones that subordinates committed in his name—would have opened a lot of doors and hearts to him. But he could never bring himself to do that, and so he died a lonely man. Weiner actually seemed to have learned from and regretted his cyberflashing, and briefly led in the polls during his doomed comeback race for mayor of New York. But when still more sexting images of him were released—ones he'd taken and shared in the months after his resignation from Congress—most people washed their hands of him.

The learning curve for most narcissists may be exceedingly steep—obtuseness in some ways is a key feature of the condition—but that's not to say insight never occurs. My working relationship with the narcissistically volatile boss who lost his temper and threw a viewing lens across his office in my presence did not end well. A few years later, when I was still rather junior in age but rather senior in position, I was meeting with him and with two other editors who, along with me, helped supervise the rest of the staff at the magazine at which we all worked. The three of us felt overworked, underappreciated and certainly underpaid, and we wanted to discuss our grievances with him.

The conversation started off professionally enough, but as we went on, I began to be filled with a delicious sense of outrage; I became steadily more pitched and indignant, and decidedly less respectful. If I noticed that my two colleagues had grown strangely silent, I surely attributed it to their timidity, their unwillingness to take the bold stand I was taking. I definitely didn't notice the knock-it-off signals they were sending me with their eyes.

The next morning, the boss's secretary buzzed me to say he wanted to see me. This was, I assumed with satisfaction, the promotion I deserved and was now openly expecting. It was nothing of the kind. It was a summary dismissal—the only time in my life I've ever been fired. I was stunned, though I had absolutely no right to be. For about a year, I did a good job of nursing my resentment over the unjustness of it all, but I slowly began to accept—with no small amount of ex post facto embarrassment—that I had grossly overstepped. My behavior had been all about entitlement, all about narcissistic self-importance, but I had been too blinkered to see it as it was happening.

The timing of my sacking was fortunate. I was old enough that my behavior had a real and instructive impact on the arc of my career, but young enough that I could bounce back from it without too much difficulty. A number of years later still, after I had had the good fortune of seeing my book *Apollo 13* enjoy the success it did, I was talking to a friend from the days of the old magazine. She mentioned that she had run into our old boss and asked him if he had heard that the book was being made into a movie. "Yes," he answered. "I suppose he's grateful I fired him now."

She told me that story with a "Can you believe his churlishness?" eye roll. But the fact is, he was right—I *was* grateful. He was an erratic man, as charismatic and volatile a narcissist as I've ever met, but I was showing signs of following him down that road, and deliberately or not, he helped shock me in another direction. My incipient narcissism was not, as the physicians put it, a refractory case. I was capable of learning from experience, managing my behavior and seeing myself as a meaningful part of the world without having to be at the center of it. That probably made it easier for my friends who witnessed my behavior in that office to forget about it and, more important, made it possible for me to forgive myself for it.

There are, I think, lessons in that for handling both the narcissists we inevitably encounter around us and the very particular one we may find staring back at us in the mirror. In both cases, it pays to be alert to the signs. The brilliant charmer you meet at a party or at the office may indeed be nothing more than brilliant and charming. The same may hold for you in those moments that you dazzle at a meeting or hold forth at a dinner party or get a glimpse at yourself in a store window and marvel at how flat-out great you look that day. Fine, enjoy— but cautiously!

Narcissism, like strong drink, has its place and its purpose; it braces and emboldens and offers a wonderfully primal pleasure. Indulging in it too deeply, however, leaves you sorry and sick and wishing you'd been more moderate in your pleasures. We would feel poorer in a world without liquid spirits, just as we would without the manifold elements of the human spirit. But they are all volatile spirits. They effervesce and enliven or they singe and scald. The difference, as with so many things, is in knowing how to control them.

NARCISSISTIC PERSONALITY INVENTORY (NPI)

CREATED BY ROBERT RASKIN AND HOWARD TERRY

The NPI is a "forced-choice" test, which means that sometimes neither answer feels quite right but you should still check the one that comes closer to describing you. Don't overthink it; try to complete the survey in just a few minutes. The lowest possible score is 0, the highest is 40.

1. A. I have a natural talent for influencing people.
   B. I am not good at influencing people.
2. A. Modesty doesn't become me.
   B. I am essentially a modest person.
3. A. I would do almost anything on a dare.
   B. I tend to be a fairly cautious person.
4. A. When people compliment me, I sometimes get embarrassed.
   B. I know that I am good because everybody keeps telling me so.
5. A. The thought of ruling the world frightens the hell out of me.
   B. If I ruled the world, it would be a better place.
6. A. I can usually talk my way out of anything.
   B. I try to accept the consequences of my behavior.

7. A. I prefer to blend in with the crowd.
   B. I like to be the center of attention.
8. A. I will be a success.
   B. I am not too concerned about success.
9. A. I am no better or worse than most people.
   B. I think I am a special person.
10. A. I am not sure if I would make a good leader.
    B. I see myself as a good leader.
11. A. I am assertive.
    B. I wish I were more assertive.
12. A. I like to have authority over other people.
    B. I don't mind following orders.
13. A. I find it easy to manipulate people.
    B. I don't like it when I find myself manipulating people.
14. A. I insist upon getting the respect that is due me.
    B. I usually get the respect that I deserve.
15. A. I don't particularly like to show off my body.
    B. I like to show off my body.
16. A. I can read people like a book.
    B. People are sometimes hard to understand.
17. A. If I feel competent, I am willing to take responsibility for making decisions.
    B. I like to take responsibility for making decisions.
18. A. I just want to be reasonably happy.
    B. I want to amount to something in the eyes of the world.
19. A. My body is nothing special.
    B. I like to look at my body.
20. A. I try not to be a show-off.
    B. I will usually show off if I get the chance.
21. A. I always know what I am doing.
    B. Sometimes I am not sure of what I am doing.

22. A. I sometimes depend on people to get things done.

    B. I rarely depend on anyone else to get things done.

23. A. Sometimes I tell good stories.

    B. Everybody likes to hear my stories.

24. A. I expect a great deal from other people.

    B. I like to do things for other people.

25. A. I will never be satisfied until I get all that I deserve.

    B. I take my satisfactions as they come.

26. A. Compliments embarrass me.

    B. I like to be complimented.

27. A. I have a strong will to power.

    B. Power for its own sake doesn't interest me.

28. A. I don't care about new fads and fashions.

    B. I like to start new fads and fashions.

29. A. I like to look at myself in the mirror.

    B. I am not particularly interested in looking at myself in the mirror.

30. A. I really like to be the center of attention.

    B. It makes me uncomfortable to be the center of attention.

31. A. I can live my life in any way I want to.

    B. People can't always live their lives in terms of what they want.

32. A. Being an authority doesn't mean that much to me.

    B. People always seem to recognize my authority.

33. A. I would prefer to be a leader.

    B. It makes little difference to me whether I am a leader or not.

34. A. I am going to be a great person.

    B. I hope I am going to be successful.

35. A. People sometimes believe what I tell them.

    B. I can make anybody believe anything I want them to believe.

36. A. I am a born leader.

    B. Leadership is a quality that takes a long time to develop.

37. A. I wish somebody would someday write my biography.

    B. I don't like people to pry into my life for any reason.

38. A. I get upset when people don't notice how I look when I go out in public.

    B. I don't mind blending into the crowd when I go out in public.

39. A. I am more capable than other people.

    B. There is a lot I can learn from other people.

40. A. I am much like everybody else.

    B. I am an extraordinary person.

SCORING KEY

Assign one point for each response that matches the key.

1, 2, 3: A	16: A	29, 30, 31: A
4, 5: B	17, 18, 19, 20: B	32: B
6: A	21: A	33, 34: A
7: B	22, 23: B	35: B
8: A	24, 25: A	36, 37, 38, 39: A
9, 10: B	26: B	40: B
11, 12, 13, 14: A	27: A	
15: B	28: B	

- The average American scores between 15.2 and 16 on the NPI, depending on age and other factors.

- Actors have an average score of 18.45.

- Reality show stars score 19.45.

- Violent offenders in prisons weigh in at 23.

- A score of 17 or above indicates you're flirting with narcissism.

- 15 and below may indicate self-esteem issues.

ACKNOWLEDGMENTS

The world of the narcissist is not the kind of place most of us would want to spend a whole lot of time—a polar vortex of ego, arrogance, obtuseness and entitlement. The world of the people who study narcissism is a different thing. It's a place where researchers are tackling one of psychology's most intriguing and intractable conditions, with no guarantee that they'll be able to change the lot of the people and families affected by it, but an absolute certainty that the work will, at least, be fascinating.

I had the opportunity to speak to dozens of people in the past two years who are among the leaders of the field, and to read the research papers of many more. In so doing, I have developed a new appreciation for the complexity of the work and the imaginative methods they're bringing to bear in their efforts. I am indebted to those who took even a short break from that work to speak and e-mail with me, and answer more questions than I—and surely they—would probably care to count. Those generous folks were:

Mark Barnett, Kansas State University; Robert Bilder, UCLA; Amy Brunell, Ohio State University at Newark; Brad Bushman, Ohio State University; Keith Campbell, University of Georgia; Erika Christakis, Yale University; Jennifer Crocker, Ohio State University; Ben Dattner, New York University; Colin DeYoung, University of Minnesota; Robin Edelstein, University of Michigan; Joanna Fanos, Dartmouth Medical School; Nathanael Fast, University of Southern California; Peter Gray, Boston College; Peter Harms, University of Nebraska;

Wayne Hochwarter, Florida State University; Bob Hogan of Hogan Assessment Systems, in Tulsa; Marco Iacoboni, UCLA; Jerome Kagan, Harvard University; Sara Konrath, University of Michigan; Claire Kopp, Claremont Graduate University; Mark Lenzenweger, State University of New York, Binghamton; Michael Maccoby, of The Maccoby Group; Kevin McGraw, Arizona State University; Camilo Mora, University of Hawai'i; Barbara Oakley, Oakland University, Michigan; Aaron Pincus, Pennsylvania State University; Brent Roberts, University of Illinois, Urbana–Champaign; Sander Thomaes, Utrecht University and University of Southampton; Jessica Tracy, University of British Columbia; Jean Twenge, San Diego State University; Simine Vazire, Washington University in St. Louis; Karol Wasylyshyn, formerly of Widener University; Colin Young, University of Minnesota; and Mark Zimmerman, Rhode Island Hospital.

I was uniformly impressed by the depth of knowledge of all of these investigators, as well as those with whom I did not speak but whose research I read. If there are any errors in the way I synthesize and explain their work, the fault is not in their explanations, but in my understanding.

As with so many of my books, I also owe a debt of thanks to my colleagues at *Time* magazine and Time.com—particularly managing editor Nancy Gibbs—for allowing me the flexibility to tackle projects like this. (Some of the material in Chapter Eight was repurposed and adapted from a *Time* cover story on morality that I wrote in 2007.) My thanks also go to some fine *Time* journalists for answering questions particular to their fields whenever I had them. I am especially indebted to Mark Halperin, Joe Klein, Jay Newton-Small and Bill Saporito for offering their insights about narcissists in politics and business.

The Narcissist Next Door is my second project with Riverhead Books, and I hope there will be many more. For insight, patience and deft editing, not to mention helping me choose from among the almost embarrassing bounty of famous narcissists for the ones who would best help me make the points I wanted to make, I offer my thanks to Jake Morrissey. There is none better. Much appreciation, too, to Riverhead publisher Geoff Kloske, who green-lighted the idea for this book and steered it safely to publication; to Peter Grennan, who helps prove the point that copyediting is an art form all by itself; and to Ali Cardia for keeping trains running, copy flowing and offering reminders—gently—about deadlines as they approach.

While this is my second book with Riverhead, it is my ninth with Joy Harris of the Joy Harris Literary Agency—the only literary agent I've ever had and the only one I would ever want to have. If we ever leave this field, I am determined that we will Thelma-and-Louise it together or not at all. She is a wise soul and incredibly dear to me.

Finally, as always, to my wife, Alejandra—who is boundlessly supportive, loving and enthusiastic, and has believed in me in moments when even I haven't. And to my brilliant, wild, loving daughters, Elisa and Paloma, who are thirteen and eleven as of this writing, but who were babies, it seems, perhaps twenty minutes ago. Sharing their journey, and guiding it when I can, has been my greatest joy.

INDEX

Jeffrey Kluger's critically acclaimed books are a lively and engaging combination of cutting-edge science, expert reporting, and practical insights. He understands how to make complex ideas accessible and exciting for everyone, and he frames new information in an engaging narrative that he's written for anyone looking to improve their lives, their relationships, and their understanding of the world.

A groundbreaking exploration of the complex world of siblings

Nobody affects us as deeply as our brothers and sisters do. Siblings teach us how to resolve conflicts (and how not to), how to conduct friendships and when to walk away. They are the only people who truly qualify as partners for life. In *The Sibling Effect*, Jeffrey Kluger delves into this fascinating bond, looking at the impact of birth order and genes, favoritism and competitiveness, gender and sexuality, and more. Kluger takes science's new findings about siblings and helps us understand their importance in our lives.

THE SIBLING EFFECT
WHAT THE BONDS AMONG BROTHERS AND SISTERS REVEAL ABOUT US
JEFFREY KLUGER

WITH A NEW AFTERWORD BY THE AUTHOR

"HONEST AND VULNERABLE AND CARING."
—THE WASHINGTON POST

"Honest and vulnerable and caring." **—The Washington Post**

"Like Malcolm Gladwell . . . [Kluger] can fashion something addictively readable out of even the densest list of statistics without dumbing it down." **—Entertainment Weekly**

"Eminently readable and engaging . . . a page turner . . . both enjoyable and educational—a worthwhile read for anyone interested in human relationships." **—Associated Press**